Democracy and Administration

Johns Hopkins Studies in Governance and Public Management

Kenneth J. Meier and Laurence J. O'Toole Jr., Series Editors

Democracy and Administration

*Woodrow Wilson's Ideas and
the Challenges of Public Management*

BRIAN J. COOK

The Johns Hopkins University Press
Baltimore

© 2007 The Johns Hopkins University Press
All rights reserved. Published 2007
Printed in the United States of America on acid-free paper

2 4 6 8 9 7 5 3 1

The Johns Hopkins University Press
2715 North Charles Street
Baltimore, Maryland 21218-4363
www.press.jhu.edu

Library of Congress Cataloging-in-Publication Data
Cook, Brian J., 1954–
Democracy and administration : Woodrow Wilson's ideas and the challenges of
public management / Brian J. Cook.
p. cm. — (Johns Hopkins studies in governance and public management)
Includes bibliographical references and index.
ISBN-13: 978-0-8018-8522-8 (hardcover : alk. paper)
ISBN-10: 0-8018-8522-1 (hardcover : alk. paper)
1. Public administration—United States—History. 2. Wilson, Woodrow, 1856–1924.
I. Title. II. Series.
JK421.C635 2007
351.73—dc22   2006016500

A catalog record for this book is available from the British Library.

Frontispiece: Portrait of Woodrow Wilson (c. 1910–20), by Samuel J. Wolf.
Florence Griswold Museum; Gift of Mr. and Mrs. Stuart P. Feld.

Contents

Preface

Attorney David Burman stood before the U.S. Supreme Court in January 2005, representing petitioners whose real names he did not know, and about whose background and current place of residence he had only the sketchiest of facts. John and Jane Doe, a former Soviet-bloc diplomat and his wife turned reluctant spies for the Central Intelligence Agency, had sued their former employer, alleging that the agency reneged on its commitment to provide lifetime financial support following their resettlement in the United States after their spying stint ended. The basis of the couple's suit was not a claim of a broken contract, but that the CIA had violated its own procedures for handling their claim for continued support and thus had denied them their rights to due process. The CIA had decided to let the case go forward in order to establish precedent for its claim of immunity from such suits on national security grounds. It argued, in essence, that it was not accountable to the courts for how it managed its spy network or how it treated former spies.

In a unanimous decision, the Supreme Court ruled in favor of the CIA, reversing the decision of the Ninth Circuit Court. It did not matter that the couple's claim was for a fair hearing and not enforcement of their "espionage contract." In his opinion for the court, the late Chief Justice William H. Rehnquist held that the precedent established in 1876 in *Totten v. U.S.* (92 U.S. 105) barred any judicial review of claims against the federal government that might risk revealing the existence of contracts with secret agents. Rehnquist stressed that the success of contracts for clandestine operations depended on their absolute opacity even to the eyes of the judiciary. Reporting on the case for the *Washington Post*, Charles Lane observed that the Supreme Court's decision in *Tenet v. Doe* "confirmed the latitude that intelligence agencies have traditionally claimed to recruit foreign agents beyond the normal margins of the law" (2005, A3).

Although the case was not itself spurred by the events of September 11, 2001, the outcome in *Tenet v. Doe* readily conformed to the striking changes of the past quarter century in the relationship between the American people and their government, and in government's operational practices. These changes have sharply accelerated in the wake of the terrorist attacks. Of particular significance is the increased flux and change in the contours of public control and accountability in the exercise of administrative power brought on not by a *brave* new world, but a *fearful and anxious* new world of public preoccupation with cost, complexity, and governability, but most of all external threats. The American people seem to have passed through the looking glass into a world in which they have embraced virtually unconstrained executive power at the expense of their long-run preference for power modulated by deliberation over the expression and achievement of shared purposes.

The changes and their consequences have been especially acute in connection with entities, like spy and surveillance agencies, that exercise administrative power "beyond the normal margins of the law." Just how much operational autonomy within this realm of legal and political ambiguity can liberal-democratic states allow and still maintain something reasonably resembling public influence and political accountability? Is there any guidance we can gather from ideas out of the past that may help us cope with the extraordinary demands and challenges of exercising administrative power while sustaining self-government in an age of seemingly un-paralleled turmoil, danger, and uncertainty?

In his most expansive conceptions of public administration in a modern constitutional democracy, Woodrow Wilson characterized the work of administrative agencies as strongly anchored to the law, but extending into areas beyond where the law could formally reach. Administration, in Wilson's view, was thus not just subject to the law; it was also a "constant source" of public law. The consequence was that administration had a formative influence on the law, on political institutions, and ultimately on the polity. Wilson recognized that this reality posed a significant legitimacy challenge in a political regime based on popular control and governance through representative institutions. He argued that the dominance of questions about how administrative power should be deployed required careful attention to and adjustments in the theory, structure, and practice of politics and administration in the United States.

This book offers an interpretive synthesis of Wilson's ideas, and his practices in juxtaposition to his ideas, that together defined his endeavor to successfully harmonize modern democratic rule and modern administrative practice within the peculiar confines of the American system of government and politics. The book also brings forward the substance of that synthesis to show the continued relevance and present consequences of Wilson's ideas and practices for public management and governance in what appears to be an era of social, economic, and political transformation on par with Wilson's own.

As scholar and practitioner, Woodrow Wilson was centrally concerned with the effective and responsible wielding of administrative power. He pursued this concern by developing ideas and practices aimed at organizational, institutional, and political integration that would stimulate and reinforce the development of national political habits and aspirations well-anchored in the bedrock of core political principles. His designs for securing the legitimacy of modern administrative power, especially its operation beyond the normal margins of the law and the formative effects that resulted, centered on statesmanship, especially the binding link between policy design and administrative execution that political leadership would provide. In Wilson's view, separated powers and checks and balances did not ensure that political authority wielded administrative power effectively and responsibly. Such mechanistic arrangements produced mostly fragmentation and conflict, exacerbating already-existing tendencies in the regime. The long-run survival and prosperity of the regime required, instead, political cooperation and synthesis, and institutional integration into an organic whole, all under the guidance of national leaders concerned with national purpose and national greatness.

Yet another book in which Wilson's ideas, rhetoric, and actions figure prominently is likely to struggle mightily for light in the thicket of previous scholarly and popular treatments. Indeed, it is nearly impossible to conduct research and write about Wilson's political thought and public actions without traversing ground already covered by many scholars. I nevertheless believe this book adds a distinctive interpretation of Wilson's scholarship and practice to the rich vein of material on his thought, speech, and public action and its relevance to democratic governance. First and foremost, I contend that the standard representation of Wilson's core ideas about public administration and its relationship to democratic rule is at best accurate in only a superficial sense. It misses the nuances, reservations, and complex progression in Wilson's thinking and action evident across his scholarship, public lecturing, political rhetoric, and presidential decision making. What I try to deliver, specifically with respect to the nexus between democracy and administration, is a detailed and comprehensive analysis and interpretation of Wilson's ideas as manifested in his scholarly writing and lecturing, public rhetoric, and political action.

Furthermore, I argue that as a subject of both empirical investigation and normative argument, administration was much more central to the development of Wilson's political thought than most past and current scholarship has accepted. As president, moreover, Wilson consciously attended to his words and actions about administrative matters, and thus he laid down key conceptual and institutional foundations that remain remarkably consistent with the theory and practice of public management in a modern democratic polity prominent in the United States today. Both scholarly inattention and subsequent developments have obscured the links between Wilson's ideas and actions and today's thinking, however. They deserve recovery and reflection as scholars and practitioners continue to grapple with what it means to govern in and manage the affairs of a twenty-first century liberal democracy.

Finally, I contend, this book's effort to link a comprehensive reconsideration of Wilson's ideas and practices to currently prominent thinking about public management reinforces the importance of maintaining the connection between the practical and immediate matters of administrative structure and managerial technique and broader questions about design requirements and normative principles for a working regime. These are exactly the kinds of questions one finds central to older understandings of what was required for a functional science of politics. This perspective is especially crucial today given the prominence of public management concerns that heavily orient the study and practice of administration in a democracy toward matters of structure and technique, diminishing systemic considerations, especially regarding the effective and responsible exercise of power. But what is public management if not the design and deployment of resources and techniques to harness the power of organization and coordinated effort—the power of administration—in service to the public good? For Woodrow Wilson, questions of structure and technique, institutional and systemic design, and public purpose—questions, that is, of democracy and administration—were inseparable. The answers to these questions had to treat such concerns as centrally relevant to the health of the regime. To understand public administration and management today and continue the work to refine it for a better future for American self-government, we must see it in the context of regime design and the nature of political leadership peculiar to that regime. That is the binding link I seek to illuminate.

"Books are constructed immorally," Woodrow Wilson once observed. "You start out with enough knowledge to write a chapter but as one chapter would not satisfy the publisher you then write all but one chapter borrowed from some other person." This book is the product of a peculiarly solitary scholarly venture. Borrowing from some other persons—many others, in fact—was nevertheless a conspicuous feature of that endeavor.

In the middle of my work on this project, Charles Goodsell, one of the outstanding scholars of public administration of his generation, sent me an inscribed copy of the fourth edition of *The Case for Bureaucracy*. In response, I asked him to provide me with emergency feedback by reading major portions of early drafts of the manuscript in a very short span of time. Good deeds never go unpunished, Charles. Professor

Goodsell's comments and criticisms on the initial chapters, and later on the second half of the manuscript, confirmed my own assessment of the value, and flaws, in my synthesis and interpretation of Wilson's ideas, helping me to keep the project on track at two crucial stages. I am thoroughly in his debt for this assistance. Ken Meier read the entire manuscript, providing a thorough critique that pushed me to reinforce my analysis at critical junctures, especially with respect to Wilson's governing practices. Larry Terry also read the entire manuscript, providing guidance for strengthening connections to current public administration scholarship, and insisting that I take extra care in my portrayal of Wilson's scholarship and practice. I thank both these prominent scholars for their strong support for the publication of this work. Alas, Larry will never read these words of appreciation. His untimely death in June 2006 was a tragic loss for the public administration discipline and for the academy. Kendrick Clements kindly tolerated my entreaties for feedback on several of my arguments as they were in development. He offered valuable insights and learned assistance, much of which, I'm sure he will conclude, I failed to follow.

The reference librarians at Clark University's Goddard Library once again provided me with efficient, expert help in finding vital material, including a lost volume of the Wilson papers. But they also provided opportunities for pleasant, calming conversations before and after the sometimes intense hours of research and writing. I especially thank Mary Hartman for her sense of humor, which helped me to keep an eye on life's bigger picture and defuse the artificial sense of seriousness that often builds up around research and writing projects.

With great pleasure I once again thank Executive Editor Henry Tom for giving me another chance to publish with the Johns Hopkins University Press. I also thank Ken Meier and Larry O'Toole for welcoming the book, when it was only a rough idea, into their series on governance and public management. And they subsequently stuck with that decision even though the book proved not to be, strictly speaking, a work of original empirical research. My thanks also to Martin Schneider for his expert copyediting, which rescued the text from many of my most embarrassing limitations as a writer.

My family, friends, and faculty colleagues were a constant source of support and encouragement. They endured my frequently recurring bouts of crankiness as the project telescoped far beyond the original projected completion date. Although it was not likely to have been evident to them, I especially enjoyed their subtly clever efforts to find out how the project was going without actually asking me directly. I especially thank Tammi Flynn, a very close friend who is also Director of Marketing at the Florence Griswold Museum, for keeping me informed of new discoveries about Woodrow Wilson's visits to Miss Florence's home along the Lieutenant River in Old Lyme, Connecticut, including the museum's acquisition of the rarely seen Wilson portrait that appears as this book's frontispiece. To my loving daughters Meredith and Lauren and my wife Ruth, all I can say is beware; it will not be another ten years before I start on the next one. A special "bravo!" also goes to Lauren for helping me organize and compile the list of references when I desperately wanted to avoid letting another self-imposed deadline slip by. Lauren also helped prepare the final revised manuscript for submission.

A generous sabbatical leave from Clark University, along with income from consulting for ABC News, the U.S. Environmental Protection Agency, and the Kettering Foundation, made a year away from my regular, full-time teaching duties financially feasible. The Harrington endowment in the Government Department at Clark provided support for preparation of the index.

I dedicate this book to two men who exemplify the best qualities of scholarship and practice in public management. The late Gerald Garvey, professor of politics at Princeton University, incorporated some of my earlier scholarship into his courses at the Woodrow Wilson School and gave me a campus tour during a summer visit many years ago. More important, however, he showed me how it was possible to combine hard-nosed scholarship and demanding teaching with generous collegiality. Jerry introduced me to one of his former students, Rob Brenner, principal deputy assistant administrator for air and radiation at the U.S. EPA. Rob gave me numerous opportunities through a year-long IPA and subsequent consultancy to observe and be a part of national air quality policy making and policy management. And I was honored to be able to observe how he embodied the best characteristics of the dedicated public servant, including unwavering integrity, grace under pressure, and unstinting support for the professional and personal development of his staff. To Rob and the many fine professionals who were my colleagues in the Office of Policy Analysis and Review, I can only offer again my sincere thanks for their friendly tolerance of my presence in their midst.

The scholars, practitioners, and others from whom I freely borrowed ideas, named above or remaining unnamed, bear no liability, moral or otherwise, for the flaws and errors of content and construction this book may contain. Unlike some of the most prominent members of the current generation of political and military leaders, I accept full responsibility.

Democracy and Administration

Power and Public Management

Sheldon Wolin begins his rich and stimulating account of Alexis de Tocqueville's political thought with an assessment of the emergence of modernity and the ties between modern political theory and modern power. The proliferation of the volume and forms of power was one distinctive milestone in the birth of modern society. In classical and medieval worldviews, power was finite. Individuals and various social groups contended for this scarce resource so that they could enforce their particular conceptions of the well-ordered society (Wolin 2001, 13). The ascent of western civilization, including advancements in science and technology, in economic organization, and in world exploration, along with the growth of populations energized by new social, economic, and political ideas, brought a shift in perspective "from the acquisition of power to its production." Further, whereas classical political theorists had to contend primarily with the problem of how to preserve and ration power to stave off the chaos of an otherwise uncivilized world, modern political theorists faced the problem of "a growing sense of helplessness amid a world bursting with new forces" (15). The challenge was to bring the profusion of powers into harness. "The modern project was not to renounce the commitment to increasing power but to find a saving formula whereby it could be rendered ever more predictable, ever more obedient" (18). That project of modern theorists involved hierarchical organization and extensive administrative arrangements dedicated to the "pursuit of truth" under centralized direction and control (26). This in turn defined the lives of individuals in modern society around their roles "as workers, employees, administered beings, and occasional citizens" (30).

In Wolin's view, the project of modernity—of modern theorists—was to expunge "the political" from society. Many and diverse individuals politically engaged meant that power would be uncontrolled and fragmented, and conflict rampant. The aim of developing politically thoughtful, politically mature *citizens* could in the end only undermine good social order. Wolin thus depicts a developmental dynamic for human society in which individuals first lived in subjugation to the singular power held by a family, clan, or absolute monarch. Then, in the modern age, with power multiple and abundant, the lives of individuals became defined by the influence of multitudinous powers consolidated in the hands of a central state and its similarly centralized and bureaucratized appendages of economy and technology—principally the corporation and the university—which were meant to ensure the continuous generation of power as nearly an end in itself. This is a tale told best by Karl Marx. Yet even Marx "envisaged . . . a system for exploiting the power potentialities of modern science and industry, a system that held a promise of the continuous reproduction of power" (18).

Wolin's biography of Tocqueville is built on his well-established concern for the waning prospects that modern society will choose an alternative path to a demonstrably more democratic, more participatory, more *political* future. His emphasis is on Tocqueville's titanic and ultimately failed struggle against central elements of the modernity project. Tocqueville sought to preserve valuable vestiges of "the classical notion of culture as shared and publicly accessible, a preparation for participation in the polity, and hence inseparable from civic life" (29) and to reconcile them with the reality that modernity, including the rise of the idea of mass democracy, had forever changed the world. Without such a theoretical reconciliation, however, the great mass of the people would find no collective pathway to control of hierarchical power but would instead remain subjugated to it in their multiple, fragmented roles requiring only occasional citizenship. Through the lens of Tocqueville's theoretical journey, Wolin thus sends us a clear warning that our identity as politically self-aware beings, energetically engaged in self-rule and the shaping of our collective future prospects, is rapidly vanishing from common experience.

WOODROW WILSON'S MODERNITY PROJECT

In his second book, *The State,* based to a considerable extent on his first set of lectures on administration, Woodrow Wilson offered his own rendition of the drama related by Wolin. In Wilson's version, the first act had much the same plot. Families, clans, and tribes were part of the developmental ascent of human civilization to nation-states, with individuals merely subjects serving the state as embodied by absolutist monarchs. Wilson's second act introduced a striking twist, however. He recounted what he called the "modern de-socialization" of the state (Wilson 1890, 645–46). The relationship between the state and the individual had turned upside down, such that " 'The individual for the State' had been reversed and made to read, 'The State for the individual' " (Wilson 1890, 646; see also Link et al. 1968, 5:688). The result was the emergence of "new ideas as to what constitutes social convenience and advancement." In adopting many such ideas, the modern state's aim was "to aid the individual to the fullest and best possible realization of his individuality, instead of merely to the full realization of his *sociality*. Its plan is to create the best and fairest opportunities for the individual; and it has discovered that the way to do this is by no means itself to undertake the administration of the individual by old-time futile methods of guardianship" (Wilson 1890, 646–47, emphasis in original).

Wilson saw the modern state as marshalling power to minister to society in accord with new "standards of *convenience* or *expediency*" (Link et al. 1968, 5:671, emphasis in original; see Wilson 1890, 638). But what was the nature of this modern power? Wilson was at best evasive on the question. Nearly two decades later, however, writing on "Education and Democracy" (see Link et al. 1974, 17:131–36), Wilson described three primary modern powers: science, or more precisely "exact science applied"; economic enterprise and the drive for competition and profit; and administration, the "coordination of organizations" in both the private and public spheres (Thorsen 1988, 176). These modern powers were progressive in the sense that they facilitated adjustments to changing conditions, but the social progress they motivated, especially the first two powers, was generally "the expression of anarchy and selfishness" (179). Administration was already bringing them under some discipline, for administration was cooperation and coordination; Wilson contended that cooperation "is the law of all action in the modern world" (Link et al. 1974, 17:135). But to integrate the three powers fully in order to constitute harmonious and cooperative national, and eventually international, progress required "the growth of a fourth power, the power of leadership" (Thorsen 1988, 179).

From the earliest steps in the progression of his political thought, Wilson had accepted the reality of a modern world of new conditions and flux in the fortunes of men, "a kinetic society, a sociogram of forces of unprecedented weight and extent, actual and latent, thrusting ceaselessly, colliding and absorbing, but always transforming and being transformed," as Wolin has described it (2001, 14). In the further development of this thinking, Wilson conceived an evolutionary ascent for democratic states characterized by the accumulation of habits and character over a long period but also the need for adaptation and adjustment to changing conditions. Such adjustments and adaptations brought with them the accumulation of social and political experience that was the basis of law. Modernity brought an unprecedented acceleration in this dynamic, with increasing demands and pressures on individuals from such forces as technological advancements, the development of large and dominating economic entities, burgeoning international migration, and rapid urbanization. Simultaneous with the very first vestiges of modernity's arrival came the embrace of the idea of mass democracy and the eventual expectation of most peoples around the world that they would have some hand in determining how society would respond to modern conditions and thus how their lives would be shaped. In the United States, the Civil War was a clear marker for the beginning of the effects of modernity. The war's end and subsequent territorial development had also brought with them the distinctive growth of an increasingly strong American nationalism and, with the completion of the settlement of western lands, the turn toward global engagement.

For Wilson, the integration and coordination of modern powers was an enterprise of creation and innovation. Such "governing power" (Thorsen 1988, 65)—what Wilson thought was the proper understanding of the meaning of sovereignty—belonged in the hands of political leaders. In his 1891 lecture on sovereignty, Wilson distinguished between power and control in the nature of democratic rule. Sovereignty "is the highest political power of a State lodged in active organs of the State for purposes of governing. Power is a positive thing; control, a negative thing. Power belongs to government, is lodged in governing organs; control belongs to the community, is lodged with the people" (Link et al. 1969, 7:339). This control concerned, of course, the selection of political leaders and by dint of that the ability to say no, at least on occasion, and thus the capacity to constrain the innovations of leaders.

In Wilson's view, then, the self-government expected by peoples experiencing modernity, especially the citizens of the United States, could not be the democracy of the local mass meeting, could not direct decisions on policy. This would be impossible at the national level for national purposes, for national greatness. Instead, modern mass democracy at the level of the nation would have to be, indeed already was, virtual. Citizens participated through thought and discussion. Political leaders stood at the center (Thorsen 1988, 62), interpreting the thought and discussion of the people, finding in or drawing out of the diverse and sometimes conflicting views a common opinion and community will. On the basis of this public opinion formed, leaders took initiative and action, to which citizens gave their active support, or at least their assent. Sometimes they expressed their dissent in the selection of others to lead.

Wilson's normative understanding of the nature of modern democracy was complex, with subtle shifts and modifications over time. But two dominant threads are evident, one political, the other social. The political one was that democracy involved the choice of leaders by citizens, which implied scrutiny and discussion of the initiatives and actions of political leaders. The social one was the absence of privilege or division into status groupings or social classes. Echoing Tocqueville, Wilson referred to this as "equality of conditions" (see Link et al. 1974, 17:81). The two threads were intertwined, for Wilson argued that one of the most distinctive features of democracy was that the reservoir of potential leaders was the society as a whole, rather than limited pools based on wealth, class status, or privilege. Those with the requisite talents and abilities would rise above their fellow citizens and be selected to lead and exercise power. This was true even in administration, under a system of merit selection; indeed, for Wilson it was important to argue that it was *especially* true in administration, which under modern conditions would be increasingly dominated by technical specialists. Merit selection thus was consistent with modern tenets of democratic representation.

For Wilson the prospect of a democratic future of increasing organization, centralization, and limited, virtual, participatory rule was positive, not negative. It was the only possible road to an appropriately modern form of political democracy at a national, and eventually international, level. It was the only possible link to and means of citizen engagement in the creation and exercise of national power and the only recognizable form of national self-government that could be preserved in the modern world. The exercise of power, or more precisely the creative coordination of modern powers by government, was safely democratic because the state was oriented toward social convenience and advancement with the individual's development in mind, because leaders came not from a special ruling class but from the people, and because statesmen could not devise and undertake actions beyond what popular thought was prepared to accept.

A particularly distinctive component of Wilson's stance on modern democratic rule was that most of the matters toward which citizen thought, discussion, and scrutiny would be directed were primarily administrative. They concerned the principles and purposes underlying national policy plans and the organization and execution of those plans. Questions concerning how the polity would be constituted had largely been settled, although the shift in national politics to an administrative center was itself an important, and necessary, reconstitution of the regime. It was a systemic reorientation that Wilson sought both to raise awareness of and to champion and guide to its proper realization.

In Wilson's view, administrative power was the central focus of modern, integrative democratic statesmanship because administration was at the center of modern democratic politics. In the main, modern democratic politics *was* administration. As a political institution, administration was intimately tied to the dynamic of democratic progress through both its foundations "laid deep in stable principle" (Link et al. 1968, 5:370) as well as its accumulation of experience from the immediate and everyday adjustment to conditions as the "daily and most constant force" (Link et al. 1970, 9:25) of the state. The creative exercise of sovereignty—governing power—would draw on the adjustments and accumulated experience of administration, transform it into changed habits, and codify it in rules, viz., statutes and, ultimately, constitutions (Thorsen 1988, 65). The organizations of administration would carry out the laws in their executive mode, but they would continue to make adjustments in response to conditions—rapidly changing in the modern age—and thus administration had "a life not resident in statutes" and was "indirectly a constant source of public law" (Link et al. 1969, 7:129, 138, emphasis deleted). As Wilson argued in both his lectures on administration and several key speeches during the 1912 presidential election, administration was especially actively engaged in defining and redefining the terms of the engagement between public and private, arguably the very essence of modern liberal democracy (Elkin 1985).

One might conclude that Wilson belongs in the pantheon of minor theorists of the modernity project. He sought to facilitate in theory *and* in practice the establishment of a modern administrative state within the American polity, which in many ways was the last democratic holdout on earth against the intrusions of modern powers and the transformation of social life into an administered existence. Yet one might also conclude that, like Tocqueville, Wilson sought to preserve some vestiges of the truly political in American culture and tradition (see, for example, Seidelman 1985, 40–44). His political thought, at least in its early to middle stages, was well anchored in Tocqueville and especially Burke, who was "a historical witness to the enduring power of traditionalism in politics" (Thorsen 1988, 37). Despite Wilson's "enduring bias against localism and sectionalism in almost any conceivable form" (180), he worked to preserve party government and the accompanying congressional prerogatives in a system of national leadership oriented principally toward the exercise of administrative power. Such effort much chagrined progressives who defined national, integrative leadership as incompatible with party leadership and as the province of the executive. It was, however, the success of democracy under modern conditions through national integration and political synthesis that was Wilson's chief concern. As he argued in *Constitutional Government in the United States*, his last major work of scholarship, "synthesis, not antagonism, is the whole art of government, the whole art of power" (Wilson 1908, 106; see also Thorsen 1988, 16).

Power is thus an appropriate theme for assessing and interpreting Wilson's ideas about democracy and administration. His modernity project was centered on getting the American polity to recognize, accept, and harness administrative power and to define its proper sphere in a democratic regime facing the pressures, fluxes, and transformations of the new age. This was, at least from Wilson's perspective, a project of progress and transformation of the political, not its exorcism. The centering of political thought and political action on administration and the positioning of the people outside the sphere of immediate and day-to-day initiative and action in governing was in Wilson's analysis the inexorable outcome of the evolution of the modern democratic state. Although there might be many practices of businesslike efficiency universally applicable across regimes, matters of social convenience and advancement—even the associated organizational arrangements and administrative practices—were fundamentally of a political nature and regime-specific. The enterprise was not just a matter of insuring the "democratic accountability" of government bureaucracy in the rather reductionist sense that seems to dominate current political thinking and practice. Political leadership would link administrative expertise, political habits and traditions, public thought, and political experience in a grand, creative synthesis that would fortify and enrich democracy—make it *more* democratic—in the only way possible under the conditions of modernity.

In all this one may find a very compelling way of understanding Wilson's forty-year project of scholarship, public rhetoric, and national and international statesmanship. But what of its relevance to modern public management?

PUBLIC MANAGEMENT AND MODERN POWER

Public management as currently conceived by many scholars and practitioners is the heir to Norton Long's effort to focus administrative theory and practice on matters of power (see Kettl 2002, 79). Long argued that "power is only one of the considerations that must be weighed in administration, but of all it is the most overlooked in theory and the most dangerous to overlook in practice" (1949, 257). Long principally focused on the deployment of power in practice, and his was a modern power orientation in Wolin's sense of the term. Long wanted theorists and practitioners to attend to the power production problem—how administrators could generate an adequate amount of power that would allow them to put public policies into effect. Administrators could not rely for their power solely on the authority granted by Congress and the president in statutes and executive orders or on the power inherent in the bureaucratic structure of hierarchy and command. In order to advance the missions of their agencies, administrators had to produce power by devising strategies, creating alliances, and neutralizing opposition.

This way of thinking about, and acting toward, public administration and management has become the principal focus of the executive management orientation in the study and practice of public management (see, for example, Heymann 1987). Its special focus is high-level political appointees. But Long made no distinction between high-level, politically appointed executives and career middle managers in his advocacy of a power orientation toward practice. Career executives and managers also had to be concerned with the matter of producing enough power to effect policy change and realize public outcomes. In an important sense, Long's orientation bridged what subsequently became something of a bifurcation in the field of public management. The currently dominant conceptualization of the field of public management in both study and practice thus can be said to combine the executive management focus on strategies and tactics aimed at advancing agency missions with the mantra of performance that places the onus for the measurement and demonstration of results on middle managers (see Rainey 1990; Brudney, O'Toole, and Rainey 2000, 4–6; Behn 2001, 23–27; but also see Maynard-Moody and Musheno 2003).

Public management thus consists of public executives and managers employing "judgment or discretion" (Lynn 2000, 15) in the design and deployment of organizational, fiscal, financial, budgetary, analytical, and human capital resources and techniques. Together the actions of executives and managers constitute the harnessing of what Wilson called the power of organization and coordinated effort—the power of administration. Indeed, in modern public management, especially under the auspices of the "New Public Management," public executives and managers attempt to harness Wilson's other modern powers—exact science applied, economic enterprise —in their efforts. But to what end is all this directed?

Presumably the "public" in public management refers to public purposes or the public good. On this basis, even individuals running purely private entities are public managers if they are engaged in pursuing a public purpose (see, for example, Behn 1997, 3–8). One might regard executives and managers of even the most private of entities—profit-making enterprises—as *public* managers because they produce goods or services people enjoy and value, and the wealth they generate directly improves the lives of those associated with their enterprises and thus indirectly improves the lives of their communities and even society at large. Many of the largest and most influential for-profit enterprises fall into a public classification—joint-stock companies are *public* corporations, chartered by state governments, and their directors have obligations to both the company owners and the relevant public authorities. More important, it was almost standard doctrine of both the populist and progressive eras that publicly chartered corporations had to operate, and have their behavior evaluated, with an eye toward the public interest. Wilson pressed this view quite strenuously, as when he envisioned in his 1910 American Political Science Association presidential address an era combining the statesmanship of thought and of action, in which "even corporations may seem instrumentalities, not objects in themselves, and the means may presently appear whereby they may be made the servants, not the masters, of the people" (Link et al. 1976, 22:271–72).

The academic literature on public management includes an extensive debate over what the differences between public and private management are, and whether they are really meaningful (see, for example, the brief treatment in Rainey 1990, 160, 161–62). Getting caught up in that debate would be counterproductive, however. It is more useful to consider the matter of public versus private management from the perspective of the exercise of power. From this we can begin to see the value of a comprehensive reconsideration and reinterpretation of Wilson's ideas as part of the continued development, especially in the United States, of scholarly and practitioner thinking about public management.

Both private, corporate managers and public managers (including those in not-for-profit entities) wield administrative power. In many instances, they wield that power for public purposes. For public managers, the public purposes for which they wield administrative power are always in contention. The public purposes for which private managers exercise administrative power also may be in contention, but that is a secondary matter because the public purposes they may be pursuing are tangential to the primary objective: making money for the owners of the organization. (This assumption about the profit motive as the prime driver of managerial behavior in firms has been the subject of significant scholarly challenges in the law and economics literature; see Malloy 2002.) This primary purpose for which private, corporate managers wield administrative power is never in contention in a liberal democracy—a political economy combining a market economy with a democratic state. Thus one distinction between public and private managers is the much greater extent of the very *public* political contention over the purposes for which public managers employ administrative power. It is a permanent feature of their operating environment, well captured by Rainey's characterization of a focus on "the purposeful, effective behaviors of public administrators discharging managerial functions in a political environment" (1990, 173–74). Here "political" clearly means conflict and contention over public goals, particularly among competing interests (see Wilson 1989).

As Norton Long insisted his readers acknowledge about a strategic, power-oriented approach to the practice of administration (and the *theory* of that practice), however, "attempts to solve administrative problems in isolation from the structure of power and purpose in the polity are bound to prove illusory" (1949, 264). This is the crucial distinction between private and public management that another look at Woodrow Wilson helps to reveal. The distinction consequently makes at least the initial case that a careful, detailed interpretation and assessment of Wilson's ideas can add to the continued development of public management thought and practice.

An executive or manager of a profit-making entity may argue that in the pursuit of wealth creation and the delivery of goods or services that people want and value, she is contributing to a broad, vital public purpose: maintaining economic vitality and the foundations of prosperity that reinforce citizen commitment to the regime, thus preserving its order and integrity. One might even argue that the efforts of private executives and managers go beyond even such significant instrumental values and effects. The efforts of some private executives and managers, some inadvertently, others intentionally, may have formative effects on the regime; they may alter some constituent elements or characteristics of social and political life. For public managers, however, the fusion of the instrumental and the constitutive is not just inadvertent or occasional, it is central, frequent, and permanent. Not only must public managers wield administrative power in service to political purposes that are always in contention, they wield that power in ways that raise questions and seek answers about what administrative power is, what public purposes are and should be, and how people's lives—their individual and group interrelationships, their interactions with social and political institutions—will be altered by those purposes and the strategies and methods used to try to achieve them. Public managers not only engage in the task of considering and reconsidering public purposes, they also consider what *public* means, and what the relationship between public and private is and should be.

This fusion of the instrumental and the constitutive most distinguishes public management. It is the struggle of public executives and managers, and front-line workers as well, to negotiate a careful and conscious recognition of the constitutive as they work to generate and deploy administrative power in pursuit of contested public purposes. The time and energy of public managers will always be devoted primarily to the strategies and tactics—as well as the demonstrations of results—that are the keys to the efficient, competent, and responsible realization of public purposes. It is what thoughtful citizens and their elected representatives generally regard as good governance. But public managers ignore the constitutive effects, the meaning of what they do for the constitution of the public and private life of the regime, at their peril and the peril of the citizens and polity they have pledged to serve. It is from this perspective that the value of attention to Wilson's ideas becomes especially clear.

Woodrow Wilson was very careful to give primary emphasis to the instrumental facet of administration as a form of power, a kind of politics, and a distinct political institution. Americans have always regarded administration as primarily an instrument of political power and the public will, and in many ways that is appropriate (Cook

1996). Yet Wilson found himself compelled to illuminate the regime-reconstituting dimension of administration. He had several prominent ideas to offer regarding organizational design and good methods of practice in governmental administration and management. But these ideas were anchored in a concern for the nature of a modern democratic regime, the United States in particular, and the legitimate place for modern managerial methods and practices in that regime. He was concerned for administration in the context of "the structure of power and purpose in the polity," that is, he sought to understand, and to promote a broader appreciation of, the appropriate place and practice of administration in a modern liberal democracy.

Within the core functions Wilson designated for administration, he saw a constitutive force or, more accurately, a *reconstitutive* force. The core functions included not just the execution of the law but also the observation of and interaction with changing societal conditions, the day-to-day necessity of responding to those conditions and changing them through public action, and the accumulation of experience from daily action that goes into the making and remaking of laws and constitutions. Because this constitutive effect particularly concerned the line between public and private, and thus involved liberty, the wielding of administrative power in the modern democracy that was the United States required a special legitimation effort. Wilson ultimately anchored this effort in his concept of the regime-integrating power of political leadership.

Not only Wilson's ideas but also his efforts and struggles once he attained a position of national political leadership are thus instructive in considering how his thinking reflects on and can advance both theory and practice in public management. An integrated exploration of Wilson's thought *and* practice concerning administrative power in a modern democracy supplies something heretofore unavailable: a public management perspective on Woodrow Wilson—and a Woodrow Wilson perspective on modern public management.

STRUCTURE OF THE ANALYSIS

Much consistency, and even repetition, is evident in Wilson's articulation of his ideas. Yet not all of his ideas about democracy and administration emerged early in his scholarly career, to receive only further embellishment and reinforcement later on. Wilson's thinking underwent recognizable developmental advances, including some conceptual dead ends. His best-known published works—*Congressional Government*, "The Study of Administration," *The State*, and *Constitutional Government* —mark key advances. Yet some of his most significant thinking emerged in his less-known published work, especially many short essays for an informed and politically attentive general readership in such vehicles as the *Atlantic Monthly*, and perhaps even more so in his many classroom lectures, public talks, and political speeches, all of which reflect even more firmly a consistent body of thought subject to constant refinement.

My interpretation of Wilson's ideas and practices hews to the rough chronology that reflects the arc of Wilson's scholarly and political career. Nevertheless, I attempt some synthesis, bringing together the ideas he developed across the several decades of his scholarship and incorporating what I see as notable further insights he achieved in his political campaign rhetoric and in his service as governor and president. I also subject Wilson's ideas to considerable stretching, tugging, compacting, and rearranging—smoothing over or even ignoring a number of contradictions, misdirections, and incongruities that scholars may find in Wilson's published papers—to tie together his ideas in at least an approximation of a logically consistent whole. I make no claims for anything approaching perfect consistency, however; there is much fodder in these pages and in the Wilson papers themselves for further scholarly analysis and debate.

My core argument is that administration was at the center of Wilson's attention from almost the very beginning of his concern for politics and political reform and for much of his scholarly and political career thereafter. Wilson saw a regime transformation already under way, first through his attention to the aftereffects of the Civil War, especially a nascent nationalism, and further in connection with the understanding he developed about the nature of the evolution of modern democratic states. Wilson viewed the regime transformation the United States was experiencing as a reflection of the forces of modernity. Democracy had to adapt to a new set of societal conditions, including considerable social and economic flux, which brought with them a new political reality dominated by administrative matters and the need to harness administrative power to cope with and, if necessary, alter those conditions. Wilson sought to guide and legitimate the transformation through the development of new political leadership theory and practice. This new kind of political leader of a modern democracy would be concerned primarily with ensuring good administration and management through the adoption and legitimation of new administrative structures and practices and, more generally, through the integration of lawmaking and execution.

In addition to developing and promoting new leadership concepts, arrangements, and practices, Wilson saw it as his particular task to develop and promote the key administrative structure and practice concepts that could be adopted to improve public administration and management and, more important, the ideas and arguments about the proper place and function of administration in a modern democracy. The new leaders would need to adopt and convey to citizens both the ideas and the practices necessary to cement the regime transition's success for the long term under the harsh conditions of modernity on a national and international scale.

After developing my interpretation of Wilson's ideas, I consider what he did upon assuming a position of political leadership himself. He attempted to follow many of his ideas and arguments about leadership and administrative legitimacy and practice, most certainly in his rhetoric but in his actions as well. In doing so, he ran into some insurmountable difficulties, which reveal much about both Wilson's own thinking and some of the long-standing challenges of democratic governance and public management. Through my effort to bring Wilson's ideas and his ideas vis-à-vis his practices to bear on public management studies and practices today, I try to reveal many of the insights and struggles evident just below the surface of Wilson's work. My broad reconsideration of his ideas thus can be the launch pad for further thought and action in the continuing effort to improve the management of the people's business and the further refinement of self-government in the United States and around the globe.

In unfolding the details of my analysis, I have divided the presentation into three parts. In part 1, I attempt a survey and interpretive synthesis of Wilson's ideas about democracy and administration. I begin, in chapter 1, by looking at the core elements of his critique of the separation of powers and his promotion of a "cabinet government" arrangement resting on the principle of "ministerial responsibility." Wilson's attack on the separation of powers doctrine was not an assault on this principle of governmental design in and of itself but rather an attempt to remove it as an obstacle to the emergence of new political leadership made necessary by the growing pressures of modern conditions that had to be confronted at the level of the nation. Thus, I interpret Wilson's initial analysis and critique as a call for the creation and nurturing of a new kind of public executive in the American regime, a new, centrally situated set of political leaders who would overcome the fragmentation and parochialism of American constitutional design and political practice by overseeing both policy formulation and policy management. In particular, these new public executives were to instruct the public about administration and to stimulate public scrutiny and criticism of public measures while at the same time keeping public opinion at arm's length from execution, especially where it involved the most purely "businesslike" activities of public management.

In this first major stage of his work, Wilson did not really come to grips with the normative implications of an administrative state, taking the central importance of administration as a given and needing only sufficient articulation and emphasis to justify either constitutional reforms or substantial alterations in established patterns of governing practice that would ensure the more effective and more responsible use of national administrative power. Wilson's permanent conviction that transformations in the institutional design and patterns of practice of modern American democracy were necessary clearly took root in this first major effort, yet his ideas about the nature of modern democracy and the proper place and legitimate and necessary practices of administration and management had only begun to germinate.

All modern public management theory and practice, at least in democratic nations, assumes a stable, settled conception of democracy in its political and social dimensions. Rarely, however, do scholars or practitioners scrutinize these assumptions. During the prolonged and chaotic birth of the American administrative state, Wilson did not have the same luxury. He took it as his task to understand the historical, philosophical, and developmental underpinnings of modern democracy and to develop a new conception, borrowed heavily from German organicism, that would be suitable for guiding the development, legitimation, and design of sound structures and practices of public administration and management under the strenuous conditions of modernity. In chapter 2, I delineate what I have found to be the central tenets of Wilson's democratic theory. The central importance Wilson placed on leadership was clearly an outgrowth of his *Congressional Government* analysis, but he subjected his ideas in this regard to much more extensive examination and development. The other major ideas in his thinking about democracy were primarily outgrowths of the purposeful effort Wilson undertook to understand the historical origins and modern character of the democratic state that followed the publication of his first book. This was largely the result of following backwards the logic of what he needed to know in order to pursue his principal objective: developing and promoting an understanding of the nature, legitimacy, and necessary structures and practices of public administration and management that political leaders needed to guide the adjustment and adaptation of American democracy to a new age.

In chapter 3 I present in detail Wilson's ideas about the nature, proper roles, and functions of administration in a modern democracy. Wilson's mature understanding went far beyond a simple instrumental notion of administration's role in the regime to reach a recognition, although not stated in quite this way, of administration's constitutive qualities. Wilson's promotion of administration as the central form of political power in a newly emerging American regime, which expanded administration's functions and roles in that regime far beyond traditional conceptions, thus posed a considerable legitimacy challenge. Thus, part of Wilson's endeavor with respect to studying administration involved making the case for its legitimacy. This he grounded in his democratic theory, particularly the organic-developmental nature of the modern democratic state and the central importance of political leadership. I include in my examination of Wilson's ideas on administration's roles and functions a review and interpretation of his thinking regarding the separation of politics and administration and the special role of and limitations on technical expertise.

In chapter 4, I present Wilson's ideas about institutional and organizational structure, policy design, and managerial practice. Wilson did not write and lecture on these matters as extensively as he did on administration's regime roles, functions, and legitimacy, but he promoted several primary ideas that rarely show up in treatments of his thinking in the public administration literature. Wilson addressed matters of hierarchy and command, centralization versus decentralization, autonomy and discretion, and responsibility and accountability, including the requirements of statutory design to increase the likelihood that public managers and front-line workers will use their discretion responsibly. Wilson's treatment of these matters was at times simplistic and moralistic, but that in itself does not make his ideas unworthy of closer consideration, and in fact they raise significant questions relevant to the concerns of public management today. Of particular note are Wilson's ideas about the structure and systemic function of cities and the need for administrative integration on a national scale.

The edifice of theories and practices associated with current public management thinking has at its core a rejection of the designs and practices for the administrative state that came to prominence in the middle of the twentieth century. Many scholars and practitioners now reject this once-dominant model as outmoded and counterproductive. They thus reject with it the Wilsonian ideas they see resting at its foundation. The representation of Wilson's ideas in the literature of this new thinking is largely the repetition of half-truths about and misperceptions of Wilson's ideas, aims, and practices long extant in the public administration literature more generally, reflecting both limited access to a more representative sample of Wilson's published and unpublished work and an insufficiently careful consideration of what Wilson actually said and did. I attempt to remedy this inadequate treatment of Wilson's ideas about administrative design and practice in parts 2 and 3. Proponents of the new thinking and practice in public management may still reject what they find, but at least they will have a broader foundation on which to base their rejection.

In chapters 5 and 6 I carry my consideration of Wilson's ideas about administration's systemic roles, functions, designs, and practices forward to an assessment and interpretation of his actions in political service. Although Wilson remains highly rated in periodic assessments of the presidents by American historians, and although he is widely recognized for several major domestic policy triumphs and the deft diplomacy he exercised during and immediately after World War I (an assessment that includes one obvious devastating political defeat), he has not fared as well in scholarly assessments of his administrative and managerial practices, whether as governor of New Jersey or as president. Scholars have criticized his lack of sustained support of and attention to his plans for administrative reform, his failure to adhere closely enough to civil service reform principles in his administrative appointments, his inconsistent relations with members of his cabinet regarding delegation of policy authority, and, most damning of all, his nearly disastrous lack of adequate organization and execution of plans for war mobilization. Overall, in the view of several scholars, Wilson failed to serve adequately as midwife to the birth of the American administrative state, leaving the nation incapable of coping with the demands of a modern world.

I look at what Wilson said and did, primarily as president, with respect to matters of administration and management, specifically in the areas of relations with his cabinet, regulation of the economy, and war mobilization. I find considerable consistency with the ideas he articulated before entering public service. More important, his struggles with and departures from his established thinking, when confronted with the considerable and often unpredictable demands of governing, reveal a great deal about his ideas and practices as they relate to the ongoing challenges of democratic public management in a postindustrial social, economic, and political order. The shifts in his thinking about political leadership and its importance for integrating and legitimating modern administrative power and the practical problems these shifts created for Wilson and his successors are at the heart of the conclusions I draw from my analysis of Wilson's governance.

In chapters 7 and 8, I address the significant challenges for public management today that are a result of the effects of Wilson's ideas and practices, which can be seen in sharper relief in the light of the analysis I have offered. I consider the recent scholarly treatment of Wilson's ideas and the identification of intellectual crises for which scholars have held Wilson at least partially responsible. I argue that these treatments are in significant respects mistaken. I attempt to show that some of the distinctive features of the bold new thinking about public management as a new kind of governance have identifiable antecedents in Wilson's ideas and governing practices and that the emphasis on public management today can itself be traced back to Wilson. This developmental legacy reveals that Wilson's central project—securing the integration and legitimation of modern administrative structures and techniques through political leadership—remains to be completed. It remains critical because, consistent with Wilson's most profound insight, public administration can influence the very constitution of a liberal-democratic polity.

I explore in some detail which national governmental institutions might serve as the appropriate home for the cultivation of the statesmanship Wilson envisioned, including the possibility that it might arise from within public administration and management itself. I argue, however, that the leadership public administration and management needs to cement its legitimate place in the regime must arise from the national legislature. I examine what changes in Congress are necessary so that this national political leadership can emerge. Public administration and management cannot itself provide the integrating, legitimating leadership it needs to secure its place and role in the regime. Thus, I challenge those developing the audacious new ideas about public management as the "new" governance to expand their ambitions to include Congress and its design of legislation. It is only along this path that the ambitious new theories can make a vital contribution to a future polity composed not of administered beings but of fully active citizens and responsible leaders.

PART I

Wilson's Ideas

CHAPTER ONE

Remaking the Public Executive

As his junior year at Princeton was drawing to a close, Woodrow Wilson read "The American Republic" in the *International Review*. Published to coincide with the nation's centennial celebration, the article prompted a biting entry in Wilson's shorthand diary for June 19, 1876. "The American *Republic* will in my opinion never celebrate another Centennial. At least under its present Constitution and laws. Universal suffrage is at the foundation of every evil in this country" (Link et al. 1966, 1:143, emphasis in original). In his entry of July 4, Wilson reiterated the statement about centennials, this time adding, "The English form of government is the only true one" (149).

The very young Wilson's condemnation of universal suffrage would not seem to bode well for his becoming a champion of democracy at home or, later, across the globe. Yet less than two years after recording these acerbic reflections on American politics and government in his diary, Wilson initiated a series of published and unpublished works scrutinizing the separation of powers as the center of weakness within the American constitutional structure and launching the development of his ideas about democracy, including the vital importance of a proper structure for universal suffrage and mass opinion within the regime. In this early work, Wilson proffered a diagnosis of the debilitating effects of the separation of powers on the capacity of American self-government to cope at the national level with the stresses and strains of industrialization, urbanization, and accelerated social change. More important, he promoted structural changes that he insisted would improve both the design and the implementation of national policy through the leadership of a different type of national public official.

At the tender age of twenty-one, Wilson had embarked on an intellectual sojourn through the heart of the scholarship, ideas, and public debates about the nature, purposes, and structural necessities of modern democracy in the United States. It is especially important to recognize that Wilson directed his concern and attention toward administration from nearly the very beginning of his interest in politics and government. Frustrated by what he saw as both the corruption and ineptitude in the workaday operation of American government, he sought alternative arrangements that would not just purify and invigorate American government and politics but would also enable the government to do what he regarded as its most critical function in the years to come, namely, administer its affairs efficiently, nimbly, and justly. Those affairs were already expanding, Wilson observed, and he expected that they would do so at an accelerating pace in response to the emergent forces of modernity and the concomitant growth of a national orientation in American public philosophy.

Although Wilson soon joined the rising chorus of demands for civil service reform, he advanced as his primary alternative a proposal for "cabinet government," an adaptation of British parliamentary arrangements and practices to the American constitutional structure. Wilson pursued his Anglophilic reform agenda with increasing sophistication over the course of a decade. Because his true interest centered on administration and its centrality to the success of democracy in a dynamic new age, however, his reform crusade merely laid the foundation, even if a highly influential one, for his deepest, most intense scholarly work, on the historical development and internal dynamics of the modern, "mature" democratic state and the place and practice of administration therein.

CONSTITUTIONAL REFORM

Wilson first attacked "the entire and almost fatal separation of power and responsibility" of the American system (Link et al. 1966, 1:348) in his unpublished January 1878 essay "Some Thoughts on the Present State of Public Affairs." He condemned the ability of sectional and party interests to use the committee system in Congress for their own purposes, for example, crafting a budget and imposing it on a presidential administration, the consequences for which voters could hold no one responsible. The conduct of vital national affairs, especially those concerning commerce and industry, thus had to be brought out of the shadows of party and committee machinations.

Cultivating national political leadership was central to the treatment Wilson offered for his diagnosis. Wilson thus stressed the importance of ensuring that talented young men could and would devote their careers to politics, increasing the odds in favor of the emergence of true parliamentary leaders. The main barrier to this was party politics, because it used "popular constituencies" and "our peculiar institutions . . . to seize upon the administration of government at the earliest opportunity only that they may win the *spoils*" (351, emphasis in original). But leadership anchored in "avowed principles and opinions which have stood the test of practice" (354) could retrieve popular government from the debasement of a party politics without principle, such that "universal suffrage will prove the blessing it is capable of becoming" (353).

Cabinet Government

By the time he had his Princeton diploma, Wilson had articulated, at least in initial form, two of the three primary components of his critique of American government and politics. He had exposed the separation of powers as the source of the fragmentation and irresponsible use of administrative power, and he had pointed out the critical need to foster national political leadership in a system of legislative dominance. Wilson publicized his ideas for the third component—an institutional restructuring that would both overcome the debilitating effects of the separation of powers and promote truly national political leadership—in "Cabinet Government in the United States," published in the August 1879 *International Review.*

Voters had to recognize, Wilson argued, that the vital question they needed to ask was "What plans of national administration shall we sanction?" He further contended that it was vital to get party platforms to mean something along these lines, rather than being "constructed only to deceive and bewilder." For both to occur, true national leadership and "the intelligent formation of opinion on the part of the nation at large" had to emerge (Link et al. 1966, 1:502). And Wilson argued that both *would* emerge from constitutional changes permitting cabinet government, for two reasons. First, Congress would return to "the main object of a representative assembly, . . . the discussion of public business" (494). This would happen because cabinet government would do away with committee government, in which standing committees oversaw all legislation, particularly "the shaping of the national policy in the several departments of administration" (496). By placing several members of Congress as heads of executive departments while holding their congressional seats, these members could rise during legislative sessions and demand scrutiny of and debate about any legislation affecting the policies and operations of their departments. Second, in the midst of the deliberation and spirited public debate over the merits of legislation, those who could publicly argue their points most effectively and offer the most broadly appealing conceptions of what would best serve the effective administration of national policies would become leaders, helping to guide the legislature

to responsible policies, to instruct public opinion about the choices, and to enunci-
ate a program of national progress. Clear lines of responsibility for the consequences
would be established, for these leaders would be centrally involved in both shaping
policy and carrying it into effect.

Motivating Wilson's attention to the advantages he saw in cabinet government
with respect to leadership, the instruction of public opinion, and responsible government were his concerns about improving governance—specifically policy-making
and implementation—in response to societal developments that were national in
scope and import. Thus, many of the most salutary effects of cabinet government
would come in the form of increased capacity and competence in administration
and, intertwined with that, improved design of the laws. "None can so well judge of
the perfections or imperfections of a law as those who have to administer it" Wilson
argued. Further, "the heads of the departments would also have every opportunity to
defend their administration of the people's affairs against unjust censure or crippling
legislation. Corruption in office would court concealment in vain; vicious trifling
with the administration of public business by irresponsible persons would meet with
a steady and effective check . . . ; wild schemes of legislation would meet with a cold
repulse from ministerial authority" (502).

Enumerating the administrative improvements emanating from the elimination
of backroom congressional meddling in administration, Wilson pointed to "the
increased effectiveness of our now crumbling civil, military, and naval services; for
we should no longer be cursed with tardy, insufficient, and misapplied appropriations" (503). Furthermore, Wilson's formula that cabinet government equaled responsible government, which entailed both government practiced in "the bracing
air of thorough, exhaustive, and open discussions" (495) and accountability for
consequences, figured directly in the behavior of top administrators through the
"principle of ministerial responsibility,—that is, the resignation of the Cabinet upon
defeat of any important part of their plans" (498).

Although it was quite early in the development of his ideas, Wilson had already
established a clear concern for the interplay of public opinion and administration.
Niels Thorsen (1988, 38) has suggested that Wilson saw cabinet government as the
means to cultivate untutored American democracy into the ways of effective government. Wilson's own arguments about improvements in administrative capacity and
performance suggest, however, that he was also concerned with how effective government could ultimately be made consonant with popular thought. Thus he gave
considerable emphasis to the importance of the open discussion and debate of
administrative initiatives in Congress, not only so that leaders of the government

could instruct the public on what was important but also so that members of the public could scrutinize and criticize proposed policy designs and express their collective judgment about administrative plans through their representatives.

Wilson followed up on "Cabinet Government" with an essay, "Congressional Government," completed in October 1879, and "Government by Debate," a book-length manuscript completed in December 1882. Neither of these works reached publication. However, Wilson excerpted and refashioned portions of "Government by Debate" into the essay "Committee or Cabinet Government?" The essay appeared in the *Overland Monthly* in January 1884. Therein he vigorously promoted the notion of linking the executive and the legislature structurally in order to overcome the fragmentation and irresponsibility-inducing effects of the separation of powers. The result would be the clearer definition and distinction of legislative and administrative functions, which would enable a nonpartisan civil service to come fully into effect. More important, marked improvements in the design of statutes and the management of public policy would follow.

By the early 1880s, then, Wilson had already begun to crystallize in his political thought what seemed to him to be a central dilemma of modern democratic governance: how to reconcile the aspirations for self-government and mass popular participation with the reality that the emerging forces of modernity had, in a maturing nation, created a politics dominated by matters of administration. Inspired by the work of Walter Bagehot, Wilson turned to the British parliamentary system as the model of a democratic nation well governed—that is, well administered. In his work leading up to the composition and publication of *Congressional Government*, Wilson was quite impassioned in his call for a variety of constitutional changes that would allow cabinet government to come into operation in the United States. However, as many scholars have noted, and as Wilson himself admitted, *Congressional Government* left out "all advocacy of Cabinet government—all advocacy, indeed, of *any* specific reform" (Link et al. 1967, 4:465, emphasis in original). Nevertheless, "Wilson [did] not give up. *Congressional Government* presents an unrelenting attack on separation of powers that unmistakably favors the cabinet alternative" (Rohr 1984, 34). In the extension and elaboration of his critique of the separation of powers, the standing committee system in Congress it spawned, and the implications for the design and implementation of public policy the book encompassed, Wilson produced what he called a "very much more thorough and more sober" exegesis (Link et al. 1967, 4:465). He also produced a clearer and more complete executive management–oriented analysis supporting his reform agenda. And he signaled the directions in which his ideas about administration and democracy would subsequently develop.

Congressional Government

In the preface to *Congressional Government*, Wilson crisply articulated the analytical contrast he sought: "The most striking contrast in modern politics is not between presidential and monarchical governments, but between Congressional and Parliamentary government. Congressional government is Committee government; Parliamentary government is government by a responsible Cabinet Ministry" (Wilson 1981, 24). More than implicit in this contrast was the core of Wilson's structural critique. A system predicated on a separation of powers promoted the division and fragmentation of governmental authority. As a result, political responsibility was obscured. This in turn fostered the development of institutional arrangements dedicated to keeping political responsibility hidden, namely the standing committee system in Congress and its co-conspirator, the party system. What were the dangers of such arrangements? Certainly, the inability of the voters to make informed electoral choices and to hold officials accountable for their decisions. But the dangers of committee government ultimately stemmed from the ill-informed and often irresponsible control of the kind of political power that was now at the heart of the day-to-day social, economic, and political life of the nation. That power was administration.

Also in the preface, Wilson announced as his chief aim for the book to make "as plain as possible the actual conditions of federal administration." He identified "two principal types" of administration "which present themselves for the instruction of the modern student of the practical in politics: administration by semi-independent executive agents who obey the dictation of a legislature to which they are not responsible, and administration by executive agents who are accredited leaders and accountable servants of a legislature virtually supreme in all things" (Wilson 1981, 24). Wilson employed this analytical dichotomy in his assessment of both the internal structure and operations of Congress and, in turn, its institutional relations in the federal system. He aimed to sort out the administrative and legislative functions under the Constitution as it had actually been operating and to establish the primacy of Congress in the system on a firmer foundation in order to give the peculiarly American brand of national self-government the capacity to cope with the stresses and strains of accelerating industrialization, urbanization, and social change.

Wilson began his effort by signaling that he was engaged in the task of describing the operation of the American constitutional system not in theory but in fact—the reality of how it operated in his time. He characterized the development of the system first in organic terms, a mode of thought and style of expression that would become more prominent in his later work. He referred to government in the United States as "a living and fecund system." The Constitution was its "tap-root" but "only the sap-centre of a system of government vastly larger than the stock from which it has branched" (Wilson 1981, 29). A national identity and a bond between citizens and the national government, "a steady and unmistakable growth of nationality of sentiment" (42), had emerged. The engine was the "principle of implied powers," and states had diminished in influence and consequence as a result. Wilson characterized this transformation principally in administrative terms. "Of course every new province into which Congress has been allured by the principle of implied powers has required for its administration a greater or less enlargement of the national civil service." But the outcome had been "not a foreign but a familiar and domestic government whose officer is your next-door neighbor, whose representatives you deal with every day at the post-office and the custom-house, whose courts sit in your own State, and send their own marshals into your own county to arrest your fellow-townsman" (Wilson 1981, 38–39).

Wilson also assessed to a limited extent the wisdom of this centralization of administration and its effects on the states, in a manner reminiscent of Tocqueville's critique of the "enervating" effects of administrative centralization (Tocqueville 1988, 88). Although questioning the "policy of internal improvements" because of the unequal balance of expenditures and taxation in pork barrel projects, Wilson expressed greater concern for the policy's "moral effects in rendering state administrations less self-reliant and efficient, less prudent and thrifty . . . ; to depending upon the national revenues, rather than upon their own energy and enterprise, for means of developing those resources which it should be the special province of state administration to make available and profitable" (Wilson 1981, 40).

Yet Wilson was, of course, principally concerned with the centralization of power in Congress and thus its control over this newly nationalizing administration. Early on, Congress devised its organizational structure of standing committees and "set itself through these to administer the government." Subsequently it "entered more and more into the details of administration" with its principal vehicle the parceling out of "executive work" and administrative responsibility to the secretaries of the executive departments (49). The secretaries, then, became "no longer simply the counselors of the President" but "integral parts of the machinery of administration," with the effect that Congress had gotten "into the habit of investigating and managing everything." Wilson thus confirmed the historical tendency of Congress "to subject even the details of administration to the constant supervision, and all policy to the watchful supervision, of the Standing Committees" (50).

Wilson admitted that "the enlarged powers of Congress are the fruits . . . of an

immensely increased efficiency of organization, and of the redoubled activity consequent upon the facility of action secured by such organization" (50). Wilson's concern was animated not by "any definite and consistent scheme of conscious usurpation" on the part of Congress, but by "the pressing problems of the present moment
regard[ing] the regulation of our vast systems of commerce and manufacture, the
control of giant corporations, the restraint of monopolies, the perfection of fiscal
arrangements, the facilitating of economic exchanges, and many other like national
concerns" (54). These forces fed "a distinct movement in favor of national control of
all questions of policy which manifestly demand uniformity of treatment and power
of administration" (55).

Wilson saw in the American system of his time serious deficiencies in the capacity
to govern rooted in a strong tradition of localism, which was the source of the power
of the parties and which aggravated the division and fragmentation of authority and
political responsibility inherent in the separation of powers. In case the reader had
not gotten the message about "the conditions of public life in this country" (136) that
Wilson saw as requiring adjustments in the structures and patterns of governance, he
characterized them unequivocally in his chapter on the Senate: "we are left to the
unexciting but none the less capitally important business of every-day peaceful
development and judicious administration to whose execution every nation in its
middle age has to address itself with what sagacity, energy, and prudence it can
command" (141). Wilson developed in the four central chapters of the book his
detailed characterization of the operating conditions and patterns of practice of
government in the House and Senate, especially in their relations with the executive.
He also constructed his case for a revised set of arrangements that would ensure
attention to the "quiet, business-like matters" that had become central to sustaining
the American nation for the long term.

Wilson saw the standing committee system as deficient because the speeches and
debates that took place in the committees, where the legislative action really occurred, were contests of interests, not principles. As such, they would not help
inform public opinion even in cases where the public *was* paying attention. Wilson
insisted that debates could be informative and attractive to public attention only if
they took place before the whole legislative body and involved "pressing question[s]
of administration or of law" (73) in which the positions of power and the influence of
a leader or party were at stake. In short, the system afforded few such opportunities
and provided no consistent leadership that could help the public attentively and
enthusiastically confront the issues of governance that had become so central in this
new administrative age.

A second element in Wilson's case was that the legislature interacted with the administration in only an indirect, haphazard way rather than in the intimate, coordinated manner necessary for good governance. Congress was thus deprived of the "administrative knowledge and training" that would be helpful in the drafting of legislation. Unlike the British houses of Parliament, the U.S. House and Senate were unable to "sit as it were in committee on the management of the public business." As part of such a grand committee on public management, chief administrators would have the opportunity to promote policy designs informed by their administrative experience and to defend their management of existing policy. In an arrangement lacking the interdependence of legislators and administrators, however, policy managers did not have the opportunity to ensure "not only that their policy be defensible, but that it be valiantly defended also" (92).

In the first four chapters of *Congressional Government*, Wilson reiterated the diagnosis of the ills of American national governance that he had developed over the previous seven years. Although he now resisted openly advocating cabinet government, his fully developed diagnosis remained anchored in his argument that cabinet government, or a structural arrangement organized around the concept of "ministerial responsibility," would generate a number of beneficial effects in policy design and policy management. Policy design would improve because first, it would be influenced by the presence and extensive legislative participation of experienced administrators and second, administrative heads would seek to influence legislation to produce policy that could be effectively administered. As a result of these first two effects, public debate would be centered on the pressing public problems the nation faced and what policies and programs would best address them.

In parallel, policy management would be improved because heads of departments would seek to demonstrate their administrative prowess and successes in order to gain or sustain their positions of leadership. Further, the operation of the executive departments would be subject to extensive scrutiny in open public debate, and the legislature would be more effectively organized to exercise its oversight function in a responsible manner. Legislators would, moreover, no longer have the incentive to interfere with the personnel and spending decisions of executive agencies since they could no longer hide such efforts behind the closed doors of standing committee meetings. A nonpartisan civil service could be fully put in place as a result, and department heads would be better able to improve administrative effectiveness as a means of maintaining their positions of power. Finally, policy management would improve because policy would be designed better in the first place and thus more easily administered.

To this point, in his work leading up to the book and in its first four chapters, Wilson had conceived the remaking of the public executive in American national government. These new executives would be ministers in the parliamentary sense, both legislators and administrators, engaging the external environment of their departments by both defending and promoting departmental endeavors, including new ideas for advancing the welfare of the nation. The skills of these new executives would include both public debate and oversight of the work of career department managers. But most significantly, the new executives actually had not just persuasive power but also actual legal authority to shape the larger policy and political environment of their departments. This came from their holding seats in the legislature and also seats in the cabinet, and thus positions of national leadership in the policy areas of their departments.

If, however, administrative politics and the exercise of administrative power were as central to the modern American regime as in Wilson's analysis, he then faced the need to go beyond his existing analysis and reform proposals to an assessment of administration in its own right, not merely as a reflection of legislative structure and behavior. He had to spell out more fully the contrast between the existing form of the public executive and the new one he envisioned, and he had to be more forthcoming about the position and role of these new executives in the national government. This Wilson began to do in *Congressional Government* with the fifth chapter, devoted to "The Executive." The chapter is the chief advancement in his own thinking Wilson achieved with the writing and publication of the book. Although the chapter is principally about congressional relations with the executive branch, it reveals Wilson's further thinking about the role of the national executive in a modern democratic state, and its appearance signaled Wilson's turn to more direct attention to administration as a political institution in its own right.

The chapter on the executive showed that Wilson had fully internalized his conviction that administration had become the central mode of politics and governance in an American regime emerging into modernity. Hence the chapter was not about establishing the central importance of administration in modern American politics—that was a given. The chapter instead marked the beginning of Wilson's exploration of the proper structure and institutional status of administration under a popular constitutional regime.

Wilson concerned himself first with questions about the proper training, preparation, and experience of administrators. He praised the apparently increasing tendency for presidents to come from the ranks of the states' governors rather than from the ranks of senators, who mostly arrived in their positions through "promotions" from the House. This was to be applauded because of the better training and preparation for the presidential office that service as a governor supplies. Because of his much more expansive views on the presidency, developed late in his scholarly years, and because of his own behavior as president, Wilson's relegation of the office of the president in *Congressional Government* to "*mere* administration" and the notion that the president might simply be "a permanent officer; the first official of a carefully-graded and impartially regulated civil service system" (170, emphasis in original) have tended to strike subsequent generations of readers of *Congressional Government* as particularly anachronistic. The change in Wilson's thinking about the presidency after this characterization is certainly critically important to understanding the development of his ideas about democracy and administration. An exclusive focus on this contrast, however, deflects attention from Wilson's effort to give serious thought to the appropriate supportive institutional structure and proper behavioral standards for high-level government executives. This is something, as far as I can determine, to which no scholar or political leader had given much attention in the United States up to Wilson's time—certainly not to the extent that Wilson does—with the possible exception of Andrew Jackson (see Cook 1996, ch. 3). It was, however, Wilson's aim in part to find an escape from the administrative quagmire into which General Jackson had marched the American regime.

Wilson's attention to the institutional standing and administrative preparation of the president takes place in the context of his more general concern for setting national administration on a firmer footing by bringing the administrative and legislative realms into a relationship of greater cooperation and trust. Hence he argued that the separation of powers and the development of the standing committee system had produced presidents who were partisans but nevertheless frequently operated against their parties' majorities in Congress, and who selected men for the heads of departments who were partisans but, increasingly, not party leaders. Thus Congress had increasingly looked "upon advice offered it by anybody but its own members as gratuitous impertinence" (179). The ultimate effect was "the forcible and unnatural divorcement of legislation and administration" (214). This absence of interconnections left Congress with "limited and defective" means of oversight and control of administration. The independence and discretion left to administrators as a result also left them to their worst inclinations with respect to incompetence, corruption, or pursuit of their own personal objectives: "They may make daily blunders of administration and repeated mistakes in business, may thwart the plans of Congress in a hundred small, vexatious ways, and yet all the while snap their fingers at its dissatisfaction or displeasure. They are denied the gratification of possessing real power, but they have the satisfaction of being secure in a petty independence which gives them a chance to be tricky and scheming" (180).

The relationship between administrators and Congress was thus more antagonistic than it was hierarchical or collaborative. "The relations existing between Congress and the departments must be fatally demoralizing to both. . . . The departments may be excused for that attitude of hostility which they sometimes assume towards Congress, . . . [for] Congress cannot control the officers of the executive without disgracing them. Its only whip is investigation, semi-judicial examination into corners suspected to be dirty" (183).

It is remarkable how current Wilson's characterizations of congressional-executive agency relations sound. This may reflect in part what David Rosenbloom has claimed is the creation of a "legislative-centered public administration" by an increasingly professionalized, career-oriented Congress in the mid–twentieth century and its further reinforcement in the 1980s and 1990s (2000, ch. 5). At the core of this effort has been Congress's strong desire to maintain the integrity of the constitutional separation of powers, as well as its institutional prerogatives with respect to the control of administration. The other part of the current equation is a renewed and ideologically charged national partisanship combined with frequently divided party control of the national government (see, for example, Ginsberg and Shefter 1990).

Of course, as with recurring contemporary calls for overcoming the debilitating effects of the separation of powers (see, for example, Stid 1998, 174–77), for Wilson the problems of administrative-legislative antagonism were manifestations of a central design flaw: the public through its representatives ultimately could not control public policy and thus could not attend to the pressing societal demands of modernity. Constitutional structure had produced "hide-and-seek vagaries of authority . . . , roundabout paths which legislative and executive responsibility are permitted to take" (Wilson 1981, 184) and "the piecing of authority, the cutting of it up into small bits" (185). Reversing the equation of the original constitutional design by centralizing authority and policy control in a new kind of national legislator-executive, Wilson argued, would not just lead to greater competence and policy success, it would generate greater confidence and trust in the system. Americans should not fear power, Wilson insisted, but should embrace it along with clearly defined accountability: "*Power and strict accountability for its use* are the essential elements of good government. A sense of highest responsibility, a dignifying and elevating sense of being trusted, together with a consciousness of being in an official station so conspicuous that no faithful discharge of duty can go unacknowledged and unrewarded, and no breach of trust undiscovered and unpunished,—these are the influences, the only influences which foster practical, energetic, and trustworthy statesmanship" (187, emphasis in original).

Among the benefits of this arrangement of centralized authority and power and accountability would be to lay the groundwork for full civil service reform. It would result in "the drawing of a sharp line of distinction between those offices which are political and those which are *non*-political. The strictest rules of business discipline, of merit-tenure and earned promotion, must rule every office whose incumbent has naught to do with choosing between policies; but no rules except the choice of parties can or should make and unmake, reward or punish, those officers whose privilege it is to fix upon the political purposes which administration shall be made to serve" (190, emphasis in original). In the United States at the time, however, it was "extremely hard to determine where the line should be drawn" (191).

The more extensive inquiry into the nature of the executive in the constitutional system and its relationship with Congress, undertaken in *Congressional Government*, led Wilson to several conclusions that stand out as distinctive in comparison to his work leading up to publication of the book. First, he argued that reform would improve the poor public standing of the executive branch: "If the people could have, through Congress, daily knowledge of all the more important transactions of the governmental offices, an insight into all that now seems withheld and private, their confidence in the executive, now so often shaken, would, I think, be very soon established" (196). Second, Wilson believed that Congress was "fast becoming the governing body of the nation" but also that it was restricted by constitutional design to mere *legislation* by discussion, rather than *government* by discussion. But "legislation is like a foreman set over the forces of government. It issues the orders which others obey. It directs, it admonishes, but it does not do the actual heavy work of governing" (197). Hence, for government by discussion, "what is quite as indispensable as the debate of problems of legislation is the debate of all matters of administration." This was invaluable because "unless Congress have and use every means of acquainting itself with the acts and disposition of the administrative agents of the government, the country must be helpless to learn how it is being served." Declaring that the "informing function of Congress should be preferred even to its legislative function," Wilson then stated even more pointedly that "the only really self-governing people is that people which discusses and interrogates its administration." In the end, Wilson concluded, it "would be hard to conceive of there being too much talk about the practical concerns and processes of government" (198). Furthermore, administration would have a more reliable footing of security and public trust when Congress took on the "duty of understanding, discussing, and directing administration. If the people's authorized representatives do not take upon themselves this duty, and by identifying themselves with the actual work of government stand between it and irresponsible, half-formed criticism, to what harassments is the executive not exposed?" (199).

In the context of the intense focus on public management that has emerged in the past two decades, in which considerable criticism has been leveled against congressional micromanagement of administration (see, for example, Aberbach and

Rockman 2000, 119–22; Behn 2001, 101–2; Rosenbloom 2000, 96–101), it is important to understand what Wilson was driving at in this extended point about congressional involvement in government. Wilson's target was also congressional micromanagement—but micromanagement undertaken by individuals and committee barons in secret, with petty and narrowly self-interested aims. This merely led to corruption, incompetence, and shirking in administration. In Wilson's view, subjecting both the ends and the means to open public discussion and debate in Congress would expose most of Congress's fragmented efforts to control administration for the self-serving endeavors they frequently were. It would also produce a high-level public executive and more generally an administration—a national government—much more capable of responding to the burgeoning demands of the modern world. Thus, Wilson concluded, fixing administration for a new age required fixing Congress, and the result would better position administration with respect to the growing demands of modern conditions and the expressions of popular thought regarding those conditions: "The government of a country so vast and various must be strong, prompt, wieldy, and efficient." Declaring that the source of strength for the government would come in part from "its accord with national sentiment," Wilson stressed also that the government "must be steadied and approved by open administration diligently obedient to the more permanent judgments of public opinion; and its only active agency, its representative chambers, must be equipped with something besides abundant powers of legislation" (Wilson 1981, 206).

A NEW CONGRESS AND A NEW EXECUTIVE

Wilson had reached three core conclusions in his work leading up to the writing and publication of *Congressional Government*. First, modern politics was primarily administrative politics, and modern political power was principally administrative power. He offered very little detail on this point, instead accepting it as fact and as a key premise for his analysis and advocacy of reform. Second, the American constitutional system as it had developed up to his time, in the midst of the emergence of a truly national polity and facing the growing stresses and strains of a society experiencing accelerating industrialization, commercial expansion, urbanization, and other manifestations of modernity, did not lend itself to effective governance. Efficacious government required the open practice and direct public scrutiny of administrative politics and the strong and prompt deployment of administrative power. Third, reforms in the direction of cabinet government would produce more effective governance because policy design and execution would be more directly guided by and responsible to a better-informed public judgment.

With *Congressional Government*, Wilson eschewed the formal and overt promotion of cabinet government and added a fourth conclusion. Administration deserved further attention and careful scrutiny in its own right with respect to its status in the regime and its relationships with other political institutions, the nuances of its relationship to the public, and its internal structure, especially regarding the design of organizational arrangements and incentives for personnel to promote both administrative effectiveness and moral and political rectitude. In this regard, Wilson gave little attention to the supporting organizational and institutional structure and the proper behavior of career public managers and lower-level operatives, other than his suggestions that they would be part of an apolitical civil service and that their work would involve strictly business-oriented tasks and practices. Yet he had gone quite some distance toward a vision of what the upper echelons of the government should be like. "Every government is largely what the men are who constitute it," Wilson declared (191–92). The bad, old department head was largely autonomous of presidential direction; possessed skills primarily of secrecy, special pleading, and dealing through back channels with representatives and senators to get support for his department while serving the special interests of the legislator; and was willful, petulant, and often corrupt. Wilson's idea of the new executive was built on the model of the English cabinet minister. The new public executive combined administrative expertise and experience with the skills to lead a legislature in discussion and debate toward designing good policy in the area of his special responsibility. He also possessed organizational leadership capacity to ensure that his department carried out new policy honestly, efficiently, and expeditiously. And his confidence and integrity were such that he could accept ultimate responsibility for his policy program, resigning from the cabinet should the program suffer some significant defeat in Congress, whether the result of policy design or policy management. With such national leadership of skill, responsibility, and integrity from the relatively small number of executive administrators, no wonder Wilson relegated the presidency to the background.

It is clear that through the decade leading up to and including the publication of *Congressional Government*, Wilson had not developed his thinking very much on questions of the nature of modern democracy, modern power, and administration. He was obsessed with how poorly American democracy fared in comparison with Great Britain, which he regarded as the foremost model of good government and good governance. Yet out of this relatively narrow focus Wilson still managed to offer a way of thinking about governance, with special reference to the roles, skills, knowledge, and strategies necessary to the deployment of administrative power, that constituted an inescapably vital step toward the emergence of a separate and distinct public administration and management orientation in government. It is also consonant with several facets of modern public management scholarship and practice.

First, Wilson sought to increase national attention to matters of administration and policy execution and thus raise to a rough level of parity with legislative matters the political status and importance of the executive in the American regime. Second, Wilson endeavored to address critical questions about—and to offer one possible model for—the executive leadership and administrative competence necessary for good governance in a liberal democracy struggling with the conditions of modernity. Perhaps the most important of these questions Wilson raised—one that remains hotly debated among scholars and practitioners—concerns the proper relationship of the public to public administration design and operation. Third, in conjunction with raising the visibility of executive and administrative matters, Wilson stressed the close ties between administrative success and competent legislative craftsmanship. Not only did Wilson argue that most policy issues under Congress's purview were administrative in concept and effect and that statutory construction had to take into account the requisites for successful policy execution, he also signaled that the design of administration and management structures were themselves a critical object of national policy development. Finally and most obviously, Wilson contended that the organization, or more accurately the reorganization, of Congress's internal practices was essential to improving American national governance in the modern age. An understanding and refashioning of the legislative process, Wilson realized, was crucial to effective congressional oversight and broader public scrutiny of administration. This in turn was critical to the development of neutral administrative competence and the increased cultivation of managerial capacities at the national level.

The one unavoidable problem with Wilson's analysis is that he could endorse the model of ministerial responsibility only by ignoring the accompanying need for a significant change in the law and the fundamental structure of the federal government. This has been the source of much criticism of Wilson's early analysis, both during his own time and for subsequent generations of scholars, and has deflected scholars, especially those in public administration and public management, from seeing the value and continued relevance of Wilson's early ideas. Somewhat surprisingly, given the existence of such strong critiques, although his constitutional reform agenda receded from prominence in his work in the wake of the publication of *Congressional Government*, Wilson never actually repudiated either his diagnosis or his specific structural remedy for what he thought ailed American democracy. His permanent attachment to the idea of a revised national governmental structure putting the executive and legislative branches in much closer governing proximity

and transforming the role of the high-level administrator is more than a mere historical footnote. It is a reflection of his core conclusion about the centrality of administration in the political practice and exercise of political power in a modern democratic regime and his concern that American governing structures and practices
adjust effectively to that reality and take full advantage of it. Rather than abandoning
either the analysis or the remedy, Wilson integrated them into his more sweeping
assessment of the historical foundations and modern character of democracy and the
place and practice of administration in it that followed.

Again, the problem, as Wilson had initially framed it, was how to deal with a
"normal" politics (that is, one not shaped by regime founding, internal crisis, or immi-
nent external threat) that had become almost exclusively administrative in character.
This was also a question of how to harness the vast potential of administrative power.
The American constitutional system did not lend itself to coping with modern
conditions effectively. The principal barrier was the separation of powers, which
fostered fragmentation, irresponsibility, and an absence of integrative leadership.
Thus Wilson sought to develop reforms to promote effective, responsible political
leadership that would tie popular judgment to administrative politics and the harnessing of administrative power. Administration would be improved as a result, and democratic practice would be transformed. In this context, political leadership did not concern the tenets of constitutional design or the enumeration of basic rights but rather
the plans of administration that the nation as a whole could, and would, sanction.

The even more prominent attention to nationalism, progress, responsibility, and
especially leadership in the continued evolution of Wilson's political thought following the publication of *Congressional Government* is nevertheless consistent with his
initial realization about the ineluctable forces of modernization and industrialization—which, it is important to stress, were themselves enabled and driven by advances in administrative structures and techniques—and the need to harness the
administrative power that followed in their wake. Wilson's ultimate aim, from both a
theoretical and practical standpoint, was to reconcile administration and democracy
—to find a combination of ideas, institutional arrangements, and political practices
that would constitute both effective and responsible democratic government in the
modern world. In the work he subsequently undertook, Wilson turned directly to
administration as a subject in and of itself, devoting considerable attention to the
identification, comparative study, development, and legitimation of administrative
methods to improve American governmental practice. But he simultaneously
sought to expand considerably his perspective on governmental design and political
reform through the development of a sweeping reconception of the nature of modern democracy.

The Character of Modern Democracy

Congressional Government was largely the product of an intellectual agenda that predated Wilson's graduate training. Before he had even met Herbert Baxter Adams and Richard T. Ely, his principal instructors at Johns Hopkins, Wilson had already begun to focus his intellectual attention on an emergent nationalism and mass democratic politics as the primary forces of modernity driving the development—and practice—of American government. He concluded that the bedrock of political ideas and actions had shifted away from constitutions and toward administration. American constitutional design and the peculiar development of the party system had stood in the way of the American polity's ability to adapt to this tectonic shift. Wilson felt compelled to work out his critique of the system's barriers to adaptation, reform, and effective governance in what he saw as the degenerate conditions of legislative organization and operations and legislative-executive relations. Once he had completed that task with the publication of *Congressional Government*, Wilson could catch up to the ideas and materials he first encountered at Johns Hopkins (see Thorsen 1988, 99).

As the editors of Wilson's papers note, Richard Ely introduced Wilson to administration as a subject of study. Ely even claimed to have "convinced Wilson that 'the problem of our age is not one of legislation but fundamentally one of administration'" (Miewald 1984, 18, quoting Ely 1938, 114). Wilson also adopted for his own analysis and interpretation the emphasis both Ely and Adams placed on "the origins and organic development of institutions" (Link et al. 1968, 5:55), and their methods of historical and comparative analysis. To extend the advances in his own thinking achieved in *Congressional Government*, Wilson used his postgraduate years to work out the implications of the conclusions he had reached. He did so by interpreting and greatly augmenting the secondary source material, including the extensive bibliographies containing a "preponderance of German writers" (Miewald 1984, 18) he had read in graduate school. He undertook this work on two planes of investigation: democracy and administration. He developed his ideas about the nature of modern democracy largely through the vehicles of historical writing and public lectures, both aimed at general audiences. His work on administration, in contrast, remained his more purely academic pursuit, elaborated on principally in his classroom lectures and forming the predominant component of his eventual scholarly specialty in public and constitutional law.

In his work on democracy, Wilson went beyond critiques of particular constitutional forms to inquire into the nature, structures, and practices of modern democratic rule. He developed a conception of democracy rooted in an organic understanding of the state. Yet he eventually supplanted his emphasis on the evolution of the living organism of the state with a focus on political authority, sovereignty, and political leadership, ultimately finding his way to a reconception of the nature of American constitutionalism centered on the president. In parallel, Wilson considered further the refinement and improvement of American administration. His treatment of administration was most directly connected to his exploration of democracy through his concern for establishing the proper place for administration in the modern democratic state. But his ambitions for improving American administration, and thus American governing practices more generally, also drew his attention to refinements of organization and practice, especially through the Americanization of administrative methods developed outside the United States.

In further developing his ideas after the completion of *Congressional Government*, Wilson did not initially make any obvious or intentional distinction between his work on a developing conception of democracy and his ideas about the place and practice of administration within that conception. They required one grand, synthetic scheme to confront the challenges of modernity. It was only after the publication of *The State* and his dissatisfaction with the results of his attempt at synthesis in that work that some identifiable distinctions in the directions of his work on democracy and on administration emerged. To illuminate Wilson's thinking on the intertwined topics of democracy and administration, especially during the most intensely scholarly phase of his work, I isolate for analysis in this chapter the development of his ideas about democracy, covering principally his scholarship but also reaching into his political activity, to capture expressions of his ideas that show their considerable continuity across time while noting the few key changes and refinements. I then turn in the next two chapters to the development of his ideas about both the place and the organization and practice of administration in a modern liberal-democratic regime. Although the eventual divergence in Wilson's thinking allows for the treatment of his ideas about democracy and administration as two separate lines of inquiry and argument, the reader must keep in mind that synthesis was forever Wilson's core aim. For Wilson as both scholar and political leader, helping American democracy adapt to modernity meant making it more administratively adept, and making it more administratively adept meant making it *more* democratic.

THE MODERN DEMOCRATIC STATE

When the work on compiling Wilson's papers got under way in 1963, the editors uncovered an extensive unpublished manuscript Wilson had prepared in December 1885. "The Modern Democratic State" proved to be the seedbed for many of the questions, problems, and concepts about administration and its standing vis-à-vis democracy that characterized so much of Wilson's scholarly work and public lecturing over the subsequent twenty years.

In several brief "memoranda" prepared before writing the main manuscript, Wilson declared that "Democracy . . . was itself a searching analysis—of the ultimate residence of sovereignty and the intimate nature of the state." The failure of democracy to complete a synthesis of these concerns, Wilson contended, put democracy at risk of "incapacity for the great social undertakings of our modern time" (Link et al. 1968, 5:58–59). Moreover, that synthesis had to address not just governmental organization, with which Wilson had concerned himself up to that time, but also principle, and a "synthesis of principle must precede a synthesis of form and function." As he stated the point in the manuscript proper, "the sustaining principles of the ordinary active life of democracy still lack thorough synthesis" (62).

Wilson further identified historical "ages" in the development of the state and identified a "fully adult U.S." with the modern age (59) and the democratic state more generally with the "adult state" (60). But he also stressed in the main manuscript that in its middle age, democracy had become "slow, cautious, uncertain, anxious" (61) because it had fallen short of its promise as a universal panacea "for many diseases of the body politic" (62).

Most important, however, Wilson articulated a conception of the relationship between the people and the government in the mature democratic state that crystallized his early thinking and would remain central to his ideas about and public characterization of democracy throughout the remainder of his academic and public life. Recalling his early attention to universal suffrage, he declared that its "true limitation" was "limitation of *direct* control. The people should not govern; they should elect the governors: and these governors should be elected for periods long enough to give time for policies not too heedful of transient breezes of public opinion. The power of the people ought to be the power of *criticism* and of choice upon *broad* questions" (60; emphasis in original).

Wilson's conception of democracy, as expressed here, is not a notable departure from the essence of his thinking in *Congressional Government*, with its stress on the importance of debate and on criticism of administrative measures by an attentive public informed by and in communication with its elected representatives. Wilson's statement also seems nothing so much as an expression of the basic idea of representative democracy. Indeed, as he stated it in the full manuscript, "Properly organized democracy is the best [government] of the few. This is the meaning of representative institutions" (85). But Wilson had bigger ideas in mind than simply articulating anew the idea of representative democracy, and he set about developing three particular points in fuller fashion in his manuscript, reflecting what he thought was needed for democracy to complete the necessary synthesis in order to adjust successfully to modernity.

First, Wilson advanced the notion that democracy was more than "merely a body of doctrine" (63) that could be translated into a written constitution to hold together a mass of disconnected individuals, "merely a colossal crowd composed of 'all-of-us'" (69). Instead, democracy was the culmination of a long historical development and the cultivation of habits and practices stretching over many generations. Hence he rejected the embrace of written constitutions as the pinnacle of political creativity, insisting that it was time to accept "that the real foundations of political life in the United States are to be found elsewhere than in our constitutions" and that "the Constitution is but the formal symbol of a deep reality of national character" (69). In short, a polity formed first, and the constitution followed.

Wilson explicitly probed very Tocquevillian notions in the manuscript with his recurring use of the concepts of habits and practices, reflecting at least in part the Frenchman's centering of his analysis on "mores." Wilson's papers certainly provide substantial evidence that Wilson was a close and respectful reader of Tocqueville's assessment of democracy (see Link et al. 1967, 2:293–96; also Thorsen 1988, 37). Wilson's communitarian orientation, rooted in religious doctrine as well as in Tocqueville's philosophy, is strongly on display in his reference to a higher and more permanent law than the constitution "which makes us conscious of our oneness as a single personality in the great community of nations; conscious of a common interest, a common vocation, and a common destiny: . . . a spirit for all time" (69). Wilson's reference to personality also suggests his incorporation of ideas from the German political theorist, Lorenz von Stein (see Miewald 1984, 20).

A second particular point that Wilson sought to develop in the manuscript concerned the newness of democracy in the modern world. This was, again, an extension of the thinking he initiated in *Congressional Government*. More distinctively than in that first effort, Wilson argued that "absolutely prerequisite to any competent study of the development of the modern state" was the recognition that "the democracy which is now becoming dominant is a *new* democracy . . . , informed with a life and surrounded by controlling conditions altogether modern" (80). These were "not merely new conditions" but "new essences" (81). Population size and territorial expanse were much greater and the populace was better educated and informed, forcing both the governors and the governed to find new ways to communicate and interact to secure public opinion its proper place and influence. Ultimately, what most distinguished this modern democracy was that it rested on "not the rule of the many, but the rule of the *whole*" (Link et al. 1968, 5:76; see Thorsen 1988, 96).

The final special point Wilson sought to elaborate in the manuscript concerned the new political science that a modern democratic state could employ to help it cope with the character of modern democracy and the circumstances of the modern world. Wilson appears to have been engaged in a quest similar to that undertaken by Tocqueville half a century before: the development of a new science of politics that would be serviceable in a world altogether new (see Wolin 2001, 184–94). For Wilson, it could not be a science of politics, concerned only with abstract theories of representative government. It should instead be "historical, comparative,—the method of fact. Democracy owes it to itself to be scientific,—not, however, for speculative but for practical purposes" (64). "The object of all political thought should be action," and it should ultimately aim to produce "a philosophy of statesmanship" (65). Wilson thus pointed himself toward the development of a political science not constructed of "abstract theory" but rather grounded in a thorough assessment of accumulated experience, historical development, and political "experiment" (92). This was consistent with Wilson's view that what democracy had to offer was less its ideals than its political experience and with his rejection of the "dreams" of the French Revolution and "the thin and sentimental theories of the disciples of Rousseau" (Link et al. 1972, 12:181).

"The Modern Democratic State" revealed Wilson to be concerned with the "larger problem of how democratic government could be practiced, not by communities, but by nations" (Thorsen 1988, 100). His effort on this score involved reinstating "the primacy of political authority" as a binding force to prevent the old susceptibility of democracy to the anarchy of mob rule from emerging in democracy's modern incarnation. A well-developed "philosophy of statesmanship" was crucial to this endeavor. Of particular importance was the notion that "political authority is located in social emotions, not in political reason" (103). As Wilson argued in an essay in December 1887, reason was subsequent to sentiment or feeling: "Even the literature of reasoned thought gets its life, not from its logic, but from the spirit and inspiration which are the *vehicle* of its logic" (Link et al. 1968, 5:644).

A philosophy of statesmanship also had to recognize that public opinion, the core of modern democratic government, carried "some of the vestiges of political participation" associated with direct democracy, but it was diffused and fragmented. It also tended toward "both excitement and paralysis" (Thorsen 1988, 110). In the project of drawing together the diffused sentiments of the people into what Wilson called "temperate common counsel" (Link et al. 1968, 5:71), tying together sentiment and reason, and ultimately connecting public opinion to the day-to-day tasks of governing—that is, administration—statesmanship needed both a proper institutional home and a set of practices grounded in experience. Wilson's scholarly efforts following the articulation of key ideas in "The Modern Democratic State" constituted a quest for both these necessary elements. His search for the former led him through further development of his ideas about democracy, especially with respect to the nature of sovereignty, and ultimately to further development of his ideas about political leadership and democratic statesmanship. His search for the latter led him to explore the origins and essential practices of government and to focus on the organizational and behavioral requirements for effective administration, including the proper design of statutes.

THE ESSENTIALS OF MODERN DEMOCRACY

Out of the many ideas, observations, and arguments he set down in the initial manuscript and the subsequent twenty years of his writing and lecturing, six key components form the core of Wilson's conception of democracy. These components are extensively intertwined, so the discussion of one inevitably leads to the discussion of one or more of the others. Distilling them is nevertheless important, because it sets the essential context for any attempt to understand and interpret Wilson's ideas about administration. Wilson's attention to democracy was in important respects an outgrowth of his interest in administration, rather than the other way around. That is, his recognition of the centrality of administration to the success of democratic governance—especially *American* governance—in the modern age spurred Wilson to attempt to articulate a more satisfactory understanding of the nature of a modern democratic regime. As he argued in the notes for his very first lectures on administration at Johns Hopkins in 1888, he needed to delve into the question of what the functions of government were before he could explore the "narrower" question of administration: the way in which government's functions "are to be performed" (Link et al. 1968, 5:669). Establishing a satisfactory answer to that more fundamental question would allow him to respond to his own call in "The Study of Administration" for the adoption of the governing designs and practices he believed the United States so sorely needed to adopt in its adjustment to the modern world.

Democracy as Development

Primary among the central elements of Wilson's democratic theory was his view of democracy as an advanced stage in the evolution and maturation of the organic entity of the state. Democracy was the product of a long, stable development of the habits and character of a people. The summary theme of Wilson's historical and comparative analysis in *The State*, for instance, was continuity and stable evolution taking place in an inductive reality: "Political growth refuses to be forced; and institutions have grown with the slow growth of social relationships; have changed in response, not to new theories, but to new circumstances" (Wilson 1890, 575). To understand politics and government, then, and to help American democracy in its adaptation to modernity, one had to understand the nature of society, which was "compounded of the common habit, an evolution of experience, an interlaced growth of tenacious relationships, a compact, living, organic whole, structural, not mechanical" (597).

If democracy was itself an output and not an input, an effect and not a cause, then the more significant and dramatic implication was that laws, and indeed even more so constitutions, were the outcomes of this growth of habit and national character and the long-run general accumulation of experience. In a review of James Bryce's *American Commonwealth*, Wilson contended that the "complete nationality of our law, therefore, had to await the slowly developed nationality of our thought and habit. To leave out in any account of our development the growth of the national idea and habit, consequently, is to omit the best possible example of one of the most instructive facts of our politics, the development, namely, of constitutional principles outside the constitution" (Link et al. 1969, 6:74). Making the more generalized and comparative point in *The State*, Wilson concluded that the "nature of each State, therefore, will be reflected in its law; in its law, too, will appear the functions with which it changes itself; and in its law will it be possible to read its history." Public law, in particular, "is that portion of law which determines a state's own character and its relations to its citizens" (632).

Stressing the regime-specific nature of such development, Wilson further contended that the "sources whence [law] springs, therefore, are as various as the means by which an organic community can shape and express its will as a body politic" (610). In a published essay in 1892, "The True American Spirit," Wilson brought his regime-specific point further to bear on the United States, arguing that "it is worth observing that American democracy, if interpreted by its own history, is a democracy with a character quite peculiarly its own. . . . It is not a democracy which has been thought out, but a democracy which has been lived out to its present development" (Link et al. 1970, 8:8).

Wilson thus stressed that written constitutions, and even more so statutes, were not themselves political life or the initiators of it but expressions of the character of political life at a particular time. Although a constitution did embody certain core values or principles of a people, it could be so rigid as to straightjacket the subsequent growth and development of the living, breathing organism of the state. It could be cast aside if it proved to be inflexible, while the democratic entity would nevertheless remain. As he moved toward a greater emphasis on sovereignty and political authority in his ideas about democracy, Wilson nevertheless preserved this orientation toward law and constitutions. As he argued most extensively in his lecture on sovereignty in 1891, "Law is not a creative agency at all, except to a very limited extent. . . . It has originated *forms* and *means* rather than substantive conditions. Its function is regulative, formulative. It takes up the completed tendencies of the community and turns them into formal rights and duties: it transforms practices into legal institutions. But tendencies and practices are matters of evolution, not creation out of hand. . . . Constitutions also are definitive rather than creative. They sum up experiences: they register consents" (Link et al. 1969, 7:336, emphasis in original). As he hinted in *The State*, however, and as he stated more fully and emphatically in his political speeches once he had taken up the mantel of progressivism, the formalization of experience in law had when necessary to be aimed at *altering* societal conditions consistent with the polity's aspirations for self-government.

Common Counsel

The second core component of Wilson's developed conception of democracy emphasized its manifestation in a kind of national community and, more importantly, the expressed will of this community: public opinion. But public opinion did not spring fully formed from the thoughts of individuals, nor was it the aggregation of the strivings of organized interests. It required interpretation—a sort of social-psychological sculpting—by political leaders.

Further, Wilson's conception of democracy encompassed distinctive notions about the nature of the majority and of majority rule. Wilson saw the concept of interest, or rather the fragmentation of political society into *interests*, as antagonistic to success for a modern democratic regime. That citizens should think in terms of their own interests, rather than the interests of the whole, Wilson recognized as the all too likely result of social and economic development and specialization. Although he regarded democracy as an improvement because the state would enjoy the developmental advantages of "all interests" having "representation & a voice" (Link et al. 1968, 5:758), Wilson mostly treated interest-based politics as a sort of delusion that was transcendable under the guidance of true statesmen. It was the statesman's task, then, to find the commonality among the many and divergent views of the citizenry while also preserving for the regime the strength derived from differential opinion and the distinct capacities evident across the nation.

Appearing extensively in his writing, public lectures, and his political rhetoric, Wilson's idea of common counsel clearly had its roots in his strong orientation to legislative, and especially parliamentary, politics and in the idea of government by discussion. Yet it encompassed much more; it reflected "the integrative force of a national system of public opinion" (Thorsen 1988, 108) enabled by a national system of communication, and it both enabled and restrained democracy through the proper organization of government—that is, the proper arrangements for administration—and through the efforts of true statesmen (see Thorsen 1988, 108–9). These effects would be most manifest when Americans embraced the historical and comparative study of government and the lessons of experience.

Wilson had first articulated this idea with his reference in "The Modern Democratic State" to modern democracy being rule not of the many but of the whole. He elaborated on the notion in his premiere lecture on the subject. In "Democracy," he stressed that he was speaking about "*modern* democracy in which the people who are said to govern are not the people of a commune or a township, but all the people of a great nation, a vast population which never musters into any single assembly, whose members never see each others' faces or hear each others' voices, but live, millions strong, up and down the reaches of continents." Despite their vast and disconnected number, the people were "not *separate*, but standing fast in a vital union of thought and of institutions, conceiving of themselves a corporate whole: acting so, and so accepted by the world" (Link et al. 1969, 7:347, emphasis in original).

It was in an effort to give some clearer meaning and substance to this metaphysical notion of a national will that Wilson turned to an organic conception for understanding and explicating the historical evolution and distinctive character of modern democracy, which led to his adoption, from the Germans, of the idea of "the state." The state was an organic entity, distinct from government. Governmental institutions were "organs" of the state, and government overall was "merely the executive organ of society, the organ through which its habit acts, through which its will becomes operative, through which it adapts itself to its environment and works out for itself a more effective life" (Wilson 1890, 598).

Wilson understood and expressed his organicism through two distinct but related metaphors: evolution and the body. Wilson characterized the development of human society and nations in the same way that biologists might characterize the evolution of species and the development of individuals. Every nation had its own ontogeny, the developmental stages through which it passed to its present state, an approximation of adulthood or maturity. But even with individual variations, the developmental paths also reflected the common phylogeny of states—democratic states in particular. The development of every democratic state reflected in some way the evolutionary arc of its species, even if, as in the case of the United States, the development may have experienced a peculiar interruption and reinitiation.

Wilson also portrayed the functions of political and governmental entities in terms of organisms and their parts: limbs, sense organs, blood, spirit. The integration and unity that was at the center of Wilson's attention he often expressed in analogy to the working of the organs in the body. It is principally through this metaphor that Wilson identified the organic importance of administration in the democratic state.

Wilson also referred to both "Society" and "the State" in organic terms. In his popular public lecture, "Leaders of Men," he contended that "Society is not a crowd, but an organism; and, like every organism, it must grow as a whole or else be deformed. The world is agreed, too, that it is an organism also in this, that it will die unless it be vital in every part" (Link et al. 1969, 6:659). But Wilson did see a distinction. He conceived of society as something akin to what scholars now often refer to as "civil society." He characterized it as "the field of individual initiative and endeavor, and of the combination in small groups as contrasted with universal organization for common and general objects" (Link et al. 1970, 8:600). By comparison, "the state" was organic society taken to a higher plane of organized existence and benefit to the individual. Drawing heavily and directly on Stein, Wilson made the case more emphatically first in his initial cycle of lectures on administration, and then repeatedly in other lectures on public and constitutional law: "*The State, therefore, is an abiding natural relationship*; neither a mere convenience nor a mere necessity; neither a mere voluntary association nor a mere corporation; nor any other artificial thing created for a special purpose, but *the eternal natural embodiment and expression of a higher form of life than the individual,* namely, that common life which gives leave to individual life, and opportunity for completeness,—makes individual life possible and makes it full and complete" (Link et al. 1969, 7:124, emphasis in original). The state was the manifestation of a people "organized for law" (Link et al. 1970, 8:597). Law and organization mattered most because public opinion did not arise from society. It was an outgrowth of "consultation and a single, united will and purpose, . . . not of organic action or of governing efficacy until it passes through a set of coordinating organs" (601). These organs were, most importantly, the legislature and the executive, "or, more properly, the administration" (602).

Even if Wilson's organic conception of the state was ultimately an "abandoned metaphysics" (Thorsen 1988, 91) and "little more than warmed-over German theory" (Miewald 1984, 27), it nevertheless helped undergird his ideas about democracy even after he had moved to a different conceptual orientation. Wilson's organicism thus is crucial to understanding the changes in his thinking about administration over time. Further, it remained a recurring mode of expression by which he articulated and communicated his ideas, even when fully ensconced in his political career. "Society is an organism," he declared in a May 1912 speech to the Economic Club of New York, "and every Government must develop according to its organic forces and instincts" (Link et al. 1977, 24:416). For common counsel that meant "that there must be some guiding and adjusting force—some single organ of intelligent communication between the whole Nation and the Government which determines the policy of that Nation" (418). This force was political leadership.

The Governors and the Governed

The third element of Wilson's extended understanding of democracy centered on the relationship between the rulers and the ruled he had first expressed in "The Modern Democratic State." The people—the governed—exercised control and consent or dissent, but they did not govern. As he argued preliminarily in *Congressional Government* and more colorfully in "The Study of Administration," the role of the people was to be "authoritative critic" of the rulers and their official agents—the administration.

Wilson further developed his notion of the relationship between the governors and the governed in conjunction with his turn toward the subject of sovereignty near the end of *The State*. This was the first clear indication of Wilson's initial move away from a strictly organic orientation in his ideas about modern democracy. It emerged in his treatment of law and constitutions as products rather than initiators of democracy's development. The developmental dynamics of law posed a significant question: "If, then, law be a product of national character, if the power of the community must be behind it to give it efficacy, and the habit of the community in it to give it reality, where is the seat of sovereignty?" (Wilson 1890, 623). Sovereignty, and with it the meaning of political and governmental authority, became Wilson's new focus in his endeavor to understand American democracy and help adapt it to the modern world. His initial response to the question within the text of *The State* set some of the parameters of his further efforts. He contended that sovereignty "as conceived in legal theory nowhere actually exists" (624). Instead, the "sovereignty which does exist is something much more vital, though, like most living things, less easily conceived. It is the will of an organized independent community, whether that will speak in acquiescence merely, or in active creation of the forces and conditions of politics" (624–25). "Sovereignty resides in the community," Wilson concluded, "but its organs," that is, its particular ruling officials or classes, varied according to the peculiar historical development of a given nation and its people (625).

Wilson developed his conception of sovereignty much further and more fully in his lecture of 1891. He located sovereignty in a democracy in the chosen few who would govern: "We have been mistaken in looking for any unlimited power. There is no unlimited power except the sum of all powers. . . . Sovereignty, if it be a definite and separable thing at all, is not unlimited—is not identical with the power of the community. It is not the general vitality of the organism, but the specific originative power of certain organs." He pressed for a clear distinction between "the powers and processes of government" and "the relations of the people to those powers and processes," noting that "those relations are relations of assent and obedience,—and the degree of assent and obedience mark the limits,—the sphere—of Sovereignty" (Link et al. 1969, 7:333).

Wilson further characterized sovereignty as "the daily operative power of giving efficacy to laws," and it had originative, planning, and executive aspects. He insisted that free people may elect a sovereign body, but by themselves they do not constitute sovereignty. Likewise, the "sovereign, originative body must prudently regard the state of opinion," and the people's obedience to the sovereign body was neither unconscious nor automatic but "the product either of choice or of habit" (334). Ultimately, Wilson declared sovereignty to be "an active principle, a principle of command and guidance, and not merely of superintendence." Therefore sovereignty "is the highest political power of a State lodged in active organs of the State for purposes of governing. Power is a positive thing; control, a negative thing. Power belongs to government, is lodged in governing organs; control belongs to the community, is lodged with the people" (339). The particular home for sovereignty within the government was the legislature, "the highest originative or lawmaking body of the State" (340).

The first three integral components of his conception of democracy reveal Wilson's strong belief that democracy was not just rule by a disorganized mass. Instead, democracy had order, and the "control" the people could exercise was only activated, and thus useful, on the initiative of the governors. "But, after all," Wilson continued, "progress is motion, government is action. The waters of democracy are useless in their reservoirs unless they may be used to drive the wheels of policy and administration" (Link et al. 1969, 6:238). Wilson's conceptions of majorities, majority rule, and public opinion are tied to this notion. Although they are connected to his understanding of a distinguishable, collective community rooted in his organicism, he developed his ideas about the nature of majority rule and public opinion much more extensively, as he moved his orientation to the questions of sovereignty and proper political authority.

Wilson's ideas about majorities, and especially about public opinion, were truly metaphysical in the sense of there being, roughly speaking, a mind-body connection at the level of the polity. Wilson's ideas gave emphasis to the "thought" of the people. This was not some collective mind of the state but a condition better characterized as "a meeting of the minds" or "like-mindedness." As R. McGreggor Cawley (1998) has pointed out, Wilson articulated it as making up "the general mind" (see Link et al. 1969, 7:366). This condition did not occur by luck or accident; political leaders cultivated it. In "Leaders of Men," Wilson argued, "This organic whole, Society, is made up, obviously, for the most part, of the majority. It grows by the development of its aptitudes and desires, and under their guidance. . . . And all this is but a careful and abstract way of saying that no reform may succeed for which the major thought of the nation is not prepared: that the instructed few may not be safe leaders . . . except in so far as they have transmuted the thought into a common, a popular thought" (659). This also illustrates further Wilson's point about public opinion not being efficacious or organically complete without passing through the organs of the state, including administration.

Wilson sometimes spoke in fairly stark terms about the distinction between the rulers and the ruled—keeping the people in their place, as it were—and distinguished between the average and the best of the citizenry as the vital constituent material of a well-governed democracy. In "The True American Spirit," Wilson declared, "The principle of other democracies is that the majority governs and has the right to govern. The principle of our democracy is that the majority decides between parties, and even sometimes between measures, but that officers and the law govern. . . . Majorities, of course, as a matter of fact, never govern. . . . The only use of majorities is to show how the people are disposed toward those who do govern—their representatives and rulers" (Link et al. 1970, 8:37). As Cawley has suggested, seen in this context, Wilson's conception of a meeting of the minds sounds like "a strategy through which the reformer *manufactures* public opinion, and therefore, it is the *reformer's* opinion, and not the *public's*, that rules" (1998, 58, emphasis in original).

More consistently, however, and perhaps too subtly and vaguely to be of use to practitioners (Cawley 1998, 59), Wilson characterized the articulation of public opinion as a more general meeting of the minds between the governors and the governed. In his 1900 essay "Democracy and Efficiency," Wilson defined constitutional government as "a definite understanding as to the sphere and powers of government." Such an understanding came about "by frequent conference between those who govern and those who are governed." The process was "public and continuous, and conducted by those who stand in the midst of affairs, at the official centre and seat of management, where affairs can be looked into and disposed with full knowledge and authority; those intrusted with government being present in person, the people by deputy" (Link et al. 1972, 12:8).

Wilson did recognize the problem posed by the subtleties and generalities by which he spoke of common counsel and the relationship of the governors to the governed. In a public talk in 1901, "The Real Idea of Democracy," he observed that the "real problem of democracy . . . , is how to devise and maintain in full efficiency the best means of intimate counsel between those who are to make and administer the laws and those who are to obey them, and yet not destroy leadership or render government less real or less authoritative" (178). As he moved closer to stepping into the political arena as candidate and officeholder, Wilson placed more of the burden for the formation of public opinion on the citizenry. In "The Ideals of Public Life," a 1907 public address, he characterized public life as consisting primarily of "the formation of public opinion," "the guidance of public purpose," and "the promoting of progress and of the criticism of remedies." This was "the task of the citizen and not the task of the politician." Public opinion was, again, "that compound which comes from the agreement of minds and is the result of compared and expressed opinion . . . , which is comprehended by all" (Link et al. 1974, 17:499).

Wilson went on to insist that a "majority that is ready" for change and reform would be helped along by "practical thinkers, practical talkers, who don't have to win." Without them, he warned, "you are not going to have the moving force of public opinion; public opinion is going to be a plaything and not a master; politicians are going to manipulate it and not be governed by it" (500).

From a conception of society as a living organism brought to a higher-ordered existence in the form of the state, Wilson moved over the course of twenty years to a conception of democracy centered on ideas about sovereignty, public opinion, and political authority that still required an organic sense of how these elements were interconnected. The whole was greater than the sum of its parts in the same way that a living organism is something more than a mere collection of cells, tissue, organs, and systems.

One aspect of Wilson's later thinking that distinguishes it from his earlier organicism was his increased emphasis on action as part of democratic governance and away from a legislative-centered model of modern democracy, with its focus on government by discussion. This is connected in part to Wilson's "discovery" of the potentials of presidential leadership in the American system after 1900, which I touch on further below and explore more extensively in the next several chapters. He made the point initially in "The Modern Democratic State," wherein references to action are numerous. Indeed, Wilson insisted that the "object of all political thought should be action" (Link et al. 1968, 5:65). He identified action, volition, and initiative as the defining province of the state in contrast to "mere ratification of measures," which was the province of the people (75). Action then became a critical component of his conception of sovereignty. Indeed, what made the "sovereign body" sovereign was its power of action. As part of his legislative-centered orientation, he located the power of action—determining "both the tasks to be carried out by Administration and the rules to be applied by the courts"—in the lawmaking body. The executive was merely "the agent, not the organ, of Sovereignty" (Link et al. 1969, 7:340). By 1901, in "The Real Idea of Democracy," he stated succinctly that "sovereignty is not a thing merely of consent and approval, but a thing of initiative and of action" (Link et al. 1972, 12:178). And it bears stating again that for Wilson sovereignty was not complete without administration, the quintessential manifestation of government action.

By the time Wilson had made up his mind to pursue a life in politics, he placed action ahead of public thought in the process of common counsel. In an address on Thomas Jefferson in 1906, Wilson declared emphatically that "we do not take counsel with each other as fellow citizens merely to ask each other what shall we think. There is something much more important than that in hand, and that is to determine what we shall *do*" (Link et al. 1973, 16:365, emphasis in original). Delivering a presidential address on Memorial Day in 1915, Wilson firmly bound public opinion to action, declaring that "those who stand at the head of affairs have it as their bounden obligation to endeavor to express in their own actions those things that seem to rise out of the conscience and hope and purpose of the great body of the people themselves" (Link et al. 1980, 33:289).

Liberty and Equality

A fourth component critical to understanding Wilson's conception of modern democracy encompasses his ideas about liberty and equality. The two were tied together in Wilson's conception of democracy through his rejection of privilege and the division of society into classes or interests. Wilson's attention in this regard reflected his overall concern about the threat that fragmentation and disorder posed to the success of democratic governance in adapting to modernity's challenges.

Liberty—more specifically *political* or *institutional* liberty—was for Wilson a function of ordered society, and it was especially resident in the democratic state. That is, political liberty could only be realized, only made sense, within society and within the order and higher organization of the state. Wilson accepted that liberty inhered in the individual, but he argued that individuals could only realize it in the context of a national political community: the union and cooperation of all and the adjustment of public and private that was the quintessence of the mature, adult—the democratic—state that was well administered. The individual could not realize his or her full potential except within the constraints that arose out of social relationships, cooperation, and well-adjusted government control. Political liberty was not the product of thoughts "extracted from mere speculation" by the likes of Rousseau (Link et al. 1968, 5:60). Instead, political liberty was the outcome of a people's long-run development of character, habit, and experience with government. A nation could not simply adopt the arrangements securing political liberty of another nation. The arrangements would not fit the habits and character of the adopting nation, nor would the adopters have had the requisite historical experience to make the arrangements work in the peculiar conditions facing them. Wilson was also adamant that the history of the development of political liberty did not reflect a revolt against governmental control in general but only against an arbitrary control and arrangement of institutions exercised by one or a small number of men for their own benefit and not for the general interest.

Wilson seems to have initiated his articulation of this multifaceted conception of liberty in response to John Ruskin's *Seven Lamps of Architecture*, especially "The Lamp of Obedience." Wilson used with only slight variations the same extended passage in which Ruskin exclaimed, "Call it [liberty] by any name rather than this, but its best and truest test is, Obedience" (Link et al. 1969, 6:463–64; see Ruskin 1880). From this seed, Wilson harvested a lecture that addressed the nature of the modern state, political liberty, political expediency, political morality, and political progress. Frequently in the early 1890s, he delivered this lecture freestanding or inserted parts or all of it in other lectures, including his notes for lectures on administration, democracy, and constitutional government (see Link et al. 1969, 7:157–58, 364–65; Link et al. 1970, 8:406–9, 597–608; Link et al. 1970, 9:106–18). As he articulated it in the notes for his Brooklyn Institute lectures on constitutional government, "*Liberty is of Order and Union*, not of Separation or contest. It is an antimony, not of Society, but of rigid and arbitrary authority." Liberty involved constraint, but "by adjustment and cooperation" (Link et al. 1970, 8:406, emphasis in original). Hence, "*Liberty is a systematic balance between private right and public power*: between assistance and interference. *It is such an adjustment as will give* individual spirit *free play*, as a contribution to the general variety of force: not on separation, but *in cooperation*. A man is free in nothing in which he is alone" (407).

In his ideas and commentary on political liberty, Wilson did not invoke rights or explore the concept of rights in this context. Instead, he addressed the subject of rights in his work on constitutional and public law and on administration. Rights for Wilson were not natural or precedent to society and its organic development (see Thorsen 1988, 189). Indeed, Wilson stressed in his lectures on administration that bills of rights were generally stated in the negative, frequently referred to particular administrative actions, and required administration for their substantive realization (see Link et al. 1969, 7:153–58). Although Wilson was quite insistent that liberty could never be realized through administrative means, he also argued that the particular province of administration in the democratic state was the point of contact between public and private, and the constant adjustments made between freedom and interference took place there. In a very real and rather worrisome sense, then, administration determined the particular character of liberty in individual cases. I explore this more fully in chapter 3 (see also the very enlightening treatment in Rohr 1986, ch. 10).

The notion in Wilson's thinking about political liberty regarding the revolt against control by an arbitrary and privileged few resurfaced later, in the increased attention he gave to equality as he entered the national political fray with increasingly frequent public commentary on issues such as corporate trusts, union organizing, and international affairs. He invoked notions of equality of conditions, harkening back to Tocqueville, and of equality of opportunity. He invoked the ideas of government as umpire, that all should be afforded a fair and equal start in the competition of modern life. Characterizing them as principles "as old as the world" in his Jefferson address, Wilson urged his audience, "Do not conceive for yourselves a commonwealth in which the law will assist its citizens class by class, but conceive to yourselves a commonwealth in which it will preside over the life of its citizens, condescending to nobody, but umpiring every move of the contest" (Link et al. 1973, 16:368).

Wilson subsequently carried these thoughts further, tying in several aspects of his views on political liberty and railing against the political distortions of corporate power while warning against taking governmental intervention too far. He argued that "law in a free state should have as its chief object the maintenance of equality of conditions and opportunities." Forgetting this, however, Americans "destroyed the balance, the harmony, the one-time generous cooperation of . . . national life," creating classes and putting "colossal interests at clash with one another." The danger was that policy would "push government into every experimental function in order to correct the vagaries of development we foster but do not understand" (Link et al. 1974, 17:81).

The intertwining of his views on liberty and equality reflect Wilson's dualism, his essential conservatism and progressivism with respect to democracy. He viewed democracy as the outcome and embodiment of stable, orderly development, especially in the character of a people constituting a polity. But stability and order did not mean an absence of growth and change, for a democratic polity that did not progress, did not make the necessary adjustments to changing conditions, would not survive in the modern world. "But *progress is a march, not a scamper*," Wilson insisted in his lecture on democracy. "It is achieved by advance *in hosts and under discipline*, not by the running hither and thither of inquisitive crowds. It is a slow thing, of *movement together* and in united masses, a movement of *states*, not an elegant intellectual diversion of dreaming dreams and then forming societies to carry them out" (Link et al. 1969, 7:365, emphasis in original). Again, this orderly and cooperative adjustment to conditions with the advantage of experience, both with respect to liberty and equality, was an important function of administration in Wilson's system of ideas.

STATESMANSHIP AND A SUPPORTIVE SCIENCE OF POLITICS

The final two components of Wilson's democratic thought that are key to appreciating the structure of his ideas about democratic politics and government and thus about administration should be readily identifiable from the discussion so far. But they are tied together in ways that reflect the peculiarities of Wilson's conceptual framework. The first is democratic statesmanship, which Wilson saw as synthesizing the first four components and bringing them to realization. The second is a special kind of political science, which Wilson regarded as essential to an adequate understanding of modern democracy and to its successful adaptation to modernity's conditions. It is the one component that stands outside the encompassing, integrating sphere of statesmanship and provides support to it.

Leadership

Wilson's ideas about political leadership in a democracy have perhaps received more scholarly attention and scrutiny than any other dimension of his political thought and behavior. Several scholarly treatments (see especially Tulis 1987, ch. 5; Thorsen 1988, ch. 3 and pp. 228–34) make irrefutably clear that leadership was at the very center of Wilson's endeavor to forge a sweeping revision of the theory and practice of the American political regime, one made necessary by the forces of modernity. As he stated it in notes for his never-completed "philosophy of politics" treatise, "The most helpful service to the world thus awaiting the fulfillment of its visions would be an elucidation, a real elucidation, of the laws of leadership" (Link et al. 1971, 11:239).

As his arguments in his cabinet government advocacy show, Wilson was particularly concerned that an unreformed American political system would not provide the proper institutional setting for the cultivation and exercise of national political leadership (see Thorsen 1988, 46–64). He contended that a properly organized legislature in which there was intimate connection between the makers and the executors of the law, as in cabinet government, would provide the necessary institutional setting for national leadership that was lacking in American national government. Much of the discussion and debate over policies and political principles that would take place in such a setting would inevitably and necessarily be about administration. This meant that critical improvements in American administrative philosophy and methods were more likely but also that knowledge of and experience with administration would be a vital part of the leadership capacities and reputations of the men who rose to national political prominence. Wilson extended and embellished this argument while preserving its essence and incorporating it in a substantial number of his most prominent lectures and public addresses, particularly during the 1890s. Over the course of that time, and even beyond it, the legislature remained the focal point of Wilson's public pronouncements about leadership.

In his notes for his lectures on constitutional government in 1898, Wilson declared that "*Real leaders* must *pick themselves out*: and the process of self-selection cannot be carried on except *upon some public forum* where men may prove themselves with regard to the principal function they are called upon to perform." Again, the premier forum for demonstrating leadership was the legislature: "*Wherever we look*, outside the field of international politics, *we find the Legislature the only real forum* of selection to leadership in the existing world of politics,—the only place where wisdom in affairs is publicly proved by service." A specific legislative organization was also central to fostering this leadership: "We also find that *only the 'parliamentary' system*, whereby both functions of government [legislative and administrative] are entrusted to the legislative leaders, *makes leadership distinct, effective, responsible*" (Link et al. 1971, 11:14, emphasis in original).

It was at just this very moment, however, that Wilson began to turn his orientation with regard to democratic political leadership away from the legislature and toward the presidency. In the fall of 1898, Wilson arrived at the "singular conclusion that the President, who is elected by the whole people, is not a leader in the vital matters" of the nation (70). Yet he also emphasized that with the nation's new global reach, there was an expressed need for uniting "those who plan and those who execute" in order that "there may be efficiency and responsibility" (71). The search for such an arrangement of efficiency and responsibility in the face of the American arrival on the world stage led Wilson to traverse the institutional boundary in his thinking about democratic statesmanship and embrace the presidency as the center of national leadership: "Once more it is our place among nations that we think of; once more our Presidents are our leaders. . . . We are sensitive to airs that come to us from off the seas. The President and his advisers stand upon our chief coign of observation, and we mark their words as we did not till this change came. . . . It is by the widening of vision that nations, as men, grow and are made great. . . . Let us put our leading characters at the front (226–27).

What would these leading characters actually do? What would define their leadership as truly modern democratic statesmanship? "Leadership eludes analysis," Wilson contended in notes prepared in 1902. "It is only by the action of leading minds that the organic will of a community is stirred to the exercise of either originative purpose or guiding control in affairs." He defined leadership as "the practicable formulation of action, and the successful arousal and guidance of motive in social development" (Link et al. 1972, 12:365). Similarly, he characterized statesmanship as "the guidance of the opinion and purpose of a nation in the field of political action" (Link et al. 1973, 15:33). In two important respects, at the heart of this guiding of opinion and motive and purpose was the defining idea of Wilson's conception of democratic political leadership: interpretation.

First, Wilson argued that a true democratic statesman exercising leadership as interpretation had to be from and of the people. By talent and ambition, however, and especially by imagination and a special ability to sense popular thought, leaders rose above the common folk. Only merit and capacity, not class status or privilege, should play a role in the identification of leaders. "The real test," declared Wilson, of democracy's "excellence as a form of government is the training, the opportunities, the authority, the rewards which its constitutional arrangements afford those who seek to lead it faithfully and well. It does not get the full profit of its own characteristic principles and ideals unless it use the best men in it, without regard to their blood or breeding" (Link et al. 1972, 12:179). Lincoln was the exemplar in this regard. He was "of the mass, but he was so lifted and big that all men could look up to him" (Link et al. 1975, 19:42).

Second, despite what he suggested here with his description of Lincoln, he understood the democratic leader as not standing aloof or above the people but in their midst, at the center of discussion and, more importantly, action, as he had specifically argued in his lecture on "Democracy and Efficiency" (see also Thorsen 1988, 62). And what the leader worked with at the center of political society were the myriad habits and sentiments, thoughts and motives, of citizens. This is what the leader interpreted, identifying the commonalities and unities, giving voice to the common interest and purpose, and thus articulating public opinion. Wilson saw this as a subtle yet powerful process that required careful explication.

The true work of leaders, Wilson contended, was action, not thought. However, leaders worked with "the firm and progressive" popular thought and not the "momentary and whimsical" popular mood; that is what in part distinguished true leaders from demagogues. Thus, interpretation was the enterprise of reading the common thought in order to "test and calculate very circumspectly the *preparation* of the nation for the next move in the progress of politics" (Link et al. 1969, 6:659). Wilson also stressed in his conception of leadership that democratic statesmen worked with the masses, not with individuals. They had to advance ideas that were simple and easily absorbed; they had to work not through dissemination of information but through persuasion and gaining the confidence of large numbers. Leadership as interpretation did not mean that leaders told citizens what to think, however. Instead, the leaders explained to the citizens what they *would think,* based on their own inclinations and partial thoughts, if only they had the time and energy to stop and to contemplate fully the common interest and the general good.

Furthermore, popular leadership did not follow the straight line of logic but instead the more convoluted path of habit and sentiment, "the actual windings of the channel" (662). Successful leadership, Wilson concluded, was a matter not of antagonism but of sympathy, "the impulse of a profound *sympathy* with those whom he leads,—a sympathy which is insight,—an insight which is of the heart rather than the intellect" (666, emphasis in original). Although circumstances and conditions, including variations across regimes, would demand leaders of varying characteristics, as Wilson observed in his later memo on leadership, there were common elements, including sensitivity, conceptual and interpretive prowess, initiative, and "subtle persistency" (Link et al. 1972, 12:365).

Finally, constraints on the leader were a crucial component of Wilson's conception of democratic statesmanship (Thorsen 1988, 232). In his notes for "The Modern Democratic State," under the subheading "Individualism" Wilson stated, "One dare not be so individual in social activity as in art, e.g., dare not outrun or shock the common habit; dare not *innovate*. Such is not the task of leadership" (Link et al. 1968, 5:59, emphasis in original). Similarly, in *The State* Wilson warned that the "habit of the nation" was a stubborn and sometimes volatile material that would resist a leader who sought to push it too far (Wilson 1890, 661–62). In "Leaders of Men" Wilson asserted that the political leader "must perceive the direction of the nation's permanent forces, and must feel the speed of their operation. There is initiative here, but not novelty. There are old *thoughts*, but a progressive *application* of them" (Link et al. 1969, 6:660, emphasis in original).

Summarizing his thoughts on the matter a decade later, Wilson concluded, "The problem of every government is leadership: the choice and control of statesmen and the scope that shall be given to their originative part in affairs; and for democracy it is a problem of peculiar difficulty" (Link et al. 1972, 12:178). Democracy's problem was "to control its leaders and yet not hamper or humiliate them; to make them its servants and yet give them leave to be masters too, not in name merely but in fact, of the policy of a great nation" (179). Helping democracy solve its problem, and in the process helping but also restraining its leaders, was the science of politics Wilson envisioned.

The Study of Politics

Wilson's ideas about a science of politics can be found among some of his earliest theorizing. Such a science would be based on historical and comparative analysis and dedicated to practical use in government. His notions about the nature of politics and the systematic study of it were an integral component of his ideas about democracy, and he periodically probed those aspects of his ideas, including their culminating expression in his 1910 presidential address to the American Political Science Association.

Wilson argued early on that representative government, while subject to logic in the long run, was primarily governed by short-run prejudice and convenience. Thus, a purely academic orientation, with its embrace of logic and reason, was inadequate as an approach to the study of politics. The proper approach, he insisted, had to be more in tune with the nature of politics in representative government and thus of "great direct aid to [government]" (Link et al. 1968, 5:139). He characterized politics as "an experimental art" and, more significantly, as "largely an affair of management and expediency" (140). He called for a regime-specific orientation to political analysis, envisioning "inquiry, through every available channel, as to the real forces now at work in politics and the actual operation of governments of the world. This would be, not a study of systems merely, but also of the circumstances and spirit which make each system workable in its own country and amongst its own people" (140). He insisted that students of politics had to seek alternate routes to understanding that passed through the works of the giants of literature like Shakespeare, not just the works of political theorists and philosophers. Such alternative paths were essential "to penetrate to the heart of the nation's—if possible, of *each* nation's—being, laying bare the springs of action and the intricacies of acquired habit, political morality as well as political forms, political prejudice and expediency, as well as political reason and rigid consistency."

Direct observation was a critical method, so the student of politics "must frequent the street, the counting-house, the drawing-room, the club house, the administrative offices, the halls—yes, and the lobbies—of the legislatures." Especially important was to learn "how men who are not students regard the Government and its affairs." One may acquire "many valuable suggestions" but more importantly "learn the available approaches to such men's thoughts." What was the purpose? "Government is meant for the good of ordinary people, and it is for ordinary people that the student should elucidate its problems" (399). Yet Wilson pointedly argued against a natural science orientation to the study of politics. He warned those who sought to make the study of politics a science against becoming too similar to economics, which sought to emulate the structure and methods of the natural sciences. The proper concept of science for the study of politics, he insisted, was "a science whose very expositions are as deathless as itself. It is the science of the life of man in society." That meant, again, that the student of politics had to get his hands dirty or learn nothing. Studying only in the library was counterproductive, for it might lead one to "admire self-government so much as to forget that it is a very coarse, homely thing when alive," so one "may really never know anything valuable about it" (405).

One of the most distinguishing features of Wilson's political science was his absolute and unshakable insistence that a theory of political organization and political conduct generally applicable to all states could not be fashioned out of a few *a priori* assumptions and idealistic principles. To build political theory on such foundations was to be speculative and doctrinaire, which was neither useful nor safe. It missed the subtleties, intricacies, and even the illogic of society that was the true stuff of politics, and it led to radicalism and revolutionary doctrine that was destructive of the habits, character, and sentiments of a people, which constituted the only realistic foundation for truly democratic governance.

In rejecting the radical and doctrinaire in political thinking, Wilson also rejected the rigid and unadaptable. A science of politics had to be oriented toward action and not just aimed at the refinement of political thought. It thus had to be oriented toward democratic development and changing conditions at the level of the nation and national leadership, and it had to address the past, what went on in other regimes, and current conditions so as to help guide leaders in taking the next step in the progress of the regime. Wilson thus saw an ultimate connection between the student of politics and the statesman that rested in a common aim. The "task, the difficult, elusive, complex, and yet imperative task of political science," Wilson announced in his APSA presidential address, was to build the sectioning, fragmentation, disorder, the "unprecedented differentiation" of modern social conditions "into a whole which shall be something more than a mere sum of the parts." But this was "also the task of the new statesmanship, which must be, not a mere task of compromise and makeshift accommodation, but a task of genuine and lasting adjustment, synthesis, coordina-tion, harmony, and union of parts" (Link et al. 1976, 22:265, 267). Instead of labeling the enterprise political science and treating it as a science, thus examining social phenomena as pure and separate forces, Wilson preferred the label "Politics," which included "both the statesmanship of thinking and the statesmanship of action" (271). Both were engaged in interpretation and needed to have "Shakespearian range and vision" to allow them to see "things fall into their places . . . , no longer confused, disordered, scattered abroad without plan or relation." Both must also yield to men's "passion and feel the pulse of their life" (270). The ultimate aim was to ensure that law and policy were an interpretation of life as a whole.

DEMOCRATIC STATESMANSHIP AND ADMINISTRATIVE POWER

In Woodrow Wilson's political theory, national sentiment—nationalism—had to be nurtured to ensure American democracy's adaptive success in the modern world. This endeavor was not to be arrayed solely against the old town and community foundations of democracy in the United States but also, and more substantially, against the fragmenting effects of the separation of powers doctrine and the party system and the divisive, disorderly effects—the profound differentiation—of modern social and economic forces. Wilson's conception of political development had at its core the notion of a struggle for order against disorder emanating from changing conditions. In democracy, moreover, the force of disorder also stemmed in part from the striving for power of the undifferentiated mass. In the development of his ideas about democracy after the publication of *Congressional Government*, Wilson clarified his view of modernity's impact by seeing in it forces of disorder that were particularly acute because of modernity's dynamic of constant change and flux (Thorsen 1988, 209). Of particular impact were the rising tides of international migration, economic dislocation and differentiation, and corporate power.

Wilson wondered how Edmund Burke's idea of "the representation of the classes and balance of forces in a state" could be understood organically. This led him to see the "Double processes of modern nations: the disintegration of politics and the interruption of the standards of life and opinion, the growing (?) action and power of the idea of nationality" (Link et al. 1970, 9:522, question mark in original). Over the course of the most intense period of development of his ideas about democracy, the synthesis Wilson insisted democracy represented and had to realize in order to adapt successfully to the modern world came to be the province of the statesman. The man of action would be assisted by the man of thought—the political scientist. The task of action supported by thought, in the hands of the statesman, was somehow to address the obvious tension between these prominent processes manifest in the modern democratic nation. Administration was the premier form of modern power available to the statesman. But there were serious questions that had to be addressed. Was administration more the realm of logic and reason rather than of emotion and sentiment, and therefore antagonistic to politics and self-government? The basic elements of public management—budgeting and accounting, analysis, program design, and organization for efficiency and results—would not seem at first blush compatible with the nature of politics, rooted in habit, morality, prejudice, and expediency. Furthermore, methods to make management of public affairs more effective had not developed in regimes with the history, habits, or coarse and homely practices of self-government. How could those methods usefully be imported and legitimated? Wilson confronted these questions in developing his ideas about administration's proper place and its effective practice in a modern democracy.

CHAPTER THREE

Situating Administration in the Modern Democratic State

As the cabinet government analysis turned Wilson's attention directly to administration, he almost immediately confronted a complex dilemma. Could he reconcile his realization that administrative politics and administrative power were the defining features of modern governance with a system predicated on a written constitution that separated the main functions of government, said little about the structure and function of administration, and relegated it to the primarily instrumental function of executing the law? Despite the constitutional premises, the view of administration dominant in American political culture, and his own predilections, Wilson realized that administration reached far beyond just carrying out the law. And carrying out the law was itself not a mere mechanical exercise. Wilson concluded that widespread acceptance in the polity of the centrality of administrative politics and administrative power, including acceptance of the use of more modern methods and practices not homegrown, required a major effort to legitimate a new, nationalized administrative system and define its proper role and function in the regime. This role would be an expansive one, because the impact of administration in an advanced democracy would clearly reach far beyond executing the law. It was a daunting challenge.

Developing a better understanding of the nature of modern democracy and the peculiarities of democracy in its American form was a necessary prelude to the definition and legitimation effort. This was a monumental project in itself, however. As a formal, stand-alone work of scholarship, Wilson never completed it. His treatise on a "Philosophy of Politics" was to be the project's culmination, but it remained unfinished, unstarted really, at his death. Wilson's legitimation project for administration thus had to proceed alongside his more general exploration of modern democracy. Just as important, the whole intermeshed enterprise extended beyond Wilson's scholarly years, with further reinforcement and development of core ideas taking place during his first presidential campaign and in his public speech and actions as president.

Throughout the legitimation project, Wilson struggled conceptually and normatively to define the limits of the sphere of administration. To shape an understanding of administration as a political institution and form of power within the constraints of American political structure and history seemed to require that such an understanding remain as close to an instrumental conception as possible. Yet recurringly and with increasing enthusiasm, Wilson found ways to describe and understand the role and function of administration that went beyond the instrumental to include the constitutive. Indeed, a world bursting with new ideas, social agitations, and technological and commercial advances seemed to require it. This is where the link between his work on administration and the other facets of this political thought are strongest, as eventually Wilson found a resolution for the legitimacy dilemma in the integrating function of statesmanship and the interpretation of public opinion, as ultimately vested in the presidency. It is less Wilson's particular resolution, however, and more the questions he raised and the insights he generated about the nature and legitimacy of administration and its connection to political leadership that make his ideas relevant to the continuing challenges confronting the study and practice of public management.

Over the nearly forty years of Wilson's rich and varied articulation of his ideas about democracy and administration, beginning with the publication of *Congressional Government* and ending with his first inauguration, five main ideas stand out as the core of Wilson's overall conception of administration's place in a modern democratic regime properly understood. The challenge toward which Wilson directed his thinking was to find the right relationship between public opinion and administration or, more precisely, to consider the design requisites for a political regime that was both popular and well-governed. These five ideas represent the building blocks with which Wilson constructed his long-run, and never fully complete, answer to the challenge. Specifically, Wilson argued that the following five elements defined the contours of administration's proper station in and contribution to the life of the modern democratic state: (1) modern administration was the manifestation of a particular developmental progression and stage of societal and political development; (2) administration reflected the peculiar nature of the functions taken on by modern government; (3) administration was embedded in the organic character of the modern state and was an important part of the modern state's ascent toward complete integration; (4) administration was dependent on the crucial role of leadership in articulating popular aspirations and making them the harness and motive force of government; and (5) effective administration required particular qualities of institutional design and organizational structure.

ADMINISTRATION IN PROGRESSIVE REGIME DEVELOPMENT

Recall that Wilson crafted an understanding of the character of modern democracy partly in developmental terms. Modern democracy as a type, and democracies as distinctive individual regimes, ascended through several stages, moving from the "police" state, to the "law" state, and finally arriving at some version of the "constitutional" state. Administration was an important aspect of this developmental progression, for it was the emergence of administrative questions at center stage in a regime in place of constitutional questions that marked a significant advance in maturity for a given democratic state. This was, in fact, a distinctive feature of Wilson's analysis in the first section of "The Study of Administration" before he assigned specific labels to the stages in his subsequent notes for his lectures on administration.

Wilson contended in the essay that administration became a critical component and central concern of a democratic regime in the regime's development when it had exhausted most of the questions of constitutional design and when it could no longer ignore the growing pressures of modernity and the concomitant demands for governmental action in response. In the third of "three periods of growth through which government has passed in all the most highly developed of existing systems . . . the sovereign people undertake to develop administration under [the] new constitution which has brought them into power" (Link et al. 1968, 5:365). This third period arrived when the "weightier debates of constitutional principle" although "by no means concluded," were "no longer of more immediate practical moment than questions of administration" (362).

Wilson implied that as a general rule, the rise of administration was a critical and inevitable stage of democratic regime development. But he argued that the "English race" had struggled with the transition to this new stage. He reiterated several times that democratic peoples who develop constitutions before they develop administration never really give up on arguing over constitutional design matters (see esp. 366–67). They eventually must, however, move from the constitutional questions, "Who shall make the law, and what shall that law be," to the administrative questions, "how [shall] law be administered with enlightenment, with equity, with speed, and without friction" (360–61).

It is curious that Wilson did not in the essay draw on his cabinet government treatise to distinguish between the United States and England as to the relative ease or difficulty with which the transition to the third period of development was navigated because of the design of government. One might have expected him to argue that England had been better prepared to face the rise of administration and did so sooner because of its embrace of the principle of ministerial responsibility. In Wilson's broader analysis, of course, it was England's transition to a government based on a responsible ministry that enabled its developmental advance and thus its governing focus on what had become primarily administrative questions. Yet Wilson offered no such comparison in the essay, restricting his analysis to obstacles peculiar to the United States.

With respect to the possibility of a transition in the United States to primarily administrative questions, then, Wilson located a specifically American difficulty traceable to its particular historical and cultural characteristics. Therefore, Americans needed a special boost into the third period of development featuring administrative centrality. This push would have to come from a realization of the distinctive demands of modernity and the accompanying necessities of modern governance. Thus, the modern conditions of "complexities of trade and perplexities of commerce," "giant monopolies," and "perennial discords between master and workman" (361) had driven "new conceptions of state duty" followed by administration "everywhere putting its hands into new undertakings" (362). A full realization of the demands, the necessities, the appropriate responses in organization and practice would be generated by a fundamental reform in the organization of government and by an Americanized science of administration.

Administrative Science and Regime Development

As he had stressed in two of his preparatory essays, "Notes on Administration" and "The Art of Governing," free governments were those in which public opinion had authoritative influence on public affairs. Americans would have to find ways to devise and legitimate a science of administration that had largely developed in governments that were "unfree" because even in the United States, "administrative questions are now very pressing questions" (54). Hence the development of a distinctive science of administration was a key characteristic of progressive democratic development. Before considering Wilson's initial thinking in this regard any further, however, I want to take note of Wilson's reference to free and unfree governments for what it reveals about the value Wilson placed on thinking developmentally concerning administration's legitimate role in a modern democracy.

In his "Notes on Administration," Wilson at first accepted in qualified form the notion advanced by the German scholar Barthold Niebuhr that liberty was dependent on administration. Wilson suggested that perhaps the "practical facilitation of [liberty's] exercise" might depend on administration. But he immediately rejected even that modification, declaring in no uncertain terms that administration had to remain subservient to liberal self-government. "Liberty consists in enlightened, *authoritative* public opinion—consists in the realization of the purposes of active, directive popular thought. Liberty lives and moves and has its being in self-government. Because subjection is without *chains* and is lightened by every easy-working device of considerate, paternal administration, it is not transformed into liberty" (50, emphasis in original).

Despite Robert Miewald's (1984, 22) conclusion that Wilson misapprehended Niebuhr's "famous dictum" as "a plea for more efficient management," Wilson seems not to have been contemplating management organization and practice here but rather the proper position of administration in a liberal-democratic polity. In "The Study of Administration," Wilson incorporated this point into his distinction between constitutional and administrative questions, stressing that administrative methods, even very liberal ones, were not the same as liberal constitutional principles—were not the same as the liberty enjoyed through self-government.

What does Wilson's thinking about the distinctions between liberal constitutional principles and liberal administrative methods reveal? Although not in its full and final form, Wilson had stated, even before composing his now-famous essay, the essence of his aims with respect to the study of administration: to find or develop new methods that would not supplant but rather serve the cause of liberty, popular rule, and national purpose by making democracy on a national scale work better. Administration's place had to be detailed within those general parameters. The importance of the distinction between substitution and service will loom large in my analysis later in this and subsequent chapters. The focus on *study* points to the importance of seeing what Wilson saw, that administrative study was a critical aspect of the *developmental* place of administration in the modern democratic state.

Administration, Public Opinion, and a Political Administrative Science

Wilson's point concerning the historical and developmental status of administration in a democratic regime went to the heart of the question he sought to address—the relationship between administration and public opinion. Although Wilson contended that this question was nearly universal given the democratizing trend around the world, it was especially acute in the United States. The "fundamental problem" for all democratic regimes was to address adequately the question, "What part shall public opinion take in the conduct of administration? The right answer seems to be, that public opinion shall play the part of authoritative critic" (374). In a democratic regime, public administration was thus subordinate to the reign of public opinion and, in accord with Wilson's *Congressional Government* analysis, subject to its informed scrutiny. In all democratic systems, administration had to pass the barrier of popular sovereignty and become accepted by "a multitudinous monarch called public opinion" (368), which, in its role of authoritative critic, had been instructed properly. In the United States, however, the challenge of passing the barrier was especially daunting because its share of the "unphilosophical bulk of mankind" exercising popular sovereignty was both "more multifarious in its composition" (369) and more "apt to think itself quite sufficiently instructed beforehand" (374). The operationalization of the relationship, more importantly, was a theoretical and practical challenge of both constitutional design and organizational structure that a science of administration could appropriately undertake—indeed, had to undertake —for a democratic regime's developmental ascent to continue.

The prospects for administrative science in this regard were again particularly daunting in the American case because of the need for adaptation "not to a simple and compact, but to a complex and multiform state, and . . . highly decentralized forms of government" (363), all of which perpetuated "the error of trying to do too much by vote" (374). This made it even more crucial to devise a conception of democracy based on the notion of public opinion as authoritative critic and to design an administrative system that fit with that conception. Wilson's thinking about democracy and about administration were thus inextricably linked. It is helpful to see this from the perspective of the implications of Wilson's conception of administrative science for his pursuit of a new science of politics.

As Niels Thorsen argued, Wilson's "focus on administration was an outgrowth of his work on the concept of the modern state and its attendant issues of constitutionalism, leadership, and political habit. Wilson had no need for an 'apolitical science of administration'" (Thorsen 1988, 128, quoting Caiden 1984). Wilson was not seeking in the essay to invent or import a science of administration but "to consider it from the 'outside,' that is, from a general political point of view." Wilson's pursuit of an administrative science thus reflected his focus on fundamental political questions. Whatever shape that science of administration ultimately would take, it had to be animated by these questions. Thorsen also stressed that it was "worth pausing to observe the extreme cautiousness with which Wilson enters the new field" (129).

Note also that, at least according to the evidence reviewed by the editors of Wilson's papers, Wilson composed "The Study of Administration" and "Of the Study of Politics" only about a month apart, in November 1886. Both stress the historical and comparative method—Wilson was quite profuse on the subject in "The Study of Administration" (see Link et al. 1968, 5:377–80)—although in "Of the Study of Politics," Wilson also stressed the importance of careful, detailed direct observation, even immersion, in the subtle and defining characteristics of political life in the student's own nation. In both essays Wilson also stressed the practical application of formal study of their subjects with the aim of improving governance. And both essays stressed the importance of taking regime differences into account. However, whereas in his views about the study of politics Wilson placed the central emphasis on learning the differences, his emphasis in the study of administration was on identifying the commonalities in administrative organization and practice across nations with very different politics and governments, so that those common or universal features of administration could be adapted to a specific regime, with all its subtle and defining features, to help it cope with any democratic state's universal developmental imperative: confronting and adjusting to the impacts of modernity.

Thus Wilson argued in the essay on administration, "Without comparative studies in government we cannot rid ourselves of the misconception that administration stands upon an essentially different basis in a democratic state from that on which it stands in a non-democratic state." By engaging in the kind of administrative study he gave shape to in the essay, "we would [find] but one rule of good administration for all governments alike. So far as administrative functions are concerned, all governments have a strong structural likeness; more than that, if they are to be uniformly useful and efficient, they *must* have a strong structural likeness" (377, emphasis in original). And there was nothing to fear from the investigation of other systems, because "nowhere else in the whole study of politics . . . can we make use of the historical comparative method more safely than in the province of administration." Such study would be both revealing—"of ourselves, so long as we know only ourselves, we know nothing" (378)—and useful, "making what is democratically politic towards all administratively possible towards each" (379).

All of this was in important respects a developmental matter. To progress, modern democracies had to devise a new science of politics that recognized, as Wilson would later argue, that they were more like living beings subject to the laws of biology, rather than machines subject to the laws of physics. Ultimately, Wilson saw this as the need to develop a science of national political leadership, of democratic statesmanship, in response to the driving conditions of modernity. A democratic state that clung to notions of politics as primarily if not exclusively constitutional rather than administrative, clung to its old ways of allocating political authority and ordering its lawmaking and policy execution, would not long survive. A distinctive science of administration would arrive as an imperative when attention centered on "running" constitutions rather than on making them. Administrative science would serve the new political science (and the new conceptions of national democratic governance devised by political science) by answering questions about the proper design of an administrative system and the appropriate relationship between administration and public opinion. Its answers about place and practice would not be substitutes for democratic politics but enhancements. At the early stage of the development of his ideas represented by the two study essays, however, Wilson had not yet considered a crucial question: toward what were modern democratic states progressing and what functions and roles would administration thus have to fulfill? Wilson proceeded to address these questions in his lectures, which became the primary vehicle of expression for his most expansive ideas about situating administration in a modern democratic regime.

THE FUNCTIONS OF GOVERNMENT

Wilson's expanding conception of administration emerged more fully in his first set of lectures on administration, delivered at Johns Hopkins. He reiterated the ideas articulated in the lectures in the last several chapters of his second major published work, *The State*, filling in some of the sketchiness of the lecture notes and signaling the public law direction toward which he eventually took his newly expanded conception of administration.

Wilson declared at the outset of the first of four lecture topics that in order to understand administration, it was necessary to consider the subject in the context of larger questions about the functions of government. The twin aims were, first, to reach "a just conception of the importance and domain of Administration, whose problems concern always the best ways of accomplishing [government's] tasks and duties" and, second, to differentiate "the laws of *Administration* from the laws of *business*, namely the actual distinctive character of the State" (Link et al. 1968, 5:670, emphasis in original). As he had signaled in "The Study of Administration," Wilson was beginning to think of administration as more than simply the application of business practices to government. Although many of the structures and methods of public administration may be very businesslike, administration as an institution reached beyond them to touch all the functions of the organic state.

Wilson proceeded to point out that factual questions about the functions of the state—what it did in the past, what it did over the course of the development of human civilization, what it does now—were often confounded by questions of what the state ought to do. Wilson took the position that the empirical should precede the normative: "What government *does* must find its roots in what government *is:* and what government is must determine what government ought to *do*" (670, emphasis in original). Wilson then introduced a crucial conceptual innovation by identifying two distinct groups of functions: constituent and ministrant.

By constituent functions Wilson meant functions that constituted the state, that made it what it was. No government, no state, existed without them. He listed them as including the protection of life, liberty, and property, "together with other functions that are *necessary to the civic organization of society,*—functions which are *not optional* with governments, even in the eyes of strictest *laissez faire,*—which are indeed the very bonds of society" (670–71, emphasis in original). Summarizing his conception, Wilson described them as defining "what the state *does*, that it *is*"—the functions that embody its existence (671, emphasis in original). In his second lecture topic, he labeled them "genetic" (677).

By ministrant functions, Wilson meant functions that were not constitutive of the state and society but enhancements of the basic order of society, intended to take care of a society and serve the good life or the good society. These *were* optional, and "undertaken, not by way of *governing*, but by way of advancing the general interests of society, . . . being necessary only according to standards of *convenience* or *expediency*, and not according to standards of *existence*, which assist without constituting social organization" (671, emphasis in original).

Wilson enumerated examples of both functions, with ministrant functions including public utilities and the regulation of industries and labor as well as social welfare and natural resource conservation. He admitted, however, that "the line of demarcation is not always clear" between the two (672), for "even among these ministrant functions there are some which everybody recognizes as habitual with most governments" (677). This distinction in functions allowed Wilson to argue that constituent functions differed very little across modern governments but that there were substantial differences in such functions between ancient and modern governments. Those differences, such as the control or regulation of property, were differences "*of policy, not of power*" (675, emphasis in original). All states, even those constituted in a most rudimentary form, had the power and faced the necessity to organize and regulate property somehow. Questions about the *extent* of the exercise of this power were questions of principle. Principles for organizing and regulating property were obviously different in ancient than in modern times, and thus the order of society was constituted differently at different times. Again, however, these principles followed the effects of historical circumstances, and changes in principles about the extent of the exercise of constituent functions did not "change . . . the *essential* nature of the State" (677, emphasis in original).

The importance for a given system of administration in Wilson's conception of constituent functions was that it had to take heed of the underlying principles developed from experience by which its state exercised a constituent function. How the state exercised administrative power in association with a constituent function had to conform to the constituent principles that had developed with that function. Later, by associating administration with the accumulation of experience in the state, Wilson would suggest a feedback loop of sorts by implying that administration played a role in fomenting changes in constitutive principles.

The Individual, the State, and Administration

When he took up ministrant functions in his second lecture topic, Wilson argued that although some ministrant functions could be considered the result of habitual development, for the most part they were in kind the same in both ancient and modern governments. All states had to minister their societies with respect to convenience and expediency and thus toward societal betterment. (In that sense, then, they were not really optional—but they were not among the elements that gave a state the minimum requirements for existence.) The actual distinction between ancient and modern was in the "morals and the conscience of government." Although basic ministrations were much the same—even, perhaps, with respect to practices employed—they were undertaken in the context of "new ideas as to what constitutes social convenience and advancement." The individual rather than the state was now at the center, and the state had to confront the complexities and demands of modern industrial development in ways that would foster individual development. Modern governments thus could not take a paternalistic stance and attempt to "administer" the lives of individuals directly. Individuals needed autonomy and social space to develop, even as government provided support appropriate to the new ideas society had adopted and in the context of modern conditions that provided both great new opportunities for, and substantial barriers to, individual development.

Wilson's purpose for pointing out this "great and profound change" (689) in the way modern, liberal-democratic states undertook ministrant functions was to consider the implications for public administration. Thus he concluded the second lecture by arguing that although there might be some truth in the notion that public administration was "merely the *business* side of government," testing it against "standards of propriety and efficiency" (689, emphasis in original) for corporations was fundamentally misleading. He stressed that "rules of good business are not always rules of good politics. . . . The State in a large and increasing measure shapes our lives" by means of ministrant functions. This had clear implications for administration because "a body which shapes our lives must have many principles of organization necessarily unknown to a body which controls only a portion of our money." Hence administration "may and should be" businesslike, "but it is not business. *It is organic social life*" (690, emphasis in original). Wilson concluded that the study of administration was the study of how it occupied the domain of organic social life. The aim of that study was to find the organizational principles that would allow the state to realize its purposes.

Wilson incorporated much of this analysis into the text of *The State*. Interestingly, he positioned it after his chapters on "The Nature and Forms of Government" and "Law: Its Nature and Development" and before his final chapter on "The Objects of Government." In his chapter on law, he defined public law as "that which immediately concerns the being, the structure, the functions, and the methods of the state" (Wilson 1890, 632). But the functions of government were clearly precedent to law, in Wilson's view, and were linked most directly to the fundamental principles and changing conditions that shaped society. Law and constitutions were the formal culmination of society's experience with changing conditions processed through government and its functions, particularly the ministrant ones. But the relationship between public law and administration was something Wilson needed to think through much more extensively. This became dramatically obvious when, in his final chapter of *The State* on the ends of government, Wilson attempted to grapple with current issues and offered normative analysis based on his preceding historical and comparative assessment.

Reading in the history of democratic systems the dynamic of adaptive growth, Wilson declared that the purpose of government should be "*to accomplish the objects of organized society*: there must be constant adjustments of governmental assistance to the needs of a changing social and industrial organization. Not license of interference on the part of government, only strength and adaptation of regulation. The regulation that I mean is not interference: it is the equalization of conditions, so far as possible, in all branches of endeavor; and the equalization of conditions is the very opposite of interference" (660–61, emphasis in original). Pressing the point further, and aiming straight at the looming controversy surrounding the emergence of industrial and commercial trusts and monopolies in the increasingly industrialized United States, Wilson articulated a key point about liberty understood as autonomous individual growth and development. The point further encompassed social control of private economic behavior and the ordered adaptations to changing conditions the state had to make:

Every rule of development is a rule of adaptation, a rule for meeting "the circumstances of the case"; but the circumstances of the case . . . are not, so far as government is concerned, the circumstances of any individual case, but the circumstances of society's case, the general conditions of social organization. The case for society stands thus: the individual must be assured the best means, the best and fullest opportunities, for complete self-development: in no other way can society itself gain variety and strength. But one of the most indispensable conditions of opportunity for self-development government alone, society's controlling organ, can supply. All combination which necessarily creates monopoly, which necessarily puts and keeps indispensable means of industrial or social development in the hands of a few, and those few, not the few selected by society itself but the few selected by arbitrary fortune, must be under either the direct or indirect control of society. To society alone can the power of dominating combination belong; and society cannot suffer any of its members to enjoy such a power for their own private gain independently of its own strict regulation or oversight. (661)

In this passage, Wilson seems to have been expressing one sense of the dynamic tension between social and economic differentiation and political unity he saw as emblematic of modern liberal democracies. But who or what would be responsible for this balancing of public and private to ensure liberty, order, and social control in individual cases? It was a task that Wilson soon clearly designated for administration, in a state that was organically whole but with statesmen overseeing it to ensure congruence with public opinion.

THE VITAL ORGAN OF EXPERIENCE

In announcing his cycle of lectures on administration, which he commenced in February 1888, Wilson promised three or four lectures on introductory topics ranging from the functions of government to the nature and method of administrative study. He sought a "concise statement" (Link et al. 1968, 5:668) of the general principles and leading questions surrounding the subject. He then intended to move primarily to principles of organization and practice, including local government organization, special functions like sanitation and regulation of trade, and general subjects addressing reorganization, and arrangements for establishing responsibility and control. Wilson envisioned a progressive ordering of his topics, "from the existing machinery to the standing problems, the general tests, and the essential principles of Administration" (669).

The published Wilson papers suggest an initial delivery on this promise in the first cycle that was somewhat fragmented and underdeveloped. It is not fully evident whether Wilson delivered lectures on all of his planned topics. By the beginning of the second cycle in February 1890, he had produced a more organized and con- tiguous set of lecture topics. By late January of 1891, he had devised a full three-year sequence, which he repeated through 1896. Wilson did not deliver another full cycle after that, but his lecture material on administration found its way into a series of classroom lectures on public law and constitutional law as well as a substantial number of related public lectures and addresses. The lectures covered a wide range of topics represented by a dense and detailed set of notes. Indeed, Wilson's notes for the second and third cycles of lectures on administration at Johns Hopkins alone cover nearly 170 pages in the published Wilson papers. Much of this is repetitious, but some development in concepts and arguments is evident. Also, by far the bulk of the lecture material addressed matters of organization and practice, which I explore in chapter 4. It is primarily in the lecture material developed and delivered between 1890 and 1898 that Wilson articulated the idea of administration as a vital organ of the organically integrated democratic state.

Defining Administration's Reach

Wilson devoted the first seven subjects of his most advanced lecture cycle to defining the sphere of administration's reach in a democratic regime. Four reason- ably distinct components to that definition are evident in Wilson's notes. Together, they establish a remarkably wide scope of action and influence for administration that required a subtle, careful case for its legitimacy.

First, Wilson made clear that in his view administration did not consist of the mere instrumental function of carrying formal, written law into effect. It went be- yond "mere executive management" and a concern only with "the mechanism of government" (Link et al. 1969, 7:114–15). Administration was a branch of public law; it was intimately connected to the other branches, so it was grounded in fundamen- tal political principles and the historical and developmental foundations of constitu- tions. Even more important, administration was a part of the vitality of the state. Because of that it was national in scope and had to reflect and embody the peculiari- ties—the "national habit and national sentiment" (116)—of a given national state and its origins, growth, and likely future developmental directions. But administration also had "universal, international" (115, emphasis deleted) qualities. For those meth- ods of administration that could be regarded as "mere matters of business effective- ness" (116, emphasis deleted), it was possible to arrive at a single, best way. If comparative study of administration could show the "individual differences and . . . common likenesses," then it would reveal "a just conception of the usual province of the State" across regimes (115).

This first component in Wilson's conception of administration seems readily consistent with the general understanding of public management theory and practice that exists today, especially the notion of certain universal practices and techniques that could be adopted around the globe. Wilson especially emphasized administration's national scope and perspective, however. Particularly with respect to organization and practice but also regarding institutional status, Wilson put great weight on what he called administrative "integration." As an institution—an organ of the state—and as the premier form of modern power, Wilson did not accept that administration could be casually—or worse, theoretically—divided into federal, state, and local spheres. One studied municipal administration, for instance, as part of an overall study of administration in a modern democratic state. Administration had to be understood as a whole, not subdivided into disconnected parts. To do the latter would undermine the study and practice of administration aimed at national development and adaptation to modernity.

For the second component of his definition, Wilson identified administration as the realm of pragmatism, of what is possible for the state to do. It is concerned with the practical and workable, it is the sphere of action. It "sees government in contact with the people," and it "touches, directly or indirectly, the whole practical side of social endeavor" (116, emphasis deleted). Wilson thus argued that the scope of administrative power was "considerably wider and much more inclusive" than the executive power of classical liberal theory. "Besides the duty of executing positive law, there rest upon the administrative organs of every State those duties of provident protection and wise cooperation and assistance," whether "explicitly enjoined by [legislative] enactment" or not, that enabled the government to fulfill its ministrant functions. Administrative action also encompassed "the actual carrying into effect of the purpose or judgments of the State" from adjudicative bodies, and the regulation "of the carrying out of the functions of the State" (130, emphasis deleted).

The third component, of much more significant implication, was Wilson's articulation of the relationship between law and administration, and the distinctions separating administration, legislation, and adjudication. The editors of the Wilson papers argue that Wilson achieved an "intellectual breakthrough in early 1890 by defining administration as a branch of public law" (Link et al. 1969, 7:112). Yet the overall picture Wilson presents in his lecture notes is of administration as institution and form of political power that is barely held back by the restraints imposed by law. The source of Wilson's conception was Edmund Burke's pronouncement that "the laws reach but a very little way." Burke contended that "all the use and potency of the laws" depended on "the prudence and uprightness of ministers of state." Without such men, "your commonwealth is no better than a scheme upon paper; and not a living, active, effective organization" (see Link et al. 1969, 7:122n1). Wilson quoted from Burke on this score in nearly every classroom and public lecture he delivered on administration, public and constitutional law, and the democratic state. It is one of the epigrams heading chapter 1 of *Congressional Government*. Although left unacknowledged, it must also have been at least in part the basis of his observation in his final scholarly work, *Constitutional Government*, that "governments are always governments of men, and no part of any government is better than the men to whom that part is intrusted" (Wilson 1908, 17). On its basis, he portrayed administration as tethered to law but not encircled by it.

The confines of administration as an object of study were limited, Wilson admitted, because it had arrived late as a systematic science. It thus had to take the leftovers from other social and economic sciences that had already developed special methods and areas of study. The study and practice of constitutional law had in particular severely limited the acceptable purview of an administrative science. But that could not keep administrative study, and now even administration itself as an appendage of the state, from confronting "that great question" concerning the proper functions of government, because "the functions of government are in a very real sense independent of legislation, and even of constitutions." They are "as old as government and inherent in its very nature." Furthermore, the volume and detail of positive law masked the reality that "Administration cannot wait upon legislation, but must be given leave, or take it, to proceed without specific warrant in giving effect to the characteristic life of the State" (Link et al. 1969, 7:121, emphasis deleted). From that point on Wilson followed a rapid upward trajectory for his characterization of the scope and reach of administration beyond positive law.

In his treatment of the distinctions dividing administration, legislation, and adjudication, Wilson portrayed much of adjudicative activity and especially of legislative activity as in reality administrative in nature or effect. The legislature often took the first step in a long chain of actions that were really administrative. What made something formally legislative and distinct from administrative was formalization as an enactment "and thus made [a command] of the legislative organs of the State" (131). In essential as opposed to formal terms, legislation concerned "the delimitation of the rights and duties of subjects towards one another, or of their rights and duties as towards the State itself" (130). For Wilson, keeping in mind the conceptual distinction between the formal and essential senses of legislation—and adjudication as well—revealed that administration could act in legislative and adjudicative ways.

As suggested by his characterization of the essence of legislation, the only real legal limitations on administration stemmed from positive constitutional rights (recall that Wilson did not accept the idea of natural rights).

A rights-based legal limitation on administration was not all that robust either. Wilson recognized that the law did set limits on administrative action "in the recognition of a sphere of individual will and rights" (142). In exploring those limitations in the context of bills of rights, which he saw as protecting what he called "personality," or the autonomy and welfare of the individual, Wilson contended that it "is not true" that the rights stated in bills of rights "in their most abstract or general terms . . . constitute an absolute check on administrative action" (153). Even considering rights from the "first general aspect of individuality"—that is, maintaining the autonomy of the individual and considering the most protective of rights, the "inviolability of person,"—Wilson argued that they did not "prevent the use of force by administrative agents for the accomplishment of any of the legitimate objects of government" (154). When it came to considering rights protecting personality in its second, social aspect, such as citizenship, Wilson saw the realization of such rights and the "bettered and enlarged" social person they fostered as dependent on administration (156–57). Wilson also pointed out that administrative organizations acting legislatively could create rights or duties without the sanction of the legislature (136).

Therefore, administration was "indirectly a constant source of public law. It is through Administration that the State makes a test of its own powers and of the public needs,—makes [a] test also of law, its efficiency, suitability, etc." (138, emphasis deleted). To the question of to what extent law served to place boundaries on administrative action, Wilson answered that the "sphere of administrative authority is as wide as the sphere in which it may move without infringing the laws, statutory or customary, either in their letter or in their reasonable inferential meaning" (150, emphasis deleted). In short, because administration occupied the social and temporal space between social life on the one hand and formalization of habits and experience in written laws and constitutions on the other, it did not just carry out such formal law but filled in all the gaps left by law and generated abundant material central to shaping law and constitutions. To the extent that law and the institutions created by law had some formative effect on the individual in his social development, administration at least indirectly possessed constitutive power.

The fourth component is the most extensive, complex, and remarkable aspect of Wilson's conception of the place of administration in a democratic regime. Wilson portrayed administration as playing the vital role in a liberal democracy of balancing public and private. Through its actions, administration defined what does and does not constitute governmental interference in private life, particularly private economic activity: "It rests its whole front along the line which is drawn in each State between *Interference* and *Laissez faire*" (116, emphasis in original). As a result of this role, of its more general station as observer of and participant in governmental contact with the people, and of its constant "contact with the present," administration was "the State's experiencing organ." The effect on law was actually twofold. Administration was a direct source of law through administrative traditions and practices shaping customary, or common, law. Administration was also an indirect source of law, as noted above, "by way of suggestion or initiative," testing out laws on the books or taking action on cases for which no law directly and obviously applied (138, emphasis deleted). In this respect, then, as Wilson articulated it most directly in his Princeton public law lectures, "The Real Functions of the Administration are not merely ministerial: they are also adaptive, guiding, discretionary" (Link et al. 1970, 9:31).

Wilson's reasoning behind the two aspects of this fourth component—the balancing of public and private and the discretionary, experiencing, guiding function—are especially revealing of Wilson's thinking about administration's place in a modern democracy and about the route to legitimating that understanding of administration's regime status and role in the minds of the American people. Interestingly, Wilson argued that administration was the science of choice. As long as the state could do whatever it wanted, at any time, "no science of choice or wisdom" was necessary. But with the advent and growth of the liberal democratic state, with its emphasis on the autonomy and development of the individual and thus the need to define and preserve a sphere of private life relatively free from government interference, decisions by the state about what conditions justified interference, to what extent, and in what form were necessary. Administration, and thus administrative science as well, was put to the task. What it learned from its day-to-day contact with "the people" in carrying out laws and in addressing situations in which no existing law clearly applied, administration could then contribute to the process of fashioning new laws and of making constitutional changes, all of which would be part of the living, growing, adaptive life of state and polity.

Wilson's depiction of the reach and extent of administration's necessary role in a modern democracy seemingly stood in sharp contrast to the conception of administration dominant in American political culture and traditions. As Tocqueville had characterized it most pungently, "The majority, being in absolute command both of lawmaking and of the execution of laws, and equally controlling both rulers and ruled, regards public functionaries as its passive agents and is glad to leave them the trouble of carrying out its plans. . . . It treats them as a master might treat his servant if, always seeing them act under his eyes, he could direct or correct them at any moment" (1988, 253–54). Wilson would offer his own rendition of this characterization in his essay of 1900 "Democracy and Efficiency" (see Link et al. 1972, 12:16–17). But here stood Wilson, characterizing administration as a separate branch of public law, as at least a semi-autonomous institution that exercised the central form of modern power, that was subject to the bounds of existing law, but that was continuously and actively engaged not just in extending the law but in modifying and reshaping it and thus potentially refashioning constitutions as a result. Wilson's strategy for legitimating this remarkable conception was grounded in his developmental perspective on administration's place in a democratic regime and in an understanding of political liberty not limited by a foundation only in positive law.

Legitimating Administration's Extensive Role

As noted earlier in this chapter, Wilson characterized the historical development of the modern democratic state as going through several stages of increasing sophistication and organic integration of its political institutions. The last stage, the "constitutional state," was that at which "a self-conscious, adult, self-regulating (democratic) State" came into being (Link et al. 1969, 7:127). Wilson contended that England had reached that stage of development—indeed, that it was the experience of the English that made the realization of such a state possible. In contrast, the United States was still at the "law state" stage of development, in which the administration and the people were bound together in a "common system of law." The problem with this stage was that the life of the state was much more than what was captured in its laws or even in a written constitution. Laws reflected life, they did not contain it. "Law must integrate, must reflect the organic," Wilson insisted (126, emphasis deleted). This meant that it was not enough that governmental institutions in a mature democracy be bound together by law. As the living components of the principal organ of the state—the government—they had to be organically integrated, reflecting a definite understanding between the community and the government about the proper relationship between the government's powers and the life of the polity.

The essence of Wilson's legitimation argument for a broadly influential place for administration in the modern democracy the United States was becoming was that the public had no reason to fear administration's reach and influence. It would be properly integrated into the life of the state, and its scope and influence would benefit the government and the community when the American state as a whole reached maturity, in the "constitutional" stage of development. This would happen when the legislative and administrative organs were integrated under some arrangement based on ministerial responsibility or something akin to it. Legal constraints and various organizational designs and other practices, including hierarchy, would of course be employed to ensure responsible administration. But the most important guarantee was organic integration. A constitutional government was not one with a particular written constitution or organizational form or particular administrative devices, Wilson concluded. It was, instead, one "which is restrained by the recognition of Liberty." Political liberty, in turn, was "not the negation of order, but the perfection of it,—the equable and cooperative play of elements, the harmonious correlation of forces. It is action within the best order. Like health, it depends upon a nice balance of functions" (158, emphasis deleted). Administration was neither the source of nor a necessary condition for liberty. But properly integrated administration greatly facilitated the realization of political liberty in the modern age. Americans therefore had no need to fear administration as an outside, potentially tutelary power once it was fully integrated organically in a mature, constitutional state (see Link et al. 1970, 9:11). Preoccupied with their grand task of balancing public and private (the problem with which the modern liberal democratic state was most consumed) and informing legislators' policy decisions in that regard, administrators would have no interest in deploying administrative power for their own interests and dominance or for the interests of a privileged few. They would instead deploy it to foster the further development of the individual, which was the principal purpose of the modern state, and thus also for national progress and national greatness.

Wilson's conception of administration as having broad reach and influence in a modern democracy and his argument legitimizing that conception in terms of organic integration in a democratic state that had reached maturity remained relatively consistent over the decade of the 1890s across the numerous lectures he delivered on administration and on public and constitutional law. Yet his expansive conception of administration forced Wilson to struggle further with the critical issue concerning the extent of *direct* popular influence on administration. Wilson had defended "the propriety of administrative initiative in law-making" grounded in the importance of administration to the organic state beyond carrying out the law. He also accepted the "propriety of the participation of representatives of the people in certain acts of administration" on the same basis as well as on "all constitutional history" (Link et al. 1969, 7:139, emphasis deleted). But he refused to concede any direct participation of the people in administration. Although "general law" rested upon "general consent," administration specifically could "never have such an origin or foundation: and the only valid ground of objection to popular government lies on the side of administrative interference. The interference of the popular power in the field of administration can never be anything but maladroit" (Link et al. 1970,

9:31–32). Wilson was thus very wary, to say the least, about notions of popular participation in administrative actions. The people and the administration ought to be kept at some distance from one another, and the people's representatives would span that distance. (As I show in chapter 4, this arm's length arrangement was primarily relevant to *national* administration.)

For much of the time over which Wilson had developed and refined his conception of the proper place of administration in a democratic regime—the American regime in particular—he emphasized his new public executive, the responsible minister, as the people's representative he had in mind. Consistent with his *Congressional Government* critique and his idea of organic integration, he contended that the problem for the United States was that it could not be a constitutional state as long as it had a structure in which popularly elected legislators *not* responsible for administration could interfere in administration's organization and operation. Such interference damaged administration's discretionary, guiding, adapting capacities and functions as well as its signal contribution to the increased efficiency of modern democratic governance. Absent a restructuring to produce this new contingent of public executives who would be both legislative leaders and responsible administrative leaders, which despite Wilson's unceasing advocacy seemed increasingly unlikely, the United States would need some other institutional arrangement that would ensure an appropriate bond between administration and public opinion—and the proper distance. In the 1890s and early 1900s, Wilson promoted the president's cabinet, properly modified to ensure responsible party government, as the institutional vehicle through which administration and lawmaking could be bound together, thus achieving at least some form of organic integration in the American state. An administration of sweeping scope would then be responsible and trustworthy. Ultimately, however, Wilson turned to the presidency itself as the institution necessary to satisfy both the developmental requirement and the legitimation imperative for administration in the regime.

INTEGRATING LEADERSHIP: FROM CABINET TO PRESIDENCY

In an 1893 essay exploring Grover Cleveland's presidency, Wilson argued that his countrymen needed to learn from the manner in which Cleveland had structured his presidency and especially his cabinet. In his second term, Cleveland had a cabinet not "constituted . . . as a party council, but rather as a body of personal counsellors" (Link et al. 1970, 8:172). This led Wilson to pose a question reflecting a "fundamental" constitutional choice: "What kind of government are we to have?" Was it to be one with a "purely administrative cabinet, and individual choice of policy by the President" or "responsible party government, parties being made responsible not only for the choice they make of Presidents, but also for the character and motives of the men they bring forward to give him counsel" (173)? Pushing the point further, Wilson asked, "What *is* the Cabinet?" Was it, like Cleveland's, a mere extension of the sitting president, "or are the heads of the executive departments meant by the spirit of our national institutions to be real party colleagues of the President . . . ?" This was, again, "a question fundamental to our whole political development, and it is by no means answered from out of the text of the Constitution simply," said Constitution being only a "vehicle" of political life and self-government and not its source (175, emphasis in original).

Wilson then presented his case that if Americans were not willing to consider a formal, structural change to achieve the mature development of the American state and its organic integration, especially with respect to administration, they should at least consider an informal modification through the cabinet. As he had argued throughout the preceding decade, laws were better made and better administered when there was "close cooperation and an intimate mutual understanding" between executive and legislature (176). "Ours is the only country in the world of any consequence," Wilson insisted, in which a close, cooperative arrangement of this sort did not exist, but "sooner or later" recognition would come that such an arrangement was needed. Responding sooner would be advantageous, with the nation requiring "our Presidents, not by hard and fast constitutional provision, but by the more flexible while equally imperative mandates of public opinion, operating through the medium of the Senate, to call to the chief places in the departments representative party men who have accredited themselves for such functions by long and honorable public service" (177). Concluding the essay, Wilson called for "harmonious, consistent, responsible party government, instead of a wide dispersion of function and responsibility; and we can get it only by connecting the President as closely as may be with his party in Congress. The natural connecting link is the cabinet" (178).

Wilson issued much the same call in his 1897 address "Leaderless Government": "We should have Presidents and Cabinets of a different calibre were we to make it their bounden duty to act as a committee for the whole nation to choose and formulate matters for the consideration of Congress in the name of a party and an Administration; and then, if Congress consented to the measure, what they already are—a committee to execute them—make them work and approve themselves practicable and wise" (Link et al. 1971, 10:303). Wilson completed the address with the general call for "nationalization of the motive power of the government, to offset the economic sectionalization of the country." He suggested "the addition to Congress, which represents us severally, of a power, constituted how you will, which shall represent us collectively in the proposing of laws; which shall have the right as of course to press national motives and courses of action to a vote in Congress" (304).

By 1898, however, in notes for a course on constitutional government, such references to the cabinet had disappeared. Instead, Wilson advanced the idea of integrated leadership binding president and Congress and extending beyond law-making to administration. His general conclusion was that there could be "no lead-ership operating throughout the course of affairs, *without a single leadership* embrac-ing both the Presidency and Congress." He defined the "most developed form of constitutional government" as that under which "a cordial understanding between people and government . . . extends *beyond questions of fundamental law* to ques-tions of administration and policy." This could only be possible, however, "when the people's real leaders constitute the government in both its parts, the planning *and* the executing" (Link et al. 1971, 11:15, emphasis in original).

While Wilson was delivering his constitutional government classroom lectures, he was also giving public talks on the same topics. In those talks he had begun to turn the focus on the presidency as the institution with the best chance of providing integrating national leadership and solving the administrative legitimacy problem, particularly in light of the growing international demands on the nation. His principal device for making his case was a renewed stress on "efficiency and responsibility." In his 1900 essay on "Democracy and Efficiency," Wilson reiterated the point he had been making since "The Study of Administration." He argued that any polity that had "the principle of representation at the centre of its arrangements, where counsel is held and policy determined and law made, . . . can afford to put into its administrative organization any kind of businesslike power or official authority and any kind of discipline as if of a profession that it may think most likely to serve it" (Link et al. 1972, 12:17). Unlike the lack of attention to leadership in the 1887 essay, however, Wilson stressed in the later essay the painful absence "in our domestic arrangements, above all things else, [of] concentration, both in political leadership and in administrative organization." In contrast to the dispersion of authority and the minimization of leadership that prevailed in lawmaking and "administrative action," the new impera-tive was that "leadership must be single, open, responsible, and of the whole" (18).

Administrative Legitimacy and Presidential Leadership

This brings us to Wilson's last book, *Constitutional Government.* In June 1902, Wilson ascended to the presidency of Princeton University and became deeply immersed in leading the institution into a new, more academically vigorous era. Over the course of his term, several of his reform efforts engendered increasing political conflict within the institution, imposing even greater demands on Wilson's energy and attention. Wilson also was increasingly drawn to direct engagement in politics and public commentary on major issues of the day, especially concerning industrial and commercial concentration in the American economy. Increasing talk in Democratic Party circles of Wilson's potential as a candidate for office piqued Wilson's interest even more. In the midst of all this, however, Nicholas Murray Butler, his counterpart at Columbia University, invited Wilson to deliver the Blumenthal Lectures. Wilson did so in the late winter and early spring of 1907. He edited the lecture transcripts extensively before publication. Despite his disclaimer that he did not intend the published version of the lectures to be "a systematic discussion of the character and operation of the government of the United States," the volume stands as a remarkable synthesis of Wilson's political thought up to that time, leavened by a "fresh point of view" and a "fresh analysis of the character and operation of constitutional government" (Wilson 1908, v).

As Niels Thorsen's analysis of the book deftly showed (1988, 198–213), Wilson's presentation of the presidency as the proper institutional home for integrating national leadership was not a simple shift of allegiance or orientation from his long embrace of the responsible minister. Fundamental to Wilson's fresh point of view and analysis was an understanding of the nature of the new, modern American citizen. No longer was the citizen principally a critical spectator of national debates in Congress led by those responsible ministers. Now, citizens were heavily preoccupied with the demands of modern life, particularly "the pursuit of economic objectives. This implied that the new citizen was less interested in listening and more ready to ask for, or even to pressure the government for, help in the realization of material interests" (200). The most important governmental institution, in Wilson's new analysis, turned out to be the courts.

In Wilson's treatise, according to Thorsen, the courts were a critical institution of administrative integration in American constitutional development, an understanding consistent with more contemporary scholarly analyses (e.g., Keller 1977; Skowronek 1982). The new, more modernized citizen found the courts the most useful institutional vehicle for individual, primarily material, development "in an interest-ridden, competitive, litigious society with its ever-changing meaning for the terms *individual rights* and *property*" (Thorsen 1988, 201, emphasis in original). Thorsen further interprets Wilson as contending that the principal function of the courts "was to absorb, administer, authorize, and direct individual interests and energies toward the national interest" (203). By virtue of the principles, character, habits, and developmental circumstances of the polity, as embodied in the Constitution, the American democratic state was directed toward "the growth and development of national power." Although the courts "had nurtured and restrained" the energies directed toward this national development, one of the national "representative institutions" had to bring it to "self-consciousness" (204).

Consistent with his longstanding critique, Wilson did not find the Congress capable of fulfilling that need. Also, from a historical, developmental standpoint, Grover Cleveland had permanently ended any possibility for an informal approximation of cabinet government (Wilson 1908, 75–76). Hampered by localism and bossism and by the growing public distrust toward them, neither the states nor the parties could fill the need. But the "revolution of communications" and the "revolution in foreign affairs" provided the president the upper hand in becoming "the focus of national unity" (Thorsen 1988, 207). More important, the presidency embodied institutionally—and the president embodied personally—both the legitimacy of government conferred by popular rule through universal suffrage and the efficiency of the executive at the head of administration, which, again, could only be understood and accepted in national terms. As Wilson argued early in the book, "The object of constitutional government is to bring the active, planning part of government into accord with the prevailing popular thought and need, and thus make it an impartial instrument of symmetrical national development" (Wilson 1908, 14). The president embodied this accord, thus standing as a bridge to Congress, party, administration, and nation by "being spokesman for the real sentiment and purpose of the country," "giving direction to opinion," and "giving the country at once the information and the statements of policy which will enable it to form its judgments alike of parties and of men" (68).

As Thorsen also pointed out, "Wilson clearly favored the legitimating function over the executive, administrative function" for the president (1988, 207; see also Eden 1996). The president could legitimately watch over administration, since he had daily contact with it and presumably at least some experience in it. But the president ought not actually do much administering; he should instead give voice to public opinion regarding the central matters of policy and administration facing the nation: "But we can safely predict that as the multitude of the President's duties increases, as it must with the growth and widening activities of the nation itself, the incumbents of the great office will more and more come to feel that they are administering it in its truest purpose and with greatest effect by regarding themselves as less and less executive officers and more and more directors of affairs and leaders of the nation,—men of counsel and of the sort of action that makes for enlightenment" (Wilson 1908, 81). Administration as an institution could then operate with reasonable autonomy, since those "who administer the law and direct the policy of the nation in its field of action shall be strictly subject to the laws, must observe the prescribed methods and understandings of the system very precisely; but it is by no means a necessary inference that they shall be in leading strings and shall be reduced to be the mere ministerial agents of a representative assembly" (15). With such standing, administration could fulfill its important roles in the regime, including shaping the law through the fusion of its experience with presidential leadership of policymaking.

In his final scholarly treatise, then, Wilson made the case for the president as the political leader best fit to ensure that administration would fulfill the purpose that he had projected for it in the democratic state's most mature stage of development. That purpose, as he stated in his lectures, was one of "serving the State, not the law-making body in the State, and possessing a life not resident in statutes." It would be through the harmonizing, integrating effect of presidential leadership that the "administrative organs of the Community" would become "organically whole, vigorous, and full of purpose" (Link et al. 1969, 7:129). How those administrative organs would be structured and operated would have to be considered, of course. Thus institutional design and organizational structures and practices were a final key component of Wilson's conception of the normatively defensible place of administration in a modern liberal democracy.

POLITICS, ADMINISTRATION, AND THE STRUCTURE OF POWER

At least in a general way, Wilson had addressed the structure of administration's place in a modern democratic regime from nearly his earliest thinking and writing on politics and government. Certainly the general notion that a responsible ministry would supervise both legislation and administration implies a particular arrangement of administrative offices and their relationship to political authority. But Wilson's more complex, subtle, and seemingly even contradictory ideas about administrative structure have engendered perhaps the most confusion of anything in his writings, lectures, and political practices. This stems in particular from the seemingly sharp contrast between Wilson's views on the place of administration in a democratic regime I have just described and his recurring insistence, consistent with the prevailing view of his time (see Van Riper 1984, 204–7; Waldo 1984, 224; Lynn 2001), that there must be a strict separation between the political offices responsible for policy-making and the nonpolitical offices responsible for policy implementation and that politics—mostly, that is, partisan politics—should not interfere with the latter.

The politics-administration "dichotomy," as it came to be called over at least the past two generations of public administration scholarship, is now overburdened with intellectual and ideological baggage. A number of scholars over the past several decades have considered Wilson's thinking in this regard with considerable care, and the emergence of the concept in public administration "orthodoxy" cannot reasonably be traced to any contribution from Wilson (Van Riper 1984, 209–11). Many more, however, even several of considerable scholarly renown, have put forward the simplistic version of the separation idea largely as a straw man, in the process invoking Wilson as an authoritative source (again, see Van Riper 1984; Lynn 2001; for an illustrative example, see Rosenbloom 2000, 140). I shall not rehash what has itself become a virtual cottage industry in public administration and public management scholarship, but it is important in light of what I have presented so far in this chapter that I offer an interpretation of what Wilson was thinking when he insisted on a separation between politics and administration that reveals how Wilson saw administrative structure as helping to define administration's place in the modern democratic regime of the United States.

Administrative Structure and Political Legitimacy

It is important to realize that in his invocation of the separation idea, Wilson was thinking both empirically and normatively, but with much greater emphasis on the latter component. Hence, dismissals of Wilson's advocacy of the separation as inconsistent with the reality of how government and politics actually works (see, for example, the scholarship assessed in Frederickson and Smith 2003, ch. 3) are rather beside the point. Certainly, Wilson's historical-comparative research suggested to him that separating administration from political manipulation but not legitimate political control was the way administration was organized and related to political authority in some contemporary nation-states—or at least the way it might be on sufficiently close examination. More importantly, however, such separation was the way Wilson thought administration might become ordered and connected to political authority, particularly in the United States, as a result of the discoveries that would come from the new science of administration that would reveal what structures and practices were alike across all types of regimes.

Wilson thus advanced a two-part normative argument about neutral competence. First, many of the good structures and practices to be discovered, or devised, were businesslike in the obvious sense that they should be deployed to make individual programs, and the government generally, run well, irrespective of the prevailing philosophy that set the goals for the programs and the government. A good system of public accounts would serve any democracy well by handling public funds carefully and making transactions transparent, whether the ruling party was Monarchist, Re-

publican, Democrat, Whig, or Socialist. That Republicans might manipulate government accounting for their own ideological aims was already more than real
enough, to Wilson's thinking. But could anyone seriously argue, in Wilson's time or
our own, that a public accounting system *should* be organized and operated ideologically, that it somehow served democracy better than a system based on "scientific"
accounting principles?

Second, for good structures and practices to flourish, it is clearly imperative that
private interest and partisan manipulation and interference of administrative practices be kept to a minimum. This would allow administration at any level of government, but especially at the national level, to professionalize, to develop the necessary
educational and training regimens, vital technical expertise, and practical experience in the face of an increasingly complex industrial, commercial, and social
reality. Continuing partisan control of most administrative offices, and even worse,
maintaining them as elective offices, would clearly deter those who desired professional status and sought to employ their expertise—and the experience that would
require many years to accumulate—for public aims. Even more important from the
perspective of Wilson's ideas as I have presented them thus far, minimizing "political" interference would make administration more demonstrably useful in carrying
out the law efficiently and effectively. More forcefully still, administration relatively
free of political interference could better learn from the conditions of society what
immediate adjustments (through ordinance and regulation) and more formal and
permanent adjustments (through law and even constitutional change) become necessary to maintain the integrity and long-run health of the regime.

Both these facets of Wilson's thinking reflect a *political* strategy: to legitimate the
emergence of a more well-defined, powerful, far-reaching administrative system
employing new kinds of personnel and practices, all of which were foreign to American political culture and practices and the prevailing political experience of most
American citizens. The idea of a recognizable separation of political and administrative offices was thus part of Wilson's enterprise to bring about a new conception of
the proper relationship between public opinion and administrative power. Wilson
sought to convince Americans that administration properly situated with respect to
political authority would be subject to the control of political leaders who could
interpret public opinion—read the popular thought—and who thus could harness
administrative power to serve the aspirations of the people and the ends of the state.
This was a subtle and difficult calibration.

Consider the many dualities in Wilson's characterization: administration was the
business side of government, yet it was more than businesslike; it was a part of public
law, but distinct from positive, statutory law; it was separate from legislation and

adjudication, yet much of what legislative and judicial bodies did was administrative —and for its part, administration also engaged in legislative and judicial action; administration was the execution of law but it also both directly and indirectly shaped the law. The calibration Wilson sought required structure as a component of the definition of administration's place in the regime. Structure would keep administration in its proper place, organically integrated so that its value—the power of organization, coordination, and adjustment—could be fully exploited while being restrained so that it did not stray from its appropriate role and threaten to oppress or dominate the body politic. Restraint was also appropriate to ensure that administration would not go beyond its institutional capacity and become dysfunctional and ineffectual in its special role. As much as domination, this too could threaten the health of the body politic and perhaps even the existence of the regime in the long run.

As we shall see in chapter 4, Wilson promoted a systemic design and particular structural features and practices for administration, including a properly conceived and attuned separation of political and "purely" administrative offices, as enhancing democracy and the popular control of government appropriate for the modern age. The best illustration of the broad expanse of Wilson's thinking about how structure helped set administration's proper place in the regime comes not from "The Study of Administration" or earlier writings and lectures but rather from his political engagement and his ideas about the best design for business regulation.

The Political Value of Structure: Regulating Business

Perhaps the defining issue of Wilson's entry into politics, carrying all the way into the first years of his presidency, was the question of how government should deal with public utility monopolies and, more significantly, the "trusts," those large, financially complex, often economically rapacious industrial and commercial combinations that had emerged in the late nineteenth century. Wilson had expressed concerns about the social, economic, and political effects of these new entities, created for the pursuit of wealth and economic power, in his scholarship and commentary leading up to and including *Congressional Government*, in "The Study of Administration," in other essays such as "Socialism and Democracy," and in *The State*. As his thinking had progressed over the course of this work, including the first two cycles of his lectures on administration, Wilson came to conceive of the problem of economic concentration as very much a matter of policy and administration. It was a matter of administration in particular, because it concerned where society should draw the line between state interference and unfettered private (economic) behavior. And that was expressly, in Wilson's conception, the province of administration and the central concern of the liberal democratic state more generally.

In *The State*, Wilson began to crystallize his own position on the issue by synthesizing his historical, comparative analysis of the development of the modern democratic state with his developing conception of the place of administration in a modern liberal democracy. The result was his argument in favor of regulation over more direct state management of the corporate giants. He rejected the state paternalism of the pre-modern era as not conducive to full and free development of the individual's capacities and potential. But he also rejected *laissez-faire* as inconsistent with the social equality dimensions of democracy. A small group of individuals, privileged by social standing, inheritance, or chance and not chosen by society based on merit, simply should not possess such great economic power without some counterweight. Government had to be that counterweight—indeed, had to be more powerful than the trusts (see Clements 1992, 9).

Wilson made little if any further advance in his thinking on the issue in the years between 1890 and 1905. As his interest in direct political engagement (and the interest of the political establishment in him) increased, however, Wilson returned to the trust issue with greatly increased frequency and vigor. His initial position, spanning the period between the publication of his 1907 essay "Politics (1857–1907)" and the publication of his 1909 essay "The Democratic Opportunity," consisted of three key components. First, Wilson offered a diagnosis of the problem, centered on special interests, "predatory wealth," and the legal standing of corporations as persons. Second, Wilson accepted that regulation of monopolies was a necessity but that there was a choice of approaches. It was, again, an administrative design problem, a choice between regulation by law and the courts or regulation by administrative discretion and expert commission. The third component consisted of Wilson's critique of the commission approach to trust regulation, reflecting his considerable worries about the political effects of such a regulatory design, including its implications for the legitimacy and capacity of administration in the regime.

In perhaps his most finely honed statement on the matter, "Law or Personal Power," a press statement based on his speech to the National Democratic Club, Wilson argued that the same political conditions that had allowed a paternalistic system of favors to replace law—best exemplified by the tariff—had also allowed the emergence of some large industrial and commercial combinations. These entities had developed not on the basis of "business energy and sagacity" but on speculation, "playing on the credulity of others, taking advantage of the weakness of others, trading in the necessities of others." Wilson condemned all of this as "predatory wealth" (268). Neither Congress nor the courts, Wilson contended, had taken action to define precisely and then control and limit these fraudulent, speculative transactions, which threatened both the financial security of individuals and the economic health of the nation. Reformers did get legislation passed that allowed the courts to go after the corporations. But since the corporations constituted legal persons subject to prosecution, such enforcement actions simply allowed the real culprits to hide behind the shield of corporate anonymity, and the investors—the public—paid the price.

Wilson acknowledged that "the old *laissez faire*" (264) was no longer a viable policy approach. He called for "firm and comprehensive regulation of business operations in the interest of fair dealing, of a responsible exercise of power." The question was how best to structure the regulatory response. Wilson had earlier argued that reformers had convinced Congress as well as state legislatures to pass vague laws with ill-defined prohibitions and sanctions. They required the creation of commissions or other, similar administrative entities, which would use their expertise and discretion to determine which trusts and monopolies had violated the law and what penalties and changes in operations were required of the corporations as a result.

Wilson offered as the sounder alternative an approach "based upon definite law and individual responsibility" (267). Transactions rather than organizations would be the focus of the law, and transactions that were fraudulent, predatory, or otherwise inconsistent with good business practices and an economic system meant to serve the general welfare as well as individual wealth accumulation would be precisely defined in statutes. The law would also require corporations to be more transparent in their operations, so that the individuals who actually authorized or engaged in prohibited transactions could be identified and prosecuted. Wilson argued that fining corporations even large sums did little to alter bad behavior; it only punished honest investors and inconvenienced society. By targeting the Wall Street speculator or his insider accomplice, however, much of the danger to society from concentrated, irresponsible economic power would dissipate. Just as important, the law and the courts could handle this approach to regulation without the creation of new and much more invasive administrative agencies.

The question of whether it was realistic to expect that legislators could develop the clear and precise standards of business behavior that prosecutors and judges could then readily apply would recurrently plague Wilson's treatment of the trust question. His response was to promote reliance on administrative experience. Administration would reveal through experience which transactions ought to be targeted and prohibited. But in this case it would be primarily private business administration that would provide the experience and guidance, not public administration. In a speech titled "The Government and Business," Wilson suggested that the way to tap into this experience was to invite "experienced corporation lawyers" (41) to critique legislation under consideration and ask them "what the legislatures ought to do. They know what has gone wrong if anything has, and they know how to get at it if anybody does" (42). Wilson also stressed that even regulation by commission would need administrative experience, and "the only thing that experience can yield is the revelation, item by item, of the things, the particular transactions, which society wishes to control" (40). Thus an attack on bad transactions, rather than bad corporations, would in the end be the only viable strategy.

Wilson's fears about corporate regulation by independent executive commission seem in retrospect to be feverish and overblown. He may have crafted his case in a manner meant to shore up his conservative credentials in order to get the required support for an electoral run. Nevertheless, his worries and warnings still have recognizable foundations in the conception of administration's place in the regime on which he had so long been laboring. Again, these worries centered on threats to both administrative legitimacy and administrative capacity.

The Legitimacy Value of Structural Limits Regulation of trusts through expert commissions with extensive discretion to determine the specifics of wrongdoing and the appropriate sanctions, Wilson contended, meant not only direct government supervision and even management of targeted corporations but also the eventual equivalent of government ownership and control, the intermingling of public and private interests, and public and private managers. This was "a radical change in the character of our institutions and the objects of our law," and worse, it was "socialistic" (Link et al. 1974, 17:324). The overall political effect was to reinforce and expand the paternalism fostered by the tariff to an even more unacceptable and threatening extent. Wilson feared that "this same patronizing government [that produced the tariff] must play a further paternal role of special regulation, not by careful scientific definitions of law but by detailed variations of administrative process" (Link et al. 1974, 18:266).

The juxtaposition of elements in Wilson's arguments is particularly revealing. First, relating a particular administrative design to socialism would clearly lead to the American people seeing administration as associated with foreign and antithetical values and principles, undermining Wilson's whole legitimation enterprise and contradicting the developmental progression toward administrative integration and organic wholeness. It would undermine the mature life of the state and the whole *raison d'être* of the regime. Second, by contradicting the expectation about the relationship between politics and administration by suggesting that lawmaking could be "scientific" and impartial while administration could be tainted by political bias and special interest privilege if they are not guided by impartial, scientific law, Wilson at least seemed to be implying that the reformers' efforts regarding corporate regulation would undermine the larger American government modernization project by overturning the aims of its core components, especially civil service reform. The character and capacity of administration was thus thrown into question and, by extension, its legitimacy further weakened.

One of Wilson's concerns about character and capacity has become a longstanding economic critique of administrative regulation. In order to regulate corporations rather than prosecute individual transgressors, the critique suggests, regulators would have to learn in intimate detail the workings of every company so that they could issue properly tailored requirements and directives that would avoid financial injury. But regulators could never know the companies as well as profit-motivated owners and private managers. The inevitable effect would be, at a minimum, economic inefficiency, the misallocation of resources away from optimum social benefit.

A second concern Wilson articulated in his attacks on regulation by commission reemerged decades later as the regulatory "capture" thesis and later still in the literature applying principle-agent theory to politics. The essential argument from both treatments is that through the pursuit of self-interest and "rent-seeking," regulators and regulatory commissions could eventually come under the control of the regulated. Wilson's concern in this regard was not only that capture would lead to regulation serving the narrow, privileged interests of the regulated but that it would corrupt the government more broadly, further undermining administrative legitimacy and the stability of the regime. It would, furthermore, result in the replacement of administrators motivated by public spirit with bureaucrats motivated by private gain or other narrow purposes.

Overall, Wilson's concerns about the impact of regulation by commission on the character and capacity of administration centered on the corrupting effects on individual public executives and managers and on the extension of government beyond its administrative capabilities and beyond what good philosophy and practice required. Regulation by administrative commission would "create a machinery too cumbersome and unmanageable to be desired by any prudent man" (Link et al. 1974, 17:494). It would "increase the powers and temptations of those who administer government." Resisting regulation by commission would "remove from government the burden and the temptation of the actual administration of corporate undertakings" (Link et al. 1975, 19:470). Wilson saw the outcome of regulation by commission, taken to the extreme his depiction of it entailed, as impossible for the regime to contend with: "It is imperatively necessary, if government is to be kept pure and impartial, that its officers should not themselves be made partners or managers of the great corporate enterprises through which the public is served. . . . It is bad enough to have the modern overgrown corporations to restrain and control. It would be infinitely worse if they were combined with government itself, and a partnership formed which could not be broken up without attacking our very governors themselves" (Link et al. 1975, 20:301).

In April 1910, Wilson provided suggestions for the draft of the Pennsylvania Democratic Party Platform. Points three, four, and five perfectly summarized the position he had developed on corporate regulation. He argued for the "law [finding] the responsible individuals within the corporations" and having the "punishment . . . fall directly upon them." He further argued that law should regulate public service corporations "but not in such a way as to put their administration in the hands of government officials, who may in their turn prove oppressive. The control exercised by government should be judicial, not administrative" (316). Four months later, in his suggestions for New Jersey Democratic Party platform resolutions, Wilson promoted the "establishment of a public service commission with ample powers under explicit rules to regulate rates" (Link et al. 1976, 21:44). No direct evidence in the published Wilson papers points to the exact sources and reasons for what appears to be a change in Wilson's position. But the discontinuities in Wilson's positions are not quite as sharp as they appear.

First, even as he adamantly pressed his case for corporate regulation through the courts, there were signs of adjustment in his views. In "Law or Personal Power," Wilson acknowledged the legitimate emergence of regulatory commissions. He insisted, however, that they need not be "executive instrumentalities having indefinite powers capable of domineering as well as regulating" (Link et al. 1974, 18:267). Instead, they should exercise a precisely circumscribed judicial power under well-defined legal standards, thus eliminating much of the danger of unfettered executive discretion. This would seem to be well within the legitimate scope of an administration exercising limited judicial authority as Wilson had envisioned it in his lectures.

Second, in his campaign for governor Wilson put the regulation question in a broader context, promoting general goals and aspirations for corporate regulation consistent with his longstanding analysis of the development of the modern democratic state and the threats of extensive economic concentration. He called upon government to "study not only regulation but individual liberty and individual responsibility and that no regulation incompatible with the freedom and development of the individual is tolerable" (Link et al. 1975, 19:466). He promoted as a general principle, "Government, not for the sake of success at whatever cost and the multiplication of material resources by whatever process, but for the sake of discriminating justice and a wholesome development as well as regulation of the national life" (467). Further, he argued that regulation of trusts should aim "to square their whole action and responsibility with the general interest, regarding them not as objects in themselves, but merely as conveniences in our economic life and development" (Link et al. 1975, 20:300–301). He even insisted that business leaders could not afford to think only in terms of what advanced private gain. They had to think as statesman and support only pursuits of private gain that were consistent with the public interest (414–21).

Transparency and Publicity As he moved further in his acceptance of regulatory commissions, Wilson sought to maintain long-range continuity in his position on corporate regulation in the larger context of his ideas about administration's place in the regime by recentering his argument on two key points: individual responsibility and transparency or, as he sometimes referred to it, "publicity." As I show in chapter 4, Wilson's emphasis on individual responsibility was really a more general principle of administrative design and practice. But his point about transparency and publicity as the aim of corporate regulation was linked to a larger set of notions he advanced that reflected further refinement in his thinking about the role and purpose of administration in the regime.

Wilson insisted in his gubernatorial campaign that commissions regulating pubic utilities were not just boards of inquiry; they had to have the power to correct abuses of public utility rate charging. Yet he emphasized, especially late in the campaign, that the "main function of a public utilities commission, properly clothed with power, is to display to the public, by inquiry, full information concerning the affairs and the finances of the public utility corporations." He continued to insist that by virtue of such information revelation, "inequalities in service" and inequities in rates would be corrected by commission authority (Link et al. 1976, 21:496). But ultimately the aim was "a commission whose inquiries can lay the whole state of the business before us, so that we may know what is just, so that we may be convinced by the inquiry of disinterested persons that the rates charged are reasonable rates, and then we will pay them without grumbling" (571). After the New Jersey legislature's passage in the early spring of 1911 of a new public utilities regulatory statute with surprisingly little opposition, Wilson promoted it around the country on the same basis: "The thing to do with the corporations is to turn the light on them. They don't like light. Turn it on so strong they can't stand it. Exposure is one of the best ways to whip them into line" (Link et al. 1977, 23:8). The related functions of transparency and publicity were essential for regulatory agencies to undertake; indeed, Wilson argued that they were the foundation for making the practice of enforcing individual responsibility successful. Making a broader point about the importance of shining a light on corporate practices, Wilson argued during local elections in the fall of 1911 that "when we see the inside of [a] business and have the testimony of disinterested persons that it is properly and thoroughly and individually conducted, we will cease to be suspicious of it and will be glad to pay its rates, because it renders indispensable service . . . but we insist on knowing the inside, because these gentlemen control our lives" (434).

Administrative Limits and Liberty By taking the presidential plunge in 1912, Wilson again had to confront the issue of corporate regulation, this time in its more general form of control over monopolies and trusts of all kinds, not just public utilities. In particular, Wilson had to respond to Theodore Roosevelt's concrete proposal for a commission, lodged at the federal level, that would regulate monopolies. Wilson reiterated the key arguments he had been employing on the issue, but the national campaign pushed Wilson's rhetoric to a higher level, leading him to articulate a more definitive conception of the progressive nature of administration's proper place in the modern, liberal-democratic regime of the United States.

In his responses and counter-responses to the arguments and ideas about business regulation Roosevelt put forth, Wilson emphasized three key points. First, citizens of a democracy should be wary of too great a reliance on administrative expertise: "What I fear, therefore, is a government of experts. God forbid that in a democratic country we should resign the task and give the government over to experts. What are we for if we are to be scientifically taken care of by a number of gentlemen who are the only men who understand the job? Because if we don't understand the job, then we are not a free people" (78; see also, especially, Link et al. 1978, 25:151, 154).

Second, Wilson contended that Roosevelt's Progressive Party plan for dealing with monopolies actually promoted an unbridled administrative discretion insufficiently grounded in and restrained by law (see, for example, Link et al. 1978, 25:123, 226). In contrast, he argued, the Democratic Party favored the use of government power to defend the individual against "the power of combinations stronger than any possible individual can be," but it would be "power guided by knowledge, power extended in detail. Not power given out in a lump in a commission set up . . . , unencumbered by the restrictions of law (250–51). Similarly, Wilson invoked his idea of definite law as a bulwark of liberty against irresponsible discretion: "Under the Democrats, you will find this social structure of ours penetrated and sustained by the structural steel of law, wherever law is necessary, but you won't find that we are going to put in the hands of individuals or commissions the right to build the house according to their own plans and specifications. We are going to insist upon an architecture so certain, so definite, so based upon the right engineering principles of liberty, that we can be sure we can live there and not have the roof fall in" (411).

Finally, Wilson declared, administration as an institution—a vital organ of the democratic state—properly situated in the regime, its powerful features of expertise and discretion appropriately delimited, would serve the highest aspirations of a liberal-democratic polity: individual liberty, development, and social justice. Using the superb policing of public housing evident in the city of Glasgow as a symbol for administration generally, Wilson proclaimed, "I want the law in respect of all our matters to . . . send the representatives of the law inside the house, through the corridors, up the staircases, into everything except individual men's private business. And then let us see if we can't understand one another better by knowing the conditions under which we live and the what it is that we ought to do in order to help one another." He brought his audience back to the immediate matter at hand by invoking his ideas about the nature of modernity and the ultimate quest of democratic development. He called on his listeners "to realize that life is so complicated that we are not dealing with the old conditions, and that the law has to step in and create the conditions under which we live, the conditions which will make it tolerable for us to live. And the reason that you have got to be very careful in that way that you are going to vote . . . is that you are going to choose a method of justice" (259–60).

THE NATURE, SCOPE, AND LIMITS OF ADMINISTRATIVE POWER

As suggested by everything I have presented in this chapter, a Wilsonian conception of the proper place of administration in a liberal-democratic regime, and especially of its relationship to public opinion and popular rule, would seem especially to encompass several core elements. First, administration had to be public, meaning as open and transparent in its operations and transactions as possible, to allow for an informed, interested, and scrutinizing citizenry. Second, it had to be well integrated into the organic whole, the life of the state. This was best accomplished by subordinating it to the "top" political authorities—public officials who were directly in touch with public opinion, which they would read and help give it form. Third, administration had to serve the cause of enhancing self-government properly conceived for modern times. This meant not just making popular rule more efficient and well ordered but also expanding, or at least recovering, public control of government, again through the exercise of political leadership. Fourth, administration had to serve the cause of liberty, specifically individual autonomy, and growth. Fifth, it had to serve the cause of greater social and political unity, cooperation, understanding among citizens, and thus also the cause of social justice. Finally, perhaps the most far-reaching element, administration had to have sufficiently broad scope, leeway, and flexibility to operate in order to take advantage of its "natural" characteristics, namely that in carrying out the law it is in constant touch with society and the dynamic life of the state. It uses both special expertise and experience to deal with individual cases, and understanding life and translating that understanding to guide further lawmaking. Administration thus has a significant formative effect on law and on the life of the state. As a result, political leaders properly constrain administration to maintain the legitimacy and effectiveness of its use of administrative power.

A more comprehensive look at Wilson's ideas about administration as an institution and as an integral component of a liberal-democratic regime stretching across his scholarship, public speaking, and at least the early years of his direct political engagement reveals the significant continuities in his thought and the interlocking nature of his more prominent and long-lasting ideas. In turn, several distinctive insights obscured by his own casting off of some ideas during his intellectual development and by the narrow focus on just a small number of his works come to light.

Monitoring and Enabling Actions

One of Wilson's most substantial insights is contained in his conceptualization of a division of governmental functions. Wilson did not use the distinction explicitly after its recapitulation in chapter 15 of *The State*. Upon reexamination, however, it is clear that Wilson's division of functions enables a new way of seeing the distinctiveness of modern democracy and its dependence on administrative power. The distinction is *not* the same as the politics and administration dichotomy. Administration understood as a set of tasks or practices is clearly involved in both sets of functions. Regulation of property requires administration, as does civil and criminal justice or interchange with other nations, all of which Wilson listed under constituent functions (see Wilson 1890, 650). But in the modern era, in response to upheavals in societal conditions, Wilson insisted, new concepts of the "morals and conscience" of government resulted in a vastly expanded and much more prominent use of administrative power for convenience and expediency. It became morally acceptable, in other words, for governments to expand the extent to which they ministered to the needs and desires of individuals. This placed enormous burdens on administration in terms of normative theory, and in practical terms with respect to organization and methods, both of which Wilson endeavored to develop further.

Wilson offered a very perceptive view of the nature of modern society and its emphasis on the individual and of the much greater focus for the activities of the state on convenience and expediency that resulted. Societal development, he surmised, is tied to individual development, to encouraging self-development. The state is not to develop the individual directly, although there may be some instances in which such direct ministration is warranted, as through a universal education mandate. Instead, in response to new notions of convenience and expediency stemming from altered historical circumstances, the state, through its principal "executive" organ, government, is to make individual self-development easier, to reduce barriers, to eliminate inordinate threats, and to equalize conditions to allow social differentiation for society's benefit (see Thorsen 1988, 137, 139). This is in a very real sense the true triumph of liberalism and of its most successful institutional innovation, the market economy, to which society gives a large sphere of autonomous activity to encourage individual development. Accompanying this, however, are varying levels of government monitoring and coordination depending on the circumstances of "society's case."

As Americans today also know, however, even with constant "theoretical" efforts to attack "big government," to shrink the size of its workforce, and to eliminate specific administrative agencies and programs, the administrative component of government has continued to expand, at least in terms of the scope of society's activities in which it has a presence. Much of this expansion is a direct result of the focus on the individual or of government efforts to monitor or coordinate the individual developmental actions of nongovernmental institutions, again primarily the market. Concerns about and conceptions of convenience and expediency are, like wants in economic theory, infinitely expansive. The expansion is mostly not in the form of "old-time futile methods of guardianship"; it is in the form of what might be termed "enablements." For example, in the United States at least, the national state does not administer a medical system (although it does for certain segments of society, for example veterans), but it does constantly seek ways, often with great political controversy, to increase access to health care. The state thus does not administer the lives of individuals with respect to health care and wellness, but it does attempt to administer various components of society—to organize and coordinate and monitor them—to increase the chances that individuals will be able to develop themselves further with respect to their health and physical well-being. This places a burden on public administration that is as great, if not greater, than would be the case if government in the United States actually operated the health care system.

Wilson saw that all governments ancient and modern do essentially the same *kinds* of things that are ministrant in nature—and thus not *governing* in the sense of making basic, constitutive decisions and tending to the order and makeup of society. The way governments do these same kinds of things, the extent to which they do them, and the ideas about convenience and expedience to which they must respond have varied greatly over time, however, especially in response to increased demands for government action to help people cope with changing conditions. Just as Wilson argued, what government does thus cannot be a function of abstract ideas, of theories not built from facts; it is a matter of response to changing conditions, and society's collective response to the accumulation of individual claims concerning where the line defining government intervention should be drawn. Modern administration has thus assumed the responsibility for monitoring the changing conditions and, under political leadership, guiding the development of legislative responses to them. It may do so on the basis of its own expertise, experiments, and experience or by gathering the knowledge from those who do have the requisite experience and expertise. In either case, however, as Wilson anticipated and as is now obvious to even casual observers of government processes, administration is now centrally involved in policy development, even as, in the United States at least, the national legislature has endeavored to develop some independent capabilities of its own in this regard.

The Progressive Power of Administration

A second insight derives in part from Wilson's division of functions and concerns just how distinctive a form of modern power administration really is. Consider that the creative, advanced "governing power" that Thorsen (1988, 65) finds in Wilson's writings on sovereignty might be understood to consist of two components. The first, constitutional or constituent power, is conservative—it must be employed to conserve the basic order and existence of a society—to preserve a society's essential civic form. In contrast, modern administrative power is progressive, concerned with the growth and advancement of society, with the fulfillment of its ever-changing needs. Administration in Wilson's more expansive "organic" sense is thus in tune with society and the changing conditions it is experiencing from the forces of modernity. Ultimately administration reads those conditions; it experiences them through its work at the front lines of government's contact with society. Under Wilson's leadership scheme, vested first in a responsible ministry or its American constitutional equivalent and then later in the president, administration reports its experiences and the results of its "experiments" to the legislature, which fashions laws to reflect this culmination of experience and experiment. Further on in the development of his thinking, when he more fully embraced a "progressive" worldview, Wilson saw administrative power as an active force that could shape conditions—and with it social and political life.

From this perspective, administration is thus not the power to create, to make up, or to organize society and the state. It is instead the power to fulfill the purposes of society and the aspirations of a liberal-democratic polity. It may even encompass the power to alter conditions to make the realization of those aspirations more likely.

The distinction between the two kinds of political power—constitutional and administrative—was made prominent by the rise of modernity, especially its new conceptions of convenience and expediency and of state duty centered on the individual, which made administrative power more central, vital, expansive, and intrusive, which in turn produced new challenges for, and new strains on, the state's administrative capacity. Thus a third insight evident in Wilson's thinking about administration's place in a modern democratic regime follows from his recognition of the unique challenges and pressures created by the emergence of modern administrative power. The question concerns how to gain its benefits without losing public administration's institutional and systemic legitimacy or, even more seriously, without creating a tutelary power that oppresses or just as onerously saps the energy and independence of spirit of the citizenry and "deranges" (Lowi 1993b) the underlying, constitutive order of the regime. It is, in short, a matter of pinpointing the right place to draw the line on the expansion of administrative power. Wilson's insight was to argue that administration's place and its value to the regime, and thus its legitimacy and authority, did not derive primarily from the power of expertise or discretion.

The Boundary Line for Administrative Power

As a number of his speeches in the 1912 presidential election made clear, Wilson was uneasy with the commitment of Theodore Roosevelt and his Progressive Party to greatly expanded administrative autonomy checked only by an independent elected executive and reliance on a presumptively neutral expertise. Wilson argued that an independent commission of experts in fact served to insulate administrators engaged in business regulation from the full range of business interest and opinion about monopoly practices and blocked other avenues of citizen interest expression and public scrutiny of business practices, such as the courts. The president stood as the premier path for general opinion influence and public scrutiny of administration even in Wilson's own conception, following the proposal he articulated in *Constitutional Government*. But we can at least infer from Wilson's campaign rhetoric that, despite Roosevelt's image as a vigorous national leader, Wilson regarded any president or candidate who supported extensive autonomy and discretion for expert administration as unlikely to use his powers of interpretation and national opinion leadership to keep administration well integrated administratively and politically and in line with the prevailing popular thought.

Certainly Wilson did not completely discount the importance of expertise. On the contrary, he regarded it as a vital aspect of a modern administrative service. But Wilson's understanding of the relative narrowness of the worldview of the expert, some of it of long standing and linked to his ideas about the nature of politics, academia, and the characteristics of both modern political and administrative sciences, led him to insist on putting expertise in its proper political perspective, one that constrained its role and influence. He attacked what he regarded as the vesting of too much importance—and unaccountable authority and power—in administrative expertise. Again, he was concerned about regulatory capture—that the experts who would hold seats on Roosevelt's commission to regulate monopoly would come from the same monopolistic industries the commission was supposed to regulate. But Wilson's core concern was that the combination of scientific theory and technical expertise with which public administration was becoming associated not be accepted as the appropriate foundation for administrative legitimacy, nor, even more importantly, as the purpose of public administration in a liberal-democratic regime.

In his notes for lectures on constitutional government, Wilson characterized the legislative process and the "moulding and modifying power of law" as combining "the knowledge of experts and the more subtle inferences of special observation and experience." The latter came from "authoritative leadership" (Link et al. 1971, 11:20). Thus what mattered less were the "opinions of experts and experienced judges of affairs" over which the voter did not exercise "any actual acceptance" or direct assent; more important were the "character and ability of . . . leaders" in which the public put its trust.

Consistent with his long-held views about the nature of politics and the proper approach to its study, then, Wilson saw good public law and good public administration as primarily dependent on and constructed from practical experience and much less dependent on formal expertise and theoretical perfection. It was through experience that political leaders and public administrators would find the best ways to fashion and administer law for the ultimate aims and aspirations of the regime: serving popular self-government and preserving and enhancing liberty in the form of individual autonomy and development within the enabling structure of the state. As I show more fully in the next chapter, Wilson accepted that neutral, technical expertise should be one of the principles guiding the organization of administration and public management in a democratic polity. As the evidence presented in the current chapter suggests, however, it was Wilson's position that limits should be placed on the principle of neutral competence and that the pursuit of neutral competence should not lead to any confusion of means and ends. The purpose of administration was not to be expert and neutral, nor did its authority derive from such qualities. Instead, administration was to use its expertise, experience, and willingness to experiment to serve the pursuit of individual autonomy and development within the essential unity of the nation and to become an integral part of democratic politics and popular control of government through authoritative leadership.

All of these insights, along with the broad spectrum of Wilson's ideas about administration's place and purpose in a liberal-democratic regime, have significant implications for how scholars and practitioners think about public management and the continuing challenges it faces. If public managers operate, or should operate, in a context of expectations that they will aim not just toward making democratic government more efficient and effective but also toward enhancing popular control of government and individual liberty and toward fulfilling aspirations for social justice, what does this mean for the tenets of organizational structure and managerial practice central to the prominent new thinking about public management? What, in particular, is the relationship between good public management and political leadership? Before confronting these questions and many others, it is necessary to examine more closely Woodrow Wilson's own ideas about administrative organization and practice as well as his actions as administrative overseer and political leader.

CHAPTER FOUR

Enhancing Democracy through Administrative Design and Organizational Practice

What principles of good administrative organization and managerial practice are appropriate for a modern democratic state? In *Congressional Government*, Wilson answered that competent, responsible administration responsive to but not under the direct control of public opinion would be realized with the proper structure of political leadership and public authority. Leading executive-legislators would embody the close linkage between lawmaking and administration that Wilson regarded as a necessity for effective governance. These new public executives would, through the considerable knowledge to be gained in overseeing administrative departments, be able to guide the legislative process toward public policy that was designed with administration in mind and could thus be effectively implemented and managed. In turn, with direct knowledge of and involvement in legislative crafting of the policies, they could more effectively oversee and guide the public managers directly tasked with putting the laws into effect. Political responsibility would rest primarily with them, and it would be clear, direct, and personal. They would bear the greatest burden of the consequences of failures in policy design or policy management and receive the lion's share of credit for successes, through the doctrine of ministerial responsibility.

Wilson gave further thought to matters of administrative organization and managerial practice in "The Study of Administration," in which he was especially concerned with what structural arrangements and behavioral inducements would produce "public officers" with the requisite character traits and modes of behavior appropriate for an emerging administrative state. He paid attention, of course, to administrative competence. Hence he called not just for public service hiring practices based on merit but also for more technical education of public servants ranging substantially beyond the new stress on public affairs education that he claimed was becoming commonplace at the collegiate level in the United States. Wilson also gave a brief nod to the "appropriate hierarchy and characteristic discipline" that would characterize the newly "perfected" public organizations likely to emerge from administrative reform guided by the newly self-conscious and focused study of administration (Link et al. 1968, 5:375).

But Wilson was particularly concerned with the political legitimacy of an expanding administration that was likely to employ methods of organization and practice relatively foreign to American political culture. This was where his design for a new kind of public executive—new, at least, to American politics and government— again came into play. As men adept at reading the "popular thought" and thus shaping and responding to public opinion, political leaders who were engaged in overseeing both legislation and administration could best ensure that public organizations and a public service designed substantially on foreign methods would not become a "bureaucracy" suffused with "a domineering, illiberal officialism" (376). They were likely to state quite openly and even demonstrate quite publicly the values that the new organizations and newly expert subordinate officials should follow. They could justify the use of new organizational modes and highly specialized technical experts because both were subject to control by political leaders directly responsive to public concerns.

Beyond these fundamentals, Wilson argued in the last section of the essay, the development of more specific principles and methods for administrative structure and practice formed the agenda that the new, energetically self-conscious study of administration would pursue. He identified several specific items for that agenda. First, a "science of administration for America" had to be based on American political principles—liberty, equality, and pragmatism. Second, this science should be soundly and primarily comparative and historical in method. Third, administrative study should search for all methods and practices that were common across all kinds of regimes. Such practices would be universally applicable to organizing and operating an expanded administration, which was needed especially in democratic regimes, as in the United States, to cope with the growing stresses and strains of the modern age. Fourth, administrative study should give special attention to the *vertical* structure of policy-making and policy management, looking for ways to ensure both independence and interdependence among the levels of government. Finally, the study of administration had to uncover the structural arrangements and managerial devices that would induce public-spirited behavior in public administrators, thus harnessing the skills, interests, and ambitions of managers and front-line workers in service to the public good at every level of government.

In pushing forward on this agenda for administrative study himself, Wilson undertook an extensive historical and comparative examination of administrative structures and practices, heavily reliant on German sources. Beyond the realization brought about by this endeavor that he had to understand more thoroughly the nature of democracy, Wilson also took up the more substantive items on the agenda he set out in the essay. He scrutinized the vertical structure of American administration and attempted to develop normative principles of structural reform. He also gave specific attention to questions of institutional structure, proper policy design, and internal organizational structures and controls, such as hierarchy, merit selection, and professionalism, that might improve the likelihood of administrative behavior that was responsible and oriented toward vigorous defense and pursuit of the public good. In his lectures on administration and in essays, public talks, and political speeches, especially during his campaign for and after his election as governor of New Jersey, Wilson articulated a number of very specific normative arguments about administrative organization and practice. He repeatedly stressed *administrative integration* across and within the levels of government, especially an extensive reconception of the structure and role of municipal government. He explored *accountability and democratic control* through organizational structures and statutory design as well as incentives and restraints on administrator behavior that would ensure efficiency and effective use of expertise and the creation of responsible, public-spirited administrators. Finally, Wilson touched on *training and expertise*, particularly the appropriate conception of education and training for professional administrators as well as the benefits and requisite scope of and constraints on a professionalized administrative service.

ADMINISTRATIVE INTEGRATION

Wilson's concern with administrative integration stemmed primarily from the noticeable lack of it in the United States—indeed, the lack of any recognizable administrative system that would be part and parcel of the endeavor to balance national unity with the value of political and economic differentiation. Much of Wilson's attention with respect to administrative integration was directed toward cities and the challenges of municipal government in a nation lacking any systematic relationship among administrative institutions. Cities were the sites of societal differentiation, the generators of new and distinct economic interests, and thus the primary source of stress in the regime emanating from the friction between the forces of differentiation and the inexorable drive toward national unity and power. Beyond city government redesign, Wilson also promoted what he termed political and administrative *concentration*, which concerned the structure and reach of political authority and the scope and independence of "non-political" administration. Finally, his exploration of administrative integration forced him to think further about the organization of the central government executive in a democracy, which led him, over the course of two decades, to an uneasy conceptual reconciliation of his preference for a plural executive with the design of the presidency etched in the Constitution.

Reconceiving City Government

In a lecture at Brown University in January 1889, Wilson contended that efforts to address the troubles of American cities through the search for "new devices, new methods of improvement from the outside" were not succeeding. He suggested it was time "to try the subject from a different point of view." What might be needed, he proposed, was "a new analysis of self-government; new principles, instead of new mechanism" (Link et al. 1969, 6:53). Wilson concluded that American cities needed a complete reconception of historical antecedents, developmental forces, current character, and governing structure, which had to be part of a larger vision of an integrated administrative system for American government cutting across all the levels of American federalism and incorporating his reconception of national executive leadership from his analysis and critique in *Congressional Government.*

Wilson regarded modern cities as relatively recent societal inventions, combining in complex and often stressful ways both politics and commerce and following both natural and artificial developmental forces. Although they were neither the semi-independent polities of medieval times nor the relatively self-contained units for experiencing self-government that early American townships provided, modern cities were nevertheless still primarily responsible for direct citizen experience with and instruction and engagement in self-government in modern democracies, where such direct experience was not possible at the national level.

Wilson contended vigorously that cities were not simply mini-states; rather, they were administrative entities, and there was no reason to recreate within them the separation of powers design characteristic of American national and state governments. Separation of powers was, after all, the source of political fragmentation and irresponsibility in the American national state, and he even strongly hinted at the need to restructure state governments as well. Wilson argued that city councils were not legislatures but administrative planning bodies, responsible for issuing ordinances not making laws. Wilson's idea here was based in part on the distinction he made between law and ordinance (ordinances, unlike laws, did not create or specify individual rights, nor did they define or alter relations among authorities) as well as the interesting specific distinction he made between administration and execution: "Administration and executive action are not one and the same thing. Administration is a thing of plans: *execution* is the carrying out of plans" (Link et al. 1969, 6:501–2, emphasis in original). Administration was thus broader and more encompassing, and execution was an integral, subordinate part of it. Wilson therefore advocated the elimination of most semi-independent municipal boards and commissions or at least the end of direct election of their members, as well as the end of direct election of mayors as local chief executives.

From his initial premises that cities were important sources of political and economic differentiation within the essential unity of the nation and that they were administrative units (as city councils were administrative planning bodies), Wilson concluded that considerable administrative decentralization and local autonomy were warranted within American federalism. He contended that extensive central control of cities by state legislatures was nothing more than haphazard and arbitrary outside interference that fragmented planning and action and obscured responsibility. Further, decentralization that put everything "local and peculiar" in the hands of cities and city councils would better sustain civic "health and vigor" throughout the body politic (504).

Finally, and perhaps most remarkably, Wilson argued that for these benefits to accrue, extensive citizen engagement in city government—local administration—was required. He argued that it was the duty of citizens to participate directly in the administration of their cities. He envisioned this happening through an extensive system of citizen-filled committees. In earlier Johns Hopkins lecture notes, Wilson directed his aim at municipal reformers, declaring, "Take your committees of One Hundred into your [governments]; convert their transient zeal into permanent duty" (Link et al. 1968, 5:712). This engagement in local administration, he insisted, was true self-government. Voting was not enough, as it was merely a single act of selection and something of an abrogation of power at that. Direct engagement aimed "to get and hold the attention of the community for the tasks" of government. This articulation of the object of municipal reform essentially paralleled his *Congressional Government* analysis pointing to the positive consequences of moving from congressional to cabinet government in the form of increased citizen interest in and scrutiny of national administration.

Wilson's portrayal of city government as exclusively administrative, with the city council as the central planning body, required a more thorough conceptualization of its internal organizational structure as well. Wilson thus argued that various executive units would be subordinate to the city council, staffed by council appointment, and subject to civil service rules as appropriately "prescribed and enforced." As I mentioned obliquely above, this included the mayor. Wilson opposed a city governmental structure with an elected "legislature" and a separately elected chief executive. The authority of the mayor would be inadequate to achieve the necessary internal integration of administrative units and functions. This would stem in part from the competition and suspicion bred by the separate election of distinct entities. Three negative consequences would follow. The necessary consultation and cooperation that would foster integration and that could only take place within one body would be undermined. Citizen interest, engagement, and participation would be discouraged. And responsibility would be obscured. "Only one act of election on the part of the voter, that, of the members of the Council" was preferable. "A single act of election of itself simplifies and points responsibility. A multiplicity of acts of election means obscured responsibility and fatigued interest, flagging attention" (Link et al. 1969, 6:497).

Wilson thus sought a major redesign of municipal government as part of an overall enterprise to construct the systemic, institutional, and organizational structures necessary for the effective governance of a liberal democracy facing the stresses and strains of the modern age. Did Wilson's call to "seek . . . a way to harness the people to the great wagon of state and make them pull it" (Link et al. 1969, 6:53) flatly contradict his views about administration's place in the regime regarding the inadvisability of direct popular participation in administration? Although he did not address the matter directly, one can infer that Wilson thought that his idea of vertical integration largely resolved the inconsistency. The overall object was what Wilson termed *political* integration. In the municipal context, Wilson characterized it as "general, continuous interest, a sense of solidarity, pride, the organization, not of an army, but of a cooperative society with expert guidance" (495). The problem was "to create . . . community feeling and energy." The emphasis should be less on creating schemes of "delegation" and particular arrangements of administrative machinery, although these were not trivial matters, and more on generating the necessary sense of "duty" and cooperative public spirit (496).

Political integration at the local level thus required treating city government as a single, unified administrative unit for dealing with peculiarly local issues and problems while not deviating from certain principles of national unity and the integrity of the national state. Where the people had more interest in and daily experience with the problems that needed to be addressed, direct and widespread citizen engagement was both appropriate and required. On the national level, in contrast, where the participation of millions of citizens could only be virtual, the creation of solidarity, cooperation, common interest, and communal feeling was a more overtly political endeavor, and thus the responsibility of statesmen. Also, the day-to-day tasks of national administration involved bigger, broader, and sometimes more remote matters with which too few citizens had direct interest or experience. An arm's length relationship of expert administration under the supervision of political leaders who understood and articulated the popular thought was necessary. Citizens would be more informed and interested, and they would scrutinize and question (either out of public spiritedness or, as in Wilson's *Constitutional Government* analysis, out of more self-interested motives), but they would not directly control or participate in administration.

Concentration: Administrative and Political

Thus far I have offered a glimpse of Wilson's thinking on the subject of administrative integration largely from a bottom-up view of the system. The ideas he developed out of this orientation place him in the long and noble line of scholars and advocates who have pushed for greater direct citizen engagement in American government, particularly at the local level. This endeavor has become energized once again with the emergence of a civic engagement focus within the new governance thinking in public administration and public management scholarship and practice (see, for example, Kathi and Cooper 2005). A view of Wilson's thinking from the top down shows similar concepts in play—and thus consistency—but it also reveals additional distinctive ideas Wilson articulated. The focus initially remains on local government but shifts to Wilson's notions about the organization of administration at the national level.

Wilson's overall guide with respect to vertical administrative integration was the aim of organic wholeness, reflecting in institutional design and organizational structure the life of the state. Within cities, for instance, there had to be an organic wholeness and solidarity—all the parts working in coordination to ensure a healthy community—and this would be part of an interlocking system across levels, creating a nationally integrated, organic whole. The critical distinction Wilson made, which he had identified in his first cycle of lectures on administration as the key question to be scrutinized, was between centralization and concentration. He defined the former as "the direct dependence of officers of all grades and functions upon the central authorities: because appointed and subject to removal by those authorities." He defined the latter, in contrast, as "an equal integration of the service, an equally systematic and unified organization" but with respect to local administration also "a certain independence of tenure on the part of local officers . . . their local election, and . . . their exemption from removal by the central authorities. They are subject to its oversight, but they are not its creatures" (Link et al. 1969, 7:389).

The guiding principle of concentration in administrative integration resulted in supervision of local administrative authorities by central authorities but not interference or intervention in local affairs. This supervision was not even to be "presidential but prudential," yet also in the "interest of the State" rather than the interests and welfare of localities (385). Supervision that presided over localities or, worse, intervened in local affairs, even if it was enlightened and well-intentioned, amounted to "tutelage" and administrative oppression.

Wilson argued that unity, "both national and international" was "a characteristic mark of the modern time," and it was "a result of the modern cheapness, ease, and speed of intercommunication, which produce in many spheres an almost universal community of interests, conditions, and ideas." This made the problem of preserving local "variety and vitality without loss of vital integration" even more of a challenge. The ideal integration involved not central direction of local administration but only a "limiting supervision" with the aim of securing "a nice adjustment of local administration to national aims and conveniences" (390). Wilson also argued that there should be homogeneity "of make-up and interest" (385) within the levels of government and functional differentiation across levels, to be determined in part by the spatial requirements of various functions.

The core determination in all matters of administrative integration, however, was "not a question of convenience, or glory, or management, but a question of life" (388). Wilson sought the creation of a truly integrated administrative system, but its particular structure was less important than its embodiment of the life of the state, the distinctive economic, social, and political character of a given liberal democratic regime. The specific mechanics—the instrumentalities—were secondary to the aim of a wholeness and balance that, as he sometimes argued, was evident in the human body. The tissues, organs, limbs all had specific functions, some carried out quite autonomously, but they were all integrated into the whole organism. Harmony and balance in the parts and their functions constituted good health and well-being. In the case of the democratic state, this well-being was "national unity and power" (388). By giving much greater primacy to the purpose of systemic administrative integration than to the means by which it might be achieved, Wilson's thinking seems to presage the very catholic orientation to mechanisms evident in the burgeoning new governance thrust in public management scholarship and practice.

Wilson saw the organic wholeness and integration he espoused as applying within the institutional structure of the various levels of government—and even within individual administrative organizations—as well as across the entire multi-level system. With respect to the organization of administration at the national level, this did mean a separation of purely political offices and administrative "instrumentalities" because national organic integration was a political task requiring parties to articulate policy principles around which a majority—and majority public opinion— would cohere. The separated components were nevertheless directly and intimately linked by the greater political purposes of regime development and progress toward national unity and national power underlying the design.

What shaped in considerable part Wilson's emphasis on concentrating political authority over administration in a small body of political officials—preferably in the form of a cabinet operating on the principle of ministerial responsibility and exercising both administrative oversight and legislative leadership—was his recognition of the challenge of administrative and political *coordination*. Anticipating Harold Seidman's signature work on federal executive structure and political management by more than eighty years, Wilson argued that coordination was the principal source of questions about administrative organization at the central government level. He saw coordination as a particularly complex challenge, involving questions about the extent of the authority held by the head of state "over administration as a whole" as well the "organic (collegiate) union" of functions across several executive departments through a "superintending . . . council" (Link et al. 1969, 7:394). These questions led Wilson to distinguish between "political (i.e., responsible ministerial)" integration and administrative integration. The former concerned the "political life and choice of society as a whole," while the latter concerned administration "as a business." The two were "separate (and yet united) phases" of government because government was "not merely a business" (396).

Somewhat in contrast to Seidman (see Seidman and Gilmour 1986, 225), Wilson saw coordination as necessarily taking place at the top because that was where the requisite organic integration and wholeness could be achieved. Yet both Wilson and Seidman saw coordination in systemic terms, stretching across levels of government and dependent principally on proper political leadership. Political leaders would "identify and agree on . . . national goals and priorities and . . . design programs to accomplish them" (Seidman and Gilmour 1986, 245). For Wilson, this was the core responsibility of statesmanship in an administrative age. The relationship of political leaders to the instrumental aspect of administration was "merely presidential and devoted exclusively to the origination and adaptation of policy . . . and dealing directly with all [questions] of legislation." Leaders would bear exclusive political responsibility for these lawmaking and policy-making endeavors, but because they were in frequent contact with instrumental administration their goals, priorities, and program designs would be guided "by the officials of the permanent technical service" (Link et al. 1969, 7:396).

Wilson envisioned a very broad sphere for administration in the regime, and much of what we regard today as involving the exercise of political power was, in Wilson's view, administrative. Further, from the standpoint of the organizational structure of administration and management, what Wilson labeled "non-political" governmental functions under the purview of public managers and front-line workers covered a considerable range. This "double" function of the nonpolitical, business side of administration covered the "actual detailed execution of law, [the] actual performance of the business of the State" as well as "oversight or assistance directed . . . toward" individuals or other levels of government (397). This latter oversight or assistance concerned both supervision of an authoritative sort—controlling, limiting, sanctioning, or commanding individuals or other levels of government—and supervision of a "suggestive" sort, which entailed providing information or expert advice.

Wilson's broad view was that the coordination necessary for good administration and management in a modern democratic state required an organizational structure at the central level of government with a small body of political leaders at the top, which would make the hard choices about goals, priorities, and programs, and a substantial administrative apparatus proper, which would include both planning and more strictly executing functions, especially at lower levels of government, but nevertheless would be integrated into an overall system that reinforced fidelity to national policy. Especially at the national level, this administrative infrastructure would be staffed by technical experts and management specialists, who would operate with considerable autonomy and discretion, giving the structure "an independent intelligence of its own" (396). Municipal governments would have their own technical experts at their disposal, but in the larger, nationally integrated scheme, local officials were the technical experts in local affairs. If Wilson had his way, it seems, local officials would run local affairs quite autonomously as well as advise central political authorities about policy that would directly affect local conditions.

What is especially interesting about Wilson's concern for an integrated administrative system and the coordination of policy and administration it provides is that similar notions have reappeared in the focus on public management that is currently so prominent in public administration theory, empirical research, and practice. The dominant emphasis on performance and results in the public management thrust has stimulated the development of attempts to model effective performance and test the models systematically. The proponents of one such model identify integration as one of the three dimensions of management capacity. Integration links management subsystems, such as human resources and information technology, to effectiveness by intermeshing them "as part of a unified, cohesive whole with shared values, commons goals, aligned objectives, and mutually supporting tasks." One of the "three key activities" through which integration is "primarily accomplished" is "the exercise of leadership" (Ingraham and Kneedler 2000, 246; see also Ingraham, Sowa, and Moynihan 2004). This public management recognition of the centrality of integration, common goals, and leadership is based on organizations as the unit of analysis, rather the systemic or regime level that was Wilson's chief concern. The thinking is remarkably similar, however, suggesting historically deep conceptual roots for current approaches and links to Wilson that many current public administration students might never have considered.

I explore in Wilson's ideas about accountability and democratic control more of what he saw as the necessary organizational structures and managerial practices under which American public administrators would have to operate. Before leaving this consideration of Wilson's ideas about administrative integration, however, his thoughts about the structure of the national executive deserve further attention.

A Plural Executive

Wilson's references to hierarchy and subordination (e.g., Link et al. 1969, 7:150; also see Ostrom 1989, 23–25) indicate that he supported unity of command within administrative units. With respect to systemic and institutional design and an overall scheme of administrative organization, however, Wilson clearly did not support the concept of a single top executive with unity of command over a fully, politically integrated administrative system. Wilson saw a small body of political leaders with statesmanlike qualities, especially the capacity for interpreting public opinion, overseeing both administration and legislation and striving to ensure their coordination and integration so as to embody the life of the democratic state and realize its great aims. To his mind, a cabinet of responsible ministers would better integrate, politically and administratively, the governmental system and better incorporate citizen concerns into government action. Furthermore, this integrating body of statesmen could better exercise oversight and control of the "non-political" "business side" of administration because each member would head a major administrative unit corresponding to a particular state function. Yet because of their integrating and legitimating roles and the principle of ministerial responsibility, they could allow more discretion and greater flexibility to the "permanent technical service" in the implementation of public policy. Finally, a plural executive body was better suited for assisting administration in fulfilling its organic function in the democratic state because it could better coordinate the gathering of intelligence from the state's interaction with and response to societal conditions that was the essential work of administrative agencies and bring that intelligence to bear on the lawmaking process.

Wilson held to his preference for a "cabinet government" reform of American governing structures until late in his scholarly career. He seems also to have embraced it again later in his tenure as president and as part of an effort to influence the national Democratic Party platform for 1924, just before he died (see Link et al. 1994, 68:538). Yet Wilson is best known for embracing, in theory and practice, a presidency-centered conception of national governance and political leadership, one that has left a permanent mark on American political development. I have already traced the evolution of Wilson's thinking in this regard from the perspective of his ideas about the character of democracy and about administration's place in the regime. His thinking on this score deserves further review, however, from the perspective of his ideas about administrative organization and managerial practice. That perspective reveals the essence of Wilson's thoughts about what he considered the two central issues of coordination: the nature and extent of the authority of the head of state over administration as a whole and the prospects for a "collegiate union" of individual administrative units under a superintending council.

In his examination of the Cleveland presidency Wilson found that his Democratic predecessor had not filled his cabinet with party leaders who would work with him collegially to lead the party, coordinate policy, and oversee both administration and legislation. Instead, Cleveland had filled his cabinet with personal advisors providing whatever expertise Cleveland felt he needed and specializing in matters of administration and management more than in political leadership. Against Cleveland's cabinet-organizing strategy and as the second-best solution to a formal constitutional change, Wilson called for a cabinet of genuine party leaders who would serve to integrate administration by linking the executive and legislative sides of government under the presiding guidance of the president. Wilson repeated his call for this kind of governing structure in his public lecture "Leaderless Government."

By the time of Wilson's Blumenthal Lectures at Columbia in 1907, however, Cleveland's action and the press of global events convinced Wilson of the greatly diminished prospects for a cabinet organized and functioning as a true body of responsible ministers and political statesmen bringing legislative and executive activities into close and intimate linkage and organically integrating a governmental system in which, in the face of the necessity of modern conditions, administrative power was predominant. Wilson concluded that "the cabinet is an executive, not a political body." Presidents sought "political advice" from their "executive colleagues" because of cabinet secretaries' "natural good sense and experienced judgment, . . . their knowledge of the country and its business and social conditions, . . . their sagacity as representative citizens of more than usual observation and discretion, . . . not because they are supposed to have had any very intimate contact with politics or to have made a profession of public affairs." Thus members of the cabinet might "not necessarily [be] political officers at all" (Wilson 1908, 76).

The changing conditions, both domestic and international, that Wilson saw as driving this change in the status of the cabinet forced adjustments and adaptations in the constitutional system that increasingly placed the central tasks and responsibilities of national governance on the shoulders of the president. The president had become "the leader of his party and the guide of the nation in political purpose, and therefore in legal action." This Wilson regarded as "not inconsistent with the actual provisions of the Constitution; it is only inconsistent with a very mechanical theory of its meaning and intention" (60).

A conventional or "traditionalist" (see Stid 1998, 4–5, 184n13) interpretation of Wilson's conclusion in *Constitutional Government* about the modern development of the presidency and its relationship to the cabinet is that "the President should be an Americanized version of the British prime minister" (Turner 1951, 98). Many references to Wilson acting like a prime minister, supposedly consistent with the theory of executive leadership he enunciated in *Constitutional Government*, appear in the history and political science literature on Wilson (see, for example, the editors' introduction in Link et al. 1976, 22:vii). Wilson never actually made any such reference in *Constitutional Government*, however. Evidence suggesting Wilson's support for the "president as prime minister" notion comes from his 1913 letter to A. Mitchell Palmer, at the time a Democratic representative from Pennsylvania on the House Judiciary Committee. In distancing himself from the Democratic Party platform plank calling for a single six-year presidential term, Wilson used the term "prime minister" to characterize the tremendous expectations for national leadership placed on the president. His deep involvement, with the assistance of his advisors and department heads, in establishing a legislative agenda, in drafting legislation, in monitoring and intervening in the legislative process at strategic moments, in working behind the scenes with legislative leaders, and in reaching across the separation-of-powers divide in both action and rhetoric nevertheless seems to confirm his acceptance of the prime minister role as both New Jersey governor and president (Turner 1951, 104–10). In the Palmer letter, however, Wilson was describing the expectations and demands on the president, not endorsing a role conception. Furthermore, he characterized the situation as "abnormal" and likely to lead "eventually to something very different" (Link et al. 1978, 27:99; see also Stid 1998, 89).

Further consideration of Wilson's characterization of the presidency and its trans-formed function in the midst of constitutional adaptation strongly suggests that he had a very different role conception in mind. Under what one might call Wilson's "strong" conception of cabinet government, policy-making and administration, leg-islating and executing, were, if not fused, then very closely linked. Furthermore, although administration was never on an equal plane with legislation (although much legislating was in reality administration), this subordination was tempered by the impact that administration's understanding of modern conditions through its experience and experiment could have on the shape of future policy. All of this was embodied in a "strong" cabinet whose members were both legislators and execu-tives, or something closely approximate. In *Constitutional Government*, however, we find Wilson arguing for "a distinction between executive action and opinion leader-ship" (Eden 1996, 360). Much more than that, we find Wilson very clearly decou-pling the two, at least with respect to members of the cabinet. Wilson places national political leadership—the leadership of public opinion—almost solely in the hands of the president and on a higher plane of importance than that of executive action. Cabinet members, in turn, take on the executive responsibilities of the presidency.

Robert Eden finds powerful logic in Wilson's adjusted conception; it would allow "the scale and scope of administrative activity [to] expand dramatically, so that in the aggregate result, much more would be accomplished through 'executive action' at every level." Further, the "subordination of executive governance . . . makes it possible to expand the public sphere and to establish administration as a wide field for able and ambitious professional civil servants" (365). Eden also finds Wilson arguing that the burdens of national opinion leadership are so great, and the effort so important, that the president must divest himself of all but the most insignificant executive responsibilities. The presidency was thus in a transitional phase, the ex-ecutive powers granted by the Constitution "in commission," as Wilson put it (see Eden 1996, 366–67), on their way to nearly complete delegation to the heads of executive departments and subordination to the legislature (376–77). It was the president's leadership of public opinion, of party, and thus of the legislature that would insure that legislation and administration were somehow linked. In the sense in which I have presented Wilson's ideas about the structure of an integrated admin-istrative system, the legislature would superintend lawmaking and administration, but the presidency would provide the cohering, uniting political leadership and the principal source of legitimacy for a modernized administration. This is the meaning of Wilson's prediction that presidents would have to regard "themselves as less and less executive officers and more and more directors of affairs and leaders of the nation" (Wilson 1908, 81).

ADMINISTRATIVE DESIGN AND ORGANIZATIONAL PRACTICE   119

I hesitate to go as far as Eden in seeing in Wilson's thinking the complete divestment of executive power from the presidency and its subordination to what seems to me a too-narrow conception of statesmanship as opinion leadership. Part of what statesmanship meant to Wilson included the task of executive-legislative integration. To do that a statesman had to in some way *be* an executive. Indeed, Wilson claimed, "Leadership in government naturally belongs to its executive officers, who are daily in contact with practical conditions and exigencies and whose reputations alike for good judgment and for fidelity are at stake much more than are those of the members of the legislative body at every turn of the law's application" (72). Perhaps Wilson was promoting two distinct conceptions of leadership—leadership of government versus leadership of the state and nation—but nothing in Wilson's writings or public lectures provide any further evidence that he embraced such a distinction.

It is clear, nevertheless, that Wilson did shift his thinking about the proper structure of political authority over administration and the appropriate arrangements for the exercise of administrative power. A true cabinet overseeing both policy and administration, legislation and execution, responsible for both political and administrative integration, gave way to a more purely executive body, plural in structure (Eden 1996, 372), which had responsibility only for administrative integration. The president might preside over the discussion of executive matters among department heads, but the cabinet would be much less a "collegiate union" and "superintending council." In turn, the responsibility for political integration, for ensuring the expression of state life in the system, shifted almost wholly to the president. The president would also provide the link between legislation and execution, ensuring that each would adequately inform the other. But the president would not engage in either true executive or true legislative action and thus would not be a prime minister like any form of that office recognizable in existing governments around the world. Presidents would be national interpreters and enablers of the processes of legislation and administration. The burdens on incumbents would nevertheless be heroic. As I explore in the chapters to follow, the failure of presidents before, during, and after the Wilson presidency to bear those burdens successfully, especially with respect to legitimating administrative structures and methods, would contribute to fragmented autonomy and legitimacy for national administration in a system lacking most of the political and administrative integration Wilson originally envisioned.

ACCOUNTABILITY AND DEMOCRATIC CONTROL

Wilson's principal concern in his pursuit of specific designs for vertical administrative and political integration was regime adjustment. That is, he sought ways to structure government and the administration of the people's affairs to balance the forces of unity and differentiation, which were energized by the conditions of modernity. He tried to envision ways to organize political authority and arrange and distribute administrative power in order to realize the organic wholeness he considered the object of the developmental progression of the modern democratic state, necessary for the survival and progress of a liberal democracy in the modern world. Wilson intended the designs, structures, and methods he pushed to foster greater political responsibility among public officials and thus make government more responsive— responsive in a more appropriate way—to public opinion. They were necessary ingredients in the overall enterprise of progressive democratic development toward organic wholeness and integration.

In both *Congressional Government* and "The Study of Administration," Wilson had enunciated the general structural principle concerning political responsibility (Wilson 1981, 187 and Link et al. 1968, 5:373, respectively). In both, he emphasized the need to structure administration to concentrate power, authority, and responsibility at the highest levels to make accountability transparent and to match the ambitions of administrators with managerial resources so that they would be trusted—and trustworthy. His campaign to redesign the structure of political authority in American government through the promotion of cabinet government or an alternative feasible within the restrictions imposed by the requirements of a written and difficult-to-amend constitution was predicated first on his analysis of the responsibility-fragmenting and degrading effects of the doctrine of separation of powers. Following that, Wilson turned his thinking toward the specifics of the political and administrative structures and practices that could foster greater accountability among public officeholders and ensure a quality of democratic control appropriate for modern times and a progressive democracy. Wilson's ideas in this regard were most prominent across three areas: his promotion of particular municipal government reforms, which was an outgrowth of his arguments about the role of cities in an integrated administrative system; his promotion of efficiency and the incorporation of "business principles" into the structure of public organizations; and his ideas about statutory design to promote accountability, which he articulated mainly in connection with the issue of business regulation.

The Short Ballot and Commission Government

After the early 1890s, Wilson's devoted little of his written work or the material for his classroom lectures and public addresses to municipal government. In late 1898 he dusted off, reorganized, and condensed relevant material from his lectures on administration for a series of five public talks at the Brooklyn Institute of Arts and

Sciences (see Link et al. 1971, 11:74–84). A decade later, however, his ideas about municipal organization became more immediately relevant politically as he advocated adoption of the short ballot, which limited the number of local offices subject to election, in the run-up to his campaign for governor of New Jersey. During his brief gubernatorial tenure he also promoted the commission form of government, in which a small number of elected officials, usually five to seven, govern a municipality by combining legislative and administrative roles. The observations and arguments Wilson put forth in his multiple speeches on these issues revealed the refinement and subtle expansion of his thinking (with no loss of consistency) about how organizational structure could foster responsible behavior of public officials and the responsible use of broad administrative discretion.

In speeches in March and November 1909 and January 1910 and in an article in the May 1910 issue of the *North American Review,* Wilson made the case for the short ballot as a way to structure responsible administration. The heart of his argument was that the long ballot, in which voters were faced with a plethora of elective offices, produced "hide-and-seek" politics. Voters could not possibly know or obtain sufficient information about all the candidates for all the elective offices they were obliged to vote for. Neither could they keep a watchful eye on all of them to determine what these many elected officeholders had done while in office so as to evaluate their performance when they were next up for reelection. The result of this structural design for the selection of administrative personnel was that voters had to rely on the political parties for the "nominating machine" that produced the candidates on the ballots and for cues about how to vote.

The focus of Wilson's attack was not party machines per se, although he was quite vigorous in his denunciation of party bosses and machines. Instead, his primary target was the constitutional and statutory structure of government: "The structure of the government is disintegrated by the law itself, so far as its personnel is concerned" (Link et al. 1975, 20:198). This forced political and administrative integration to take place outside government, through the "extra-legal" devices of party nominations and party discipline. This party-based system could not be eliminated overnight, Wilson admitted, but it had to be addressed, because it allowed politicians operating as administrators to hide behind the party structure and the multitudinous profusion of elective offices, using their discretion for private and corrupt ends. Wilson argued that in a system allegedly designed on the principle of direct popular control—many statutory offices subject to election—the people actually exercised less control because command was in private hands rather than in the hands of many fewer public officials the people could call directly to account.

Wilson pointed out the supreme irony of the arrangement his diagnosis suggested: "Thus we have necessitated the setting-up outside the government of what we were afraid ourselves to set up inside of it: concentrated power, administrative discipline, the authority to appoint and dismiss" (198). The solution of the short ballot produced the same result that Wilson had advocated in his lectures on municipal administration more than two decades earlier: to limit the number of votes voters had to cast, thus reducing both the complexity of the electoral process and the difficulty of monitoring the performance of public officials. In municipalities, voters would cast ballots only for city councilors, either at large or through districts, depending on the size the council needed to be to match the size, complexity, and diversity of the city itself. Voters could then more readily hold city councilors accountable for their administration of the city's affairs, including the quality of their plans, the people they appointed to executive and managerial positions, and, as a result, how well the city was governed with respect to both business efficiency and political solidarity and morality.

Simplicity, Wilson concluded, was the tie that bound the structuring of private business and public administration: "Simplicity is necessary in government as in business, for unity, for responsibility, for efficiency, and for control: these four are, indeed, as a matter of experience, almost interchangeable and equivalent words. You cannot form or execute a judgment within business or in politics without some such system of coherence and simplicity" (207). To achieve greater coherence and simplicity, Wilson contended, was to facilitate the realization of "genuine democracy."

In similar fashion, once he was New Jersey governor Wilson promoted the commission form of municipal government. His arguments were much the same as those used in his advocacy of the short ballot, and at one point he actually linked the two reforms. But he pushed the commission government reform in a more sustained and vigorous way in a series of speeches from May through December 1911. Early on he made the case for it succinctly, declaring that the "commission form of government provides a government of a few men and lets them run it. There are so few we can watch them. They can't hide behind any one else. By this simplification the American people get control of their business" (Link et al. 1977, 23:92).

In promoting such major structural reforms as the short ballot and commission government, Wilson's primary aim was to shape the behavior of top officials—recall that for Wilson they were all administrators at the local government level. And he certainly foresaw a substantial behavioral impact on top administrators from these reforms: publicizing, moralizing, and democratizing their conduct. By electing "a single body which is responsible for the whole of your administration from top to bottom" (166), you "moralize the man who exercises the responsibility. He may exercise a bad judgment and appoint Mr. A when Mr. B would have been better, but he dare not appoint a man on the ground that he will be serviceable to him, or serviceable to a party, instead of serviceable to the people." Wilson concluded that the "same principle is operative all along the line." Under a structure of concentrated authority and responsibility like commission government, public opinion would control administrative appointments better than election because "the whole atmosphere 'Opinion' sustains or destroys responsible officials" (169).

In his final speech directly on the subject of commission government, delivered in Baltimore in December 1911, Wilson sought to link that structural reform not just to the value of vertical administrative integration but also to the organic wholeness and characteristic solidarity of life in the modern democratic state he had long insisted should be the guiding principle of administrative, and especially municipal, reform: "The thing we are looking for in city government, we are looking for in every kind of government in America. . . . We are seeking for responsible action, in response not to special interests or to parts of the opinion, but to the whole opinion of the nation. We are seeking to embody it in the judgment of common men." Stressing again his conviction that government structure mattered because government was part of the life of people in society, Wilson declared, "Ah! ladies and gentlemen, you cannot touch government at any point without touching the very springs of life. Government is not something set apart. Government is part of our lives. Government sets conditions 'round about our lives" (582). The structure of administration thus had to reflect political life as it continued to develop and change in a modern democracy, but administrative structure also shaped that life, especially when it was properly integrated and thus part of the organic whole that was the democratic state.

EFFICIENCY AND BUSINESS PRINCIPLES

Wilson seems to have readily accepted without much scrutiny arguments favoring the organization of public administration along lines reflecting concepts dominant in private business management. He accepted that businesses had to be efficient to survive the competition of the marketplace and thus that the principles of efficient administration and management developed in the business world ought to be applied in the political world to ensure that the government derived the maximum use from scarce public funds. Wilson also accepted that these principles had to be combined with accepted means of "securing legality in administrative action."

First among these means was administrative organization itself, meaning in particular "oversight and control: hierarchy and subordination" (Link et al. 1969, 7:150). But Wilson saw as the principal end value of the incorporation of "business principles" into public administration not the efficient use of the public treasury or even the moralization of politics, both of which he did emphasize, but rather the enhancement of democratic control, properly conceived. As he argued in his article extolling the short ballot, "It has turned out that the methods of organization which lead to efficiency in government are also the methods which give the people control. The busy owner is more effectually in control if he appoints a capable superintendent and holds him responsible for the conduct of the business than he would be if he undertook himself to choose all the subordinate agents and workmen and superintend both them and the superintendent; and the business is also better conducted —incomparably better conducted" (Link et al. 1975, 20:206).

A look at Wilson's multifaceted views about civil service reform reveal further the interesting quality of his thinking regarding the democracy-enhancing qualities of efficiency and business principles in administrative organization. As early as his unpublished essay "Government By Debate" of 1882, Wilson had espoused civil service reform for the increased efficiency it would bring to the public's business. Appointment of administrators on the basis of party favor and the spoils brought into public administration weak skills and irrelevant experience. Competent administration was nonpolitical, that is, nonpartisan, requiring skills and capacities readily applicable in private and public organizations alike. In short, a protected civil service brought neutral competence and increased efficiency. The way to get this was competitive examination and merit selection.

This was the standard wisdom Wilson repeated throughout much of his scholarly study and commentary on administration. As in his lecture "Democracy," however, Wilson also characterized a civil service system with merit selection as enhancing the representativeness of public administration as an institution by opening up the public service to all those willing to make themselves fit to serve, irrespective of wealth or social standing. And his subsequent engagement in direct political competition seems to have stimulated further refinement in his thinking about the link connecting business principles, democratic control, and responsible administrative behavior.

In the next-to-last speech he delivered in his campaign for governor, for example, Wilson questioned the wisdom of "filling offices by examination tests," which he regarded as "a little ridiculous . . . because it is very difficult to set tests along a line which has anything to do with the duties the man who is given office is to perform." The thrust of his questioning was to point out that the real meaning of merit selection was democratic control through concentration of responsibility and authority and through hierarchical organization, which he described as "holding office on a footing that cannot be controlled by men who are not superior to the persons appointed to office" (Link et al. 1976, 21:532).

In May 1912, before he received the Democratic Party nomination for president,

Wilson offered a much more extensive commentary on civil service reform, efficiency, and democratic control. He suggested to his audience, the Connecticut Civil Service Reform Association, that "we have [not] always acted very wisely in our agitation for civil service reform or . . . thought very clearly as to our objects" (Link et al. 1977, 24:167). He stressed that the "purification of government" from the corruption of patronage and private use that was the object of civil service reform was only a preliminary step toward the more important object of efficiency in government. The real problem of government was "the enormous waste in the mere organization of government. Every time you want to do anything, you have to have a new commission to do it and pay a new set of salaries" (171–72). Civil service reform hardly got at this problem, so civil service reform had to be thought of as part of a larger scheme "for redeeming your government from inefficiency" (174). The problem of efficiency in government was primarily one of "coordination in large part. It is not so much of the character and the integrity and the knowledge of the individual public servant as it is of his relation to other public servants and to his subordination in the scheme of superintendence which will bring about what the business man would regard as efficient results" (168).

Wilson went on to promote again the idea of reducing the number of administrative positions "filled by election and therefore by preliminary selection," the latter phrase referring to the choices made by private interests, principally party bosses (170). Increasing the number of offices filled by appointment would increase public opinion's control over administration by focusing it on those fewer offices that were elected. The bottom line, Wilson argued, as he had in his advocacy of the short ballot and commission government, was that government organization was at root what had to be reformed. Such reform would both reduce control of government by private interests and help harness public-spiritedness by recovering certain fundamental principles: "Government, to my mind, is nothing more nor less than organizing the general interest so efficiently that no special interest can dominate it. And we have no doubt that in America we have let our governments become so disordered in respect to their organization, that special interest could break in and we not be aware of it" (175). The disorder prevented citizens and their leaders from mastering the "problem of government," which concerned the search for "some surplus of energy that we care to spend outside the narrow circle of our own individuality" (176).

Definite Law

One additional area of Wilson's thinking about institutional design and organizational structure as a vehicle of accountability and democratic control is perhaps the most distinctive facet of his ideas on this subject. This is Wilson's notion of "definite law," by which he meant law that spelled out very specifically right or wrong conduct and insisted that those individuals who engaged in any prohibited conduct be held personally to account for such actions and, if necessary, punished. Wilson promoted this idea principally in connection with his public stand on monopolies, trusts, and business regulation. There was certainly a strong strain of moralism in Wilson's thinking in this regard, which has drawn the skepticism of scholars (see, for example, Clements 1992, 28, 49). A moral basis for business regulation also seems wholly anachronistic, not to mention simplistic and reactionary, in the great age of uncertainty and irony that is the reality of the postmodern world. Wilson's arguments about business regulation and his idea of definite law nevertheless shed further light on his thinking about the proper place for administration in a democratic regime. They are similarly revealing of his thinking about administrative organization and practice.

Part of Wilson's attack on a trade commission, which would, in Wilson's view, regulate and thus legitimate monopoly rather than prevent or punish illegal monopolistic practices, was a straightforward structural argument. Regulation by law and courts (recall his views about the courts as administrative entities in *Constitutional Government*) was preferable to regulation by an administrative commission staffed by experts in monopoly practices who would be exercising broad "individual" discretion over the operations, and even dictating the financial fate, of the businesses subject to regulation. The latter arrangement would inevitably lead, in Wilson's view, to the invasion of private interests into the public realm and, just as seriously, the reverse as well. This could lead, in Wilson's more heated characterizations, to an unholy alliance of business and government, producing domination and tyranny. This was a serious distortion of administration's proper place in the regime. So Wilson stressed that a commission approach to business regulation tended to break down the necessary arm's length relationship between government and business, undermining the structural safeguards that ensured the good behavior of administrators by protecting them from the temptation to control, dominate, and tyrannize business and, ultimately, all private citizens. In short, it would lead to administrators behaving badly and turn upside down the proper relationship between the public and public administrators, resulting in just what Wilson had for so long been arguing could be avoided: a "bureaucratic," tutelary state.

Beyond this systemic design point, Wilson's arguments about the proper approach to business regulation also addressed policy design through his idea of definite law, which aimed to fix individual responsibility for corporate or financial misdeeds, which reinforced his more longstanding arguments about the need to fix individual responsibility for public administrator behavior. In keeping with his views about administration as the "experiencing organ" of the state, he stressed that definite law should be based not on some abstract theory of economic design or governmental structure but on administrative experience, both private and public. Two especially closely interrelated dimensions of Wilson's idea of definite law—personalization and transparency—further reveal Wilson's thinking about the accountability and democratic control facets of administrative organization and practice.

Wilson contended that whatever authority and accompanying responsibility was vested in an administrative organization, or in the administrative system as a whole, that authority and responsibility should not be diffuse or hidden. It should be concentrated, transparent, and tied to the incumbent officeholder. In short, it should be personalized. In the same Morristown, New Jersey, campaign speech in November 1910 in which he wondered about the efficacy of civil service exams, Wilson observed, "Government, gentlemen, is personal, it is not impersonal." He went on to talk in very moralistic terms, concluding, "All evil doing is, of course, personal, and guilt, therefore is of course personal." But then, taking a big logical step, he argued that "by the same proof government is intensely personal. It consists in certain freedoms and certain bondages, and what we are trying to break up now . . . is political bondage. We are trying to get away from the idea that parties are intended for the dispersion of responsibility, to come around to the idea that parties are intended for the support of responsible representatives who are expected to rede [that is, advise] them in definite policies" (Link et al. 1976, 21:533; see also 501).

For a long time Wilson had been arguing that for the American people to have confidence in their government and its exercise of the great modern power of administration, those who were responsible for wielding that power had to be relatively few in number, readily identifiable as individual officeholders, and relatively easy to monitor. With his idea of definite law, Wilson added the additional requirement that behavioral consequences be simply and clearly spelled out. This would seem to apply principally to political leaders—elected representatives—but by logical extension it would also apply to those who held office by appointment to the extent that they exercised administrative power. Transparency and personalization in administrative structure would thus create the incentive environment within which the private interests and ambitions of public officials would fuse with their sense of the public good to enable them to gain the trust of their fellow citizens.

With his idea of definite law, Wilson argued that this administrative design ought to be supported by policy design, such that the same principles should apply to private businessmen through the design of business regulation. What was at stake in the design of policy and administration on the basis of transparency and personal responsibility was the maintenance of democratic control, appropriately conceived. Ambitious private interests would be prevented from getting or keeping control of the "instrumentalities" of government, and, as Wilson had argued about the design of local government, citizen interest would be engaged and civic enthusiasm for promoting the public good preserved. Wilson's idea of definite law was, then, a distinctive manifestation of his core notion that good governance required a close linkage between lawmaking and administration—an interlocking of the two, achieved primarily through political leadership but also through the conception and design of good policy and good structures for carrying policy into effect.

TRAINING AND EXPERTISE

I explored in chapter 3 Wilson's views on administrative expertise from the perspective of his concerns about situating administration in the regime. Knowledge, expertise, careful observation, experimentation, and the consequent accumulation of experience were the elements that made administrative power distinctive and characterized administration as a unique organ of the democratic state. It is reasonably clear from the evidence that Wilson had special concerns for both developing and harnessing the power of technical expertise and keeping it in its proper place. His ideas about institutional design, organizational structure, and administrative practice with respect to technical training and expertise addressed these twin concerns directly.

In notes for his lectures on constitutional government of 1898, Wilson devoted an entire section to "Expert Administration: Its functions and conditions" (Link et al. 1971, 11:23). He defined expert administration as "that which is founded on knowledge or experience,—at best, upon both knowledge and experience." This was "typified in the administration of justice: the interpretation of the law, a function universally admitted to demand professional training,—if it is to be done at its best, even profound scholarship." The aim of all such expert administration was "to put the learning, experience, and skill of the country at the disposal of the government." To gain this benefit and thus to encourage, develop, and harness the special qualities of administration and administrative power, an administrative system in a modern democracy had to meet certain "requisite conditions" or structural requirements centered on providing job security to expert administrators, to ensure their impartial appointment and promotion, and providing for their special education and technical training that went beyond what the general educational system supplied.

Wilson regarded the arguments favoring the first two as already well accepted. He contended that much greater attention to the necessities of the third requirement was needed, emphasizing in particular two key considerations. The first was the need for the development of an adequate educational and training infrastructure. The second was the need to determine which administrative functions required what kinds of education, training, and life experience.

Wilson had argued in earlier notes that for "technical training . . . to be made effectual, uniform, complete," it was necessary to create some form of government-run or government-sanctioned schools and "bureaux of instruction in connexion with the various branches of the public service" (Link et al. 1969, 7:392). Later he stressed that the "best equipped governments have even undertaken to create the skill and the intellectual acquirements needed in their service, where the ordinary educational and professional instrumentalities do not suffice to supply them" (Link et al. 1971, 11:23). Thus Wilson regarded the creation or expansion of an entire, integrated system of administrator education, training, and professional development as an essential element in the development of a modern, professional public service. This would also signify a higher level of constitutional maturity in a modern democratic state.

In exploring the "place and limits" of "popular administration," Wilson argued, as he had in earlier lectures on administration, in his most widely delivered public lecture, "Democracy," and in a number of other instances, that the selection of managers and front-line workers in the public service by merit through competitive examination was democratic so long as the opportunity was open to all and there were no restrictions based on wealth, ethnic background, or social standing. (Race and gender were, regrettably, at least partial exceptions, although Wilson never stated this explicitly.) The most "fit and capable persons" would be accepted into the public service. Wilson contended, however, that "fitness and capacity must vary with the function to be performed." He identified two key functions in this regard, the first being functions that required "expert knowledge and a special training for their proper performance" and the second being functions "for which only special kinds of bringing up and special conditions of life and environment render men fit" (21).

With respect to the latter sort of functions, Wilson explored diplomacy and consular services, considering the possibility of an "unpaid civil service" (22). Wilson's commentary here, especially his reference to "leisured society," would proba-bly confirm for many current observers and critics the sort of old money, East Coast elitism long associated with the diplomatic corps and thus seemingly a direct contra-diction to Wilson's point about the "free and universal" democratic foundation of administrative recruitment. With respect to the former functions requiring special knowledge and schooling, Wilson explored the conditions of expert administration to which I have already alluded. Wilson's treatment of both sets of functions led him back to his point about the democratic compatibility of a competitive, merit-based public service. He argued that if variations in wealth gave some individuals more resources to be competitive than others, that was an "economic, not a political, limitation put upon the theoretical equality of competition; and the remedy for that inequality, if there be any remedy, must be sought for elsewhere than in constitutions and merely political arrangements." He also pointed out, however, that wealth had its own burdens, and the poor might "outrun the rich in fitting themselves for achievement and the successful exercise of power." His more general point, however, was that considerations of fitness and capacity, training and expertise, formed a key point of contact between administration and public opinion: "The limits of popular administration lie where the need for special training or technical skill begins" (23). Thus, however the infrastructure for developing administrative expertise might be designed and operated, the organizational arrangements for harnessing that expertise had to be compatible with the proper relationship between public opinion and administration and the structures keeping them in their proper places in the regime.

In considering the structures and practices necessary to keep public opinion and administrative expertise suitably related and in their respective places in a properly progressive liberal-democratic regime, Wilson did not offer up any new designs or devices. He relied instead on the structures he continually promoted. First and foremost was a system thoroughly integrated, both politically and administratively, with concentrated political authority, uniform law, and the centralization of law and knowledge, but with plenty of decentralization and local flexibility in the actual application of administrative power. Second was the combination of other structures and practices that fostered administrative behavior in favor of the public good. Third was the design of administrative schemes, including the types of organizations and institutions deployed to achieve particular public policy aims, which would not exceed administration's institutional capacity, keeping it within its true character and role in the regime. Combined with his scholarly critique of expertise, Wilson carried this last structural argument with him into the presidential campaign arena where, during the debate over business regulation in the 1912 election, he argued that effectively harnessing administrative power for progressive ends did not mean that Americans had to turn over the running of their lives, and the larger life of the state, to technical and scientific experts (see, for example, Link et al. 1978, 25:69–79). Institutional designs and organizational structures, Wilson intimated in both his lectures and on the campaign trail, should maximize the benefit and minimize the threat of increased expertise in government.

GOOD PRACTICE, MORE DEMOCRACY

John Rohr has argued that Wilson promoted a governmental scheme in which the separation between politics and administration was prominent as a way to "rescue government from the vortex of popular sentiment." Further, "Wilson hoped enlightened administration would replace separation of powers in the noble task of saving democracy from its own excesses" (1984, 44). Dwight Waldo preceded Rohr's interpretation with the more general observation that the ubiquitous but reviled politics-administration dichotomy was "an attempt on the part of public administration to work with and/or around the separation of powers" (quoted in Frederickson and Smith 2003, 40). These interpretations suggest that Wilson saw a governing system carefully and formally separating political and administrative functions as a preferable substitute for the Founders' scheme for controlling the mischiefs of majority faction. With the separation of powers constantly in his sights, and with so much of his commentary on democracy and on administration stressing the limitations of mass popular rule, the need to understand the proper relationship between governors and the governed, and the need to situate administration at least one step away from direct public control, it is difficult to escape the plausibility of Rohr's summation of Wilson's thinking and the consequence for theory Waldo suggested.

One cannot help but be struck, nevertheless, by the extent to which Wilson's analysis and normative argumentation, particularly regarding specific institutional arrangements, organizational structures, and managerial practices for public administration, were aimed quite explicitly at reenergizing and reengaging citizens in self-government, making American government what Wilson saw as more genuinely democratic. What this means exactly might still be interpreted in the way Rohr proposes—proper democracy is properly *restrained* democracy. Yet there is no denying that Wilson justified many of his ideas about administrative organization and practice in terms of increasing public or democratic control, primarily funneled through the popularly elected political authorities at the "top" of an integrated administrative system.

Wilson certainly embraced the administrative and managerial "good practices" of his day. Without extensive analysis or critique, he accepted the advisability of hierarchy and the orderly arrangement of superior and subordinate positions, the unity of command, organizational discipline, "scientific" principles and practices in financial and other forms of management, merit selection, professionalism, specialized education and training, the cultivation and functional deployment of technical expertise, and even the fostering of organizational *esprit de corps,* although this had to be carefully constrained. Wilson accepted all of these modernizations in structure and managerial technique, but they were not really his principal interest or aim in his reform endeavor. He regarded them all as enhancing efficiency in public administration and management. This was a good thing in and of itself, but Wilson promoted the efficiency enhancements principally for what they would do to strengthen the influence of public opinion, and by this he meant majority opinion. In a very real sense, he saw improvements in the efficiency of public administration and management as tilting the system in favor of public, majoritarian democracy and against private, special-interest democracy.

The same logic undergirded Wilson's more prominent structural ideas and reforms. He advanced his ideas about the proper role and structure for municipal government and the proper structure of "peak" political authority on the same premise: they would reengage the citizenry in government, especially critical since in the modern age administration had moved to center stage in governance, increasing citizen interest in (and scrutiny of) their representatives' administration of the public's business and enhancing public control of aims and outcomes. The desired effect was the same for Wilson's idea of definite law and for the other designs he promoted for concentrating public authority and responsibility and making them transparent. Wilson may have conceived and advanced an idea of mass popular rule that he regarded as more appropriately constrained for the modern world, but he was not hesitant about elevating the reach and presence of that new kind of democracy. And he saw the elevation and reconstruction of public administration and management as a central element in such an enterprise.

To consider Wilson's ideas as having value in confronting the current and continuing challenges of public management, it is, however, appropriate to ask how he governed according to his own ideas—what public administration and public management was like under Wilson—and what consequences followed. To what extent did he seek to maintain, even strengthen, local administrative autonomy and vitality while at the same time creating a more fully integrated national system of administration subject to central policy control? Did he succeed in guiding the development of a technically expert, neutrally competent administration restrained by political authority but not debilitated by partisan interference? To what extent did he introduce mechanisms for greater coordination and efficiency into national administration? How far did he go in pressing for the design of public policy that would clearly define responsible and irresponsible conduct and give clear and definite guidance to administrators? The authority of technical expertise versus popular control through political leadership, the preservation of local variety and vitality versus national policy integration, the coordination of policy implementation in a fragmented system, and the proper level of detail in policy design to guide administrative action remain prominent quandaries for policymakers, practicing public managers, and scholars alike. Wilson's own ideas about these matters and a host of related problems have value to the extent that we can assess and understand the governing *actions* he fashioned in response. It is toward such an assessment and understanding that we now turn.

PART II

Wilson's Practices

CHAPTER FIVE

Administrative Reform and Expansion

In his compact, illuminating biography, John A. Thompson contends that there are two contrasting views that must be taken into account in considering Woodrow Wilson's governing practices. One view is that Wilson was a "conviction politician," that is, "Wilson's actions and utterances arose directly from his beliefs, with the implicit corollary that attempts to explain them should focus on his own intellectual formation" (2002, 7–8). In this view, Wilson's long academic career more firmly cemented his convictions. The alternative view "deeply held by some of Wilson's contemporary political opponents" was that "as a practicing politician, he traveled with very little ideological baggage, adopting and abandoning positions as they suited his political interests at the time, and deftly using his exceptional rhetorical ability to cover his tracks" (8). Thompson's own analysis uncovers considerable support for the latter view, leading him to conclude that Wilson was not a rigid idealist forced by the regrettable necessities of politics to accept sharp discontinuities between his beliefs and his actions. "In terms of the types of leadership he identified in his own early writings," Thompson argues, "we may say that his successes were those of a skilled and pragmatic practitioner of the art of politics" (243).

Daniel Stid has identified within Wilson himself a struggle between two political personas similar to the competing external perspectives Thompson has identified. Stid perceives a "troubling dialogue," existing between "Wilson the reformer" striving for the establishment of responsible government and "Wilson the realistic student of political life," aware of the need to adjust his reform vision to the "political inertia embodied in the American regime" and the practical political challenges the reformer as president would face (1998, 65). In Stid's view, the dialogue began in earnest with Wilson's reconception of the locus for the binding force of responsibility and the integration of legislation and execution from the cabinet to the president, which continued into his service as an elected executive. Stid finds that Wilson managed at times to maneuver successfully through his competing predilections by exploiting the flexibility contained in his idea of interpretive statesmanship, with its subtle balance of anchoring principles and acceptance of expediency, as in Wilson's successful shift to advanced progressivism in 1916 (111). Stid concludes, however, that in some of the most important instances—fighting the war and structuring the peace, in particular—Wilson did not succeed in fitting his practices to both the demands of his reform ideas and the realities of governance in the political order spawned by the Constitution, especially with respect to spanning the separation-of-powers divide (175–79; see also Rohr 1986, 74–75; Tulis 1987, 146).

Wilson himself acknowledged the tension between ideas and practices and the untoward consequences that followed. Only a year into his first term as president, in one of a series of letters to a close friend describing the pressures and demands he had to abide, Wilson referred to the "all but unbearable strain" of the office. "This is the penalty," he concluded, "for having held since I was a youngster a distinct theory of what a President ought to be and ought to attempt. One ought not to write books until he knows whether he will be called on to do what they say ought to be done" (Link et al. 1979, 29:211–12).

Around the centennial of Wilson's birth, historians and political scientists were making quite favorable judgments about Wilson's record in dealing with the strain. The broad consensus about the distinctive achievements of Wilson's governing practices is evident in the scholarship from that time (e.g., Turner 1951, 1956; Link 1956; Latham 1958). Echoes of this consensus are also evident in more recent general treatments of Wilson (e.g., Heckscher 1991; Clements 1992) and in treatments focusing specifically on public administration (Walker 1989). The centennial consensus centered mainly on Wilson's ideas as expressed in *Constitutional Government*, emphasizing in particular two aspects of Wilson's performance vis-à-vis those ideas. First and foremost was the success of Wilson's prime ministerial leadership of the legislature, both in New Jersey and nationally, combining interpretive statesmanship with an aggressive synthesis of close communications and intimate personal interactions with legislative leaders, which allowed him to set the policy agenda, propose legislation, and oversee its formulation and final enactment. Second was Wilson's concomitant delegation of authority to his department heads covering both policy within their domains and, especially, internal management, with virtually no interference except for certain appointments (either in response to pressure for patronage or to fend it off) and to ensure consistency with his policy agenda.

In the generation following the emergence of this centennial consensus on the nature of Wilson's success, a more complex and critical series of assessments ensued, both in political science (see the works cited in Stid 1998, 184n14; see also Yates 1982) and in public administration (e.g., Rabin and Bowman 1984; Rohr 1986, chs. 5–6; Ostrom 1989), over the meaning of Wilson's legacy, primarily regarding theory but also with some attention to practice. The interpretation and assessment of Wilson, and attempts to link him to current and future problems of governance, continues (e.g., Kettl 2002, esp. 38–43, 80–98, 108–10). In this chapter and the next, I take a closer look at Wilson the *practitioner* through the lens of several existing scholarly assessments and some of Wilson's own rhetoric and in light of his ideas about administration and the interpretation of those ideas I have offered. In doing so, my principal aim is to sift through some of the evidence, sort out alternative perspectives, and, with some additional observations of my own, offer a multifaceted portrait of Wilson's governing practices. Along the way I draw my own conclusions about Wilson's enterprise and its connection to the ongoing challenges of public administration and management in a democracy.

I begin with a brief but more complete representation of the "traditional perspective" on Wilson's governing performance (Stid 1998, 4–5), with particular attention to scholarship that has stressed the administrative and management dimension. I then consider both reinforcing and countervailing views and evidence by concentrating on several facets of Wilson's rhetoric and behavior in office that correspond to his ideas about administration highlighted in previous chapters. In this chapter, I focus on Wilson's efforts aimed toward administrative reform. The subject encompasses several subcomponents, including party patronage and the merit system, mechanisms for improving coordination and administrative efficiency, vertical administrative integration and state and local autonomy, and reform and expansion of administrative structures at the national level. In the following chapter, I continue the focus on administrative expansion, integrating it into a primary focus on Wilson's efforts to adhere to his notion of definite law. I then move on to consider Wilson's governing practices with respect to his ideas about cabinet government and, finally, interpretive leadership. These various facets of Wilson's governance have received the most concentrated attention in the history and political science literature, but I emphasize the administration and management dimension commensurate with the focus of my presentation and interpretation of Wilson's ideas. I conclude the two chapters by identifying what I believe to be the core challenges public management currently faces in the United States in light of Wilson's governing struggles.

THE TRIUMPH OF EXECUTIVE LEADERSHIP

At the heart of the consensus view of Wilson's governing success is the conclusion that Wilson followed closely and with great accomplishment his theory of executive leadership and opinion management as articulated in *Constitutional Government.* He carried out his conception of the president (and governor) as prime minister, bridging the executive-legislative divide with both inspiring rhetoric and concrete overtures and actions. These actions entailed setting a specific and limited policy agenda, preparing legislation within the executive branch and getting it introduced by congressional supporters, rallying public sentiment in its favor, using individual department heads to help guide legislation through the formulation process, and interacting with Congress, especially legislative leaders of his party, to get major new policies enacted (see, generally, Turner 1951). One political scientist even found that in putting his prime ministerial theory of executive leadership into practice at the state level in New Jersey, Wilson proposed near the end of his abbreviated gubernatorial term a new state constitution "with a parliamentary type of government" (Turner 1956, 252).

In this celebratory view, Wilson's primary success in carrying into practice his theory of executive leadership produced a chain of additional successes tied to his vision of reform and modernization of national governance. Through his leadership, Wilson succeeded in redistributing national political power from Congress to the executive "so that the government of the United States would be enabled better to meet the problems of the twentieth century" (Turner 1951, 114). Most significant in this redistribution was Wilson's success in gaining broad, general grants of discretionary policy authority in key statutes, with only "the subject to be regulated or the end to be achieved" specified (112). Perhaps even more significant in this regard than the emblematically broad, general authority to fight monopolistic trade practices granted to the Federal Trade Commission (see the further discussion in the next chapter) was the almost unlimited authority to reorganize the executive branch Congress ceded to Wilson in the form of the Lever Food Control Act and the Overman Act, both enacted during the mobilization for and engagement in World War I.

Concomitant with these broad delegations of authority was Wilson's success in expanding the number and variety of agencies. Many of these were temporary organizations to meet the wartime emergency and, in keeping with the nature of the delegations of authority to the executive, they operated under strict and direct presidential control. Several of the most important new entities were meant to be permanent, however, including the FTC, the Federal Reserve, the Federal Power Commission, and the United States Shipping Board (Turner 1956, 253). Albeit created ad hoc, the successful structural innovation these entities represented was in many respects the opposite of the temporary wartime agencies. Although both the temporary and permanent agencies were situated outside the cabinet department hierarchy, the permanent establishments moved away from rather than closer to direct presidential control. In apparent consistency with Wilson's longstanding scholarly privileging of practice and experience over abstract theory in political action, "the administrative issue about departures from hierarchy does not seem to have been raised and decided in broad, theoretical terms. Special circumstances were in play in connection with each of the entities created in a period of innovative zest" (Macmahon 1958, 115–16). This established, post hoc, a precedent, if not a theory, for structuring and situating within the federal government a particular kind of administrative entity: the economic regulatory commission. The consensus view of Wilson's success also encompasses his achievements in expanding the activities the federal government was engaged in, from agricultural extension to child labor regulation, and in accelerating the centralization of policy and administration in the federal government, largely at the expense of the states (Turner 1956, 252).

The traditional perspective on Wilson's governing achievements highlights in particular his success in fulfilling his conception of the role of department heads and other administrators as he revised it in *Constitutional Government*. Wilson gave his departmental secretaries considerable autonomy and delegated to them substantial executive authority over internal management in their organizations and even granted some control over policy. He did work closely with most of his department heads on specific policy matters on an individual basis such that "larger questions of policy were to be determined by Wilson in consultation with department heads" (Turner 1956, 253; see also Macmahon 1958, 113). Wilson did take much more comprehensive personal control over policy formulation and execution in foreign relations, pre- and postwar diplomacy, and conduct of the war (although not in the sense of dictating strategic or tactical decisions to military professionals). This made extensive delegation on the domestic front even more imperative. Indeed, in this assessment of Wilson's governing practices, Wilson could not have reached his heights of achievement in public policy or diplomacy without the strategically wise decision to rely on his department heads to take over much of the policy management associated with regular government operations. Moreover, in this view, Wilson readily succeeded in fulfilling his vision, outlined in "The Study of Administration," of the separation of "policy politics" (Rosenbloom 1984, 104) from the more businesslike, technical, expert-dependent dimensions of public administration and management.

Wilson's success in his approach to administration through substantial delegation of executive authority was, according to this celebratory perspective, the result of his success in administrative appointments. Although he had to appoint several department heads primarily on grounds of political expediency in order to reinforce his claims to party leadership, "in every department Wilson appointed at least one of the top officials because of his 'special fitness for the great business post' to which he had been assigned" (Turner 1956, 253, quoting Wilson 1908, 76). It is at this point, however, that the celebration largely ends. The traditional scholarly consensus leavened its overall assessment of Wilson's status as a "great" or "near-great" president with some minor reservations and caveats.

The traditional perspective acknowledges that Wilson fell short in the area of personnel management, both because he was not able to resist sufficiently the deluge of patronage demands from the stalwart wing of his party, and because in general he "initiated few personnel reforms" (Turner 1956, 254). Wilson also failed in his management of his cabinet advisors because he was temperamentally unable to tolerate disagreement with his decisions (Turner 1956, 255–56; also see Link 1956, 67–70; Fenno 1959, 39). Finally, Wilson also largely failed in pushing for and achieving general administrative reforms, including systematizing the federal budget and reorganizing the executive branch to reduce fragmentation and increase efficiency (Turner 1956, 254; Macmahon 1959, 119–22; also Clements 1992, 11–12; 1998, 325–28). Wilson nevertheless did gain for future presidents a key precedent: a broad shift of power in favor of the executive (for a dissenting view, see Arnold 1998, 52).

Many of the scholars who have praised Wilson's governing practices have nevertheless acknowledged intermittent dark clouds in the otherwise bright sky of Wilson's accomplishments. Among the standard referents are, first, Wilson's endorsement of increased racial segregation in the federal civil service, the result at least in part of the substantial autonomy and delegation of internal management authority Wilson granted his department heads. The effect of this scourge was thus spread unevenly, depending on the predilections of particular department managers and executives. But Wilson defended the more egregious efforts, insisting at one point that "by putting certain bureaus and sections of the service in the charge of negroes we are rendering them more safe in their possession of office and less likely to be discriminated against" (Link et al. 1978, 28:65). A second standard criticism is that Wilson signed into law several statutes that instituted restrictions on civil liberties during the war, including considerable surveillance and monitoring of political speech and the rooting out of disloyal or subversive elements (see Clements 1992,

152–56). Finally, and the blackest cloud of all, Wilson failed to persuade the Senate to ratify the League of Nations treaty.

The overall conclusion is nevertheless that Wilson's political brilliance, representing a close congruence between his ideas and his actions, produced achievements in policy, administration, and regime reconstruction that are not diminished by the sporadic shadows. In the view of one political scientist a half-century ago, "Few of our Chief Executives have had a more profound effect on the scope and functioning of our national administrative system" (Turner 1956, 257).

The traditional assessment of Wilson's governing success comes from a time when the values of concentrated executive power; of large, centralized public undertakings; and of vigorous regulation of economic enterprise were ascendant. Such values are much less in vogue today; indeed, they may be in wholesale retreat if not already defeated, and that is important in considering the relevance of Wilson's ideas and practices to public management today. But for our immediate purposes it is more important first to consider Wilson's practices and perceived successes in light of the additional scrutiny to which they have been subject and the full range of ideas he developed and articulated, not just those ideas he presented in *Constitutional Government*. There is some risk with respect to the latter task, of course, because Wilson did regard a number of his earlier ideas as outmoded, at least during the apex of his political engagement, particularly with respect to the roles of the president and cabinet. He also accepted, partly as a dimension of his conception of leadership, the need to modify reform ideas to make them politically feasible. Once in public office, he clearly sought to follow much of the advice conveyed in his Blumenthal Lectures.

Yet the value of considering some of Wilson's signature practices and positive judgments about them in the context of the full spectrum of his ideas, especially with respect to administration and management, is that it raises all sorts of interesting questions about the meaning of some of his ideas, the continuities and discontinuities in his political thought, and the challenges of translating ideas into politically effective action. Most important are questions about the significance of Wilson's successes and failures for the continued development of theory and practice, since public administration and public management now appear to be operating in an entirely new world, one far removed from Wilson's ideas and practices.

I consider a set of interrelated Wilson practices that received at least some criticism in the otherwise brightly positive centennial consensus on his governing success. These practices encompass a variety of efforts at mostly structural administrative reform, touching on expansion of administrative capacity and the federal government's reach into American society, including intergovernmental relations. More specifically, these efforts cover expansion and further institutionalization of the merit system and specific reform measures regarding the structure and operational methods of government administration. I also look at the development of new administrative entities, most prominently with respect to mobilization and war.

PATRONAGE AND MERIT

Scholarly assessments of Wilson's governing practices consistently mention his failure to push with enough consistency the continued expansion and reinforcement of the merit system and principles of neutral competence. Wilson thus fell short in fulfilling a key administrative design idea he had strongly endorsed, as a result weakening the quality of public service. The standard scholarly judgment on this failure is that it epitomized the internal clash Wilson experienced, between the idealist reformer and the political pragmatist. As one prominent Wilson biographer stated, "Wilson did no worse than other Presidents before and after him; but his case is the more striking because he had aimed so high and been compelled so often to content himself with second-rate men. Ideals, once again, were being harshly accommodated to circumstances" (Heckscher 1991, 289; see also Link 1956, 160, 173–74). This standard judgment also accepts, however, that Wilson's use of patronage and his delegation of appointment authority, both of which delayed and even reversed expansions of the merit system in some instances, was a reasonable, pragmatic political accommodation to his aim of establishing his leadership of the Democratic Party in government (e.g., Milkis and Nelson 1999, 230).

Wilson's Patronage Struggles

Wilson expressed anxiety over the reputational impact of his practice of making patronage appointments. Yet he also acknowledged the necessity of such appointments in advancing the progressive cause. Edward House noted in his diary concerning the appointment of Albert Burleson as postmaster general that Wilson "thought Burleson would build up a machine. I replied that if he did it would be a Wilson machine, and he could be restrained from even doing that. He was rather distrustful of Burleson being able to hold down the place" (Link et al. 1978, 27:111). In a note to his personal secretary Joseph Tumulty early in 1914, Wilson declared himself "deeply disturbed" by the apparent political manipulations of promotions and demotions in the Public Printing Office: "I shall have to ask the Civil Service Commission to make a careful investigation and report to me. The single and most threatening danger to our party just at this moment is that it will yield to the 'spoils' impulse and make a partisan use of the power of appointments to office and of promotion and demotion in the departments" (partially quoted in Link 1956, 175; see Link et al. 1979, 29:100). In reply to a letter from Charles Eliot, who had expressed concern about patronage appointments in the diplomatic corps, Wilson argued that he was committed to the merit system in the consular services but that some change in the broader philosophy of the diplomatic corps was necessary: "In the matter of the diplomatic service, . . . those who have been occupying the legations and embassies have been habituated to a point of view which is very different, indeed, from the point of view of the present administration. . . . I have been genuinely distressed at the necessity of seeming to act contrary to the spirit of the merit system in any case in particular, but there are circumstances which seem to me to make a certain amount of this necessary at the opening of a new order of things" (Link et al. 1978, 28:280). There are a number of additional instances indicating that Wilson was less concerned about patronage activity leading to a politicized and incompetent civil service and more that without patronage he would be stuck with a civil service lacking the "right" political orienta- tion toward progressivism (see Link 1956, 157–58, 162–63, 175).

It was in appointments to the foreign service that Wilson found himself caught in the most intense struggles over patronage (see Link 1956, 97–110). Arthur Link gives Wilson some credit for trying to balance the goals of shifting administrative ideology, releasing some of the pent-up Democratic Party pressure for government jobs and at least maintaining the existing level of merit and administrative competence. Wilson "made the most important appointments" to the State Department staff himself (97). More important, Wilson made a "number of distinguished minister appoint- ments" (106) and "stood firm" against partisan raids of the consular service: "He not only insisted upon appointing consuls from the civil service list, but also continued Roosevelt's and Taft's practice of appointing secretaries in the diplomatic corps on a basis of merit" (107).

Where Secretary of State William Jennings Bryan had freer reign, however, patronage exploitation of personnel was rampant. Because of the extent of Wilson's delegation of administrative control and some policy development to his department heads, the pattern seems to have repeated itself across the executive establishment in the Wilson administration. Where a secretary had "spoilsman" predilections, as with Bryan and Burleson, patronage manipulation of personnel was widespread. Among those department heads primarily interested in good administration and faithfulness to progressive ideology, such as Agriculture Secretary David Houston and Secretary of War Lindley Garrison, "the standards of professionalism lauded by progressive reformers were advanced" (Stid 1998, 101). The policy effects thus were irregular:

"Spoilsmen were less able and often less willing to implement their president's New Freedom legislation than officials who were chosen for their talent and their commitment to progressive principles" (Milkis and Nelson 1999, 230–31).

Two Critical Perspectives

Moving beyond the conventional idealist versus realist assessment, two scholars have offered much more far-reaching assessments of the effects of Wilson's patronage policies on his reform aims and on the longer-run character and legitimacy of modern public administration and management. The more recent appears in Daniel Stid's illuminating analysis of Wilson's actions as they relate to his ideas about "responsible government." First, Wilson failed to confront the need to explain how his vision of party unity based on principle could be achieved in the face of the reality that party members would continue to seek easily distributed material benefits in the form of government jobs. Starting in New Jersey with his delegation of much of the appointing power to Joseph Tumulty and carrying that practice of delegation into the White House, Wilson created a "programmatic contradiction between the imperatives of party politics and sound administration" (Stid 1998, 99). Wilson's policy agenda as well as his individual policy designs could not satisfy both objectives well, and dedication to sound administration tended to succumb to patronage where the independent action of department heads and their chief subordinates did not act to prevent it.

Second, the ambiguities in Wilson's cabinet appointments reinforced the uneven effects of patronage on capacity and competence across the executive departments. For obvious structural reasons, Wilson could not follow his first, bolder conception of cabinet government by appointing Democratic Party leaders in Congress to cabinet posts without taking on the risk of losing Democratic seats. Yet he also failed to appoint a cabinet exclusively made up of "experienced men of affairs who would be dedicated to the president's agenda and serve as efficient administrators" (100). Instead, he selected a cabinet with varied backgrounds. There were party men with no particular interest in administrative reform and dedicated to both pursuing a narrow set of policy objectives and rewarding loyal Democrats long cut off from the spoils. There were reasonably competent administrators who nevertheless had their own policy aims in mind. And there were competent or supremely able administrators who were also fully committed to the president's program. Stid's point here is somewhat misleading, because Wilson could not have encompassed in his agenda or even in his list of domestic policy interests all of the programmatic activities in which some departments were already engaged. Thus even if Wilson had appointed a cabinet exclusively made up of loyal and competent administrative experts, his department heads could have pursued their own professional or ideological agendas, or those of their career subordinates, with little possibility of raising the president's ire or even, in most cases, his attention. The case of the Department of Agriculture is suggestive in this regard (see Clements 1992, ch. 4; Carpenter 2001, ch. 9).

Third, in his use of patronage, Wilson succumbed to the danger he had pointed out years earlier. Patronage "tended to keep the sights of legislators fixed on the mundane activities suited to gaining and keeping office and away from . . . more appropriate aims—using power for systematic and collective purposes" (Stid 1998, 101). With no apparent sense of the relevance to his own actions, Wilson argued in a newspaper interview, "It is my firm impression that patronage ruins more potentially great men than any other one political influence. By that I mean that many a man who comes into public life hampers his true development by his devotion to pa-tronage hunting. . . . [B]ut it is my firm opinion that if patronage could be eliminated we should have a bigger, broader, more patriotic and more useful body of legislators than we now have" (Link et al. 1979, 31:400).

Finally, in Stid's evaluation, Wilson's use of patronage, or at least his acquiescence to its use by members of his administration, aggravated the problem of modern administration's legitimacy in the American regime. Although Wilson never claimed that administration ought to be considered nonpolitical in every possible sense of the term, he did accept that partisan interference in the selection and evaluation of technical or professional personnel undermined the efficiency and competence of the civil service. He certainly did not intend to include the spoils among the very American values which would control the adoption of foreign administrative struc-tures and methods to make them useful to and accepted by the American public. Hence, the extent to which Wilson allowed patronage practices to flourish in his administration tended to weaken the legitimacy of his original ideas, his administra-tive leadership, and, ironically given his expressed aim, his leadership of the progres-sive cause (see Stid 1998, 98).

Stephen Skowronek's path-breaking analysis of the efforts to expand national administrative capacity during the emergence of the modern American state offers an even harsher judgment on Wilson's actions with respect to patronage and merit. Skowronek argued that Wilson's Republican predecessors, especially Theodore Roo-sevelt, used the advent of merit protection to shape "the merit civil service into an instrument of executive-centered government" (Skowronek 1982, 180). Through the work of Roosevelt's Civil Service Commission, an "executive-professional reform coalition" emerged across levels of government linking career professional admin-istrators and civil service reformers who supported executive, as opposed to legislative, control of administration as the surest path to increased administrative capacity and competence. Wilson's approach to patronage and merit, intended to support his aim of securing leadership of party and Congress and enactment of his New Freedom agenda through interpretive statesmanship, thus weakened the already existing drive for expanded capacity and competence in national administration. On that basis, Wilson acted contrary to his own reform objectives. In Skowronek's assessment, "Wilson gave up executive pretensions to independent administrative control," and he traded "the perquisites of office for party support of his legislative program. On this basis, the President became a legislative leader, and party and Congress advanced with a mixture of old administrative methods and new administrative machinery."

Skowronek acknowledged that Wilson "did resist party pressures for even more drastic reversals of civil service reform, and he never gave up rhetorical support for the professional ideal." But Wilson abandoned "the idea that administrative control required independent and imposing executive machinery." Skowronek also pointed out that most major New Freedom legislation "carried explicit provisos against the merit classification of administrative personnel" (195). The effect of Wilson's decisions to use patronage for his legislative leadership and policy aims was to shift control of administration back toward Congress with its fragmented, local party and sectoral oversight mechanisms. This directly contradicted his aims for overcoming the legislative-administrative divide and the splintering effects of back-channel congressional control of administration. Two corrosive outcomes followed.

First, Wilson's patronage practices and his ceding of significant administration control back to Congress delayed the expansion of national administrative capacity, competence, and expertise. Thus, when Wilson sought to regain executive control of administration in the face of the need for war mobilization and war management, he found his administrative agencies too weak and underdeveloped to carry the burden. He had to turn to private-sector managerial resources and expertise, which introduced a controversial element into wartime administration and raised serious questions about the legitimacy of his administrative solutions. Wilson thus also had to justify them as only temporary, emergency fixes (199–200).

Second, Wilson's patronage and merit practices produced "not a depoliticization but a repoliticization of American bureaucracy" (178). The repoliticization, Skowronek found, took two forms. More prominent was the "constitutional stalemate" (210) over control of administration between president and Congress. Again, this was exactly the opposite of what Wilson had sought through his conception of regime reconstruction and administrative reform centered on executive-legislative cooperation and coordination of policy and administration. Wilson's practices also politicized national administrative structure by introducing the characteristics of interest-group pressure politics "into the interior structure of the new bureaucratic establishment." The result was not a "strong bureaucratic state" with a "national center of power" but the advent of particularistic interests able to influence policy *and* administration "in a weak bureaucratic state" (247). The politicization of administration this approach fostered has proved far more difficult to undo than the spoils system and was in an important sense fully legitimated with the advent of a "legislative-centered public administration" (Rosenbloom 2000) after World War II.

Assessments of Wilson's presidency typically note that he turned away from patronage practices after the 1916 election, especially with the nation's entry into World War I (e.g., Stid 1998, 137; Milkis and Nelson 1999, 235–36). But this change in practice does not seem to diminish the general implications of Skowronek's perspective, which are quite damning because they portray Wilson's practices as initiating a political struggle over administration at all government levels—one that continues to this day—that has left both its capacity and legitimacy in a seriously weakened condition. Wilson's practices did not concentrate authority and responsibility for policy and administration but fostered "a proliferation of semi-independent and competing power centers at the national level" (Skowronek 1982, 247).

Leadership Trumps Merit

There is, however, another perspective from which to view Wilson's patronage practices and Skowronek's assessment, one that suggests more continuity between Wilson's ideas and his practices while not entirely ruling out the results of Wilson's practices revealed in Skowronek's analysis. This perspective stems from Wilson's peculiar relationship to civil service reform. Very early on Wilson considered himself a civil service reformer and accepted the importance of "purifying" administration by eliminating the immoral, corrupt spoils system and the partisan manipulation of public office. But as I showed in chapter 4, Wilson regarded civil service reform, especially a merit system using competitive examination for administrative appointments, as at best only a first necessary step in administrative reform. The end was not moral purity but efficiency and the greater democratic control of administration that efficient organization and methods would enable, as against private control through bossism and party machines.

Wilson pointed out the narrowness and rigidity of appointment by competitive examination. He also exhibited, in connection with his expressed views about civil service reform, his ingrained skepticism about the role of experts in public affairs even as he sought and welcomed the advice of experts. Hence it is not out of bounds to suggest that despite his public expressions of distress to the contrary, in practice the merit "ideal" was the component of his reform strategy that Wilson found the easiest to jettison, or at least very liberally to interpret. Yes, he did accept that merit protection laid the groundwork for increased administrative competence and efficiency. But he could justify the negative impacts on efficiency and technical competence in his own administration because the patronage appointments he sanctioned, or at least accepted, led to offices under the control not of private "bosses" but of a Democratic Party that he led and controlled. His ultimate standard of democratic control through national leaders interpreting public opinion was thus still maintained. To borrow a point Kendrick Clements has made (1998, 328) and to which I shall return, Wilson depended on presidential leadership and interpretive statesmanship to make an otherwise unacceptable practice—patronage—the servant of a more important aim. To the extent that political conditions eventually warranted it, Wilson moved away from his reliance on patronage, further aligning practices with his ideas.

STRUCTURES FOR COORDINATION AND EFFICIENCY

If one takes seriously Wilson's argument that increased efficiency in administrative organization and practice makes government more democratic, then one would have to expect that Wilson would pursue other enhancements to administrative efficiency with notable vigor and consistency. As my exploration of Wilson's ideas about administrative restructuring and innovations in methods indicates, Wilson proposed fairly sweeping changes in the systemic design and organizational operations of public administration in the United States. Even before his formal entry into direct political engagement, however, Wilson probably realized that his call for a wholesale breaching of the separation of powers from the top to the bottom of the system was unrealistic. He nevertheless pressed a series of reform ideas meant to concentrate political authority and responsibility, to simplify, to regularize, and to integrate administrative entities, and, albeit with much less detail or creativity, to introduce good "business" practices into the conduct of government. All this would augment transparency and efficiency and thus produce the true enhancements to democratic control that Wilson had trumpeted. Kendrick Clements has concluded, however, that Wilson failed to push with any reliability or sustained energy his reform ideas once in office or to provide astute political leadership for his more far-reaching proposals, whether in New Jersey or once he took residence in the White House.

Clements points in particular to the ambitious reform agenda Wilson proposed to the New Jersey legislature in 1912, which included a substantial list of administrative reorganization ideas and a commission to undertake further study (1998, 326–27). Wilson did not stop there, however. He went on to define the work of the commission broadly to include a possible reworking of the state tax system and, in Clements reading, sought shifts in the locus of policymaking that amounted to a sweeping shift of power from the legislature to the executive. Not surprisingly, the Wilson proposals met stiff resistance in the Republican-controlled legislature, and few of the recommendations were enacted.

Wilson issued a call the following year for administrative consolidation and improvements in economy and efficiency, without much in the way of specifics. The 1912 platform of the New Jersey Democratic Party, the principal authorship of which the editors of Wilson's papers attribute to Wilson, did include a few specifics, however. It called for "the extension of the powers of the department of labor and the state health department, . . . when their scope is enlarged they should be given an adequate number of inspectors adapted to their increased needs" (Link et al. 1978, 25:308–9). The platform also called for a number of specific fiscal management reforms, including "the installation of a uniform system of accounting for the municipalities and counties of this state" (310). Clements stresses, nevertheless, that Wilson simply did not follow through on his initial, far-reaching proposals in New Jersey, a loss of interest that carried over to the national level when Wilson became president. This may reflect the problem of Wilson's retreat to the less risky position of a "constitutional" governor (see Stid 1998, 79), which I consider further in the next chapter.

For evidence of Wilson's continuing lack of strong commitment to administrative reform once he became president, Clements points to Wilson's failure to seek continued funding of the Commission on Economy and Efficiency that President Taft had established, relying instead on his ability to lead Congress and the nation to reforms by means other than administrative. As Thomas Lynch and Maurice Rahimi have pointed out, Wilson had envisioned in *Congressional Government* the president having the "benefit of the guidance of a trained, practical financier" (1984, 99). This became reality with the passage of the Budget and Accounting Act of 1921, which created the Bureau of the Budget. But, Clements argues, budget reform was only the most minor of elements in Wilson's effort at reform leadership. Wilson offered only "tepid endorsement at the last possible minute" to the "administrative reform that commanded the widest political support" at the time (1998, 328). Lynch and Rahimi reached a much more positive conclusion, arguing that Wilson's support for an executive budget was crucial for moving the idea forward, and the initiative became law in the form Wilson supported shortly after he left office (1984,

100). Lynch and Rahimi also gave equal if not greater weight to the broader fiscal reform effects of Wilson's successful policy agenda, pointing to the restructuring of the system of public revenue and debt and the successful management of deficit financing for World War I, thanks to the newly established Federal Reserve System. Thus, in their view, Wilson's contributions to reforming the national government's financial planning capacity were significant.

Until his campaigns for and service in public office, Wilson offered few details about standards for administrative consolidation, the trimming of government organization charts, or the "scientific" and "business-like" practices that would have been so consistent with his core ideas about administrative structure and methods. One can infer from his acceptance of notions about hierarchy, administrative discipline, and professionalized methods, however, that in failing to press with consistency and energy for specific actions consistent with these general notions, Wilson in practice did not meet at least one implication of his ideas. Wilson's papers offer little evidence of his attention to and endorsement of an executive budget apparatus, an idea seemingly quite consistent with his concern for administrative and political coordination in his push for concentrated political authority and responsibility. The flurry of activity surrounding it evident in the papers comes at the time when Wilson was most debilitated by the October 1919 stroke.

The absence of a concerted push on Wilson's part in favor of an executive budget seems particularly curious in light of the core assumption on which the Commission on Economy and Efficiency had based its push for an executive budget, that is, that "the President had to assume responsibility for the coordination and control of the administrative departments, the independent agencies, and federal civil service personnel" (Skowronek 1982, 187; see his extended treatment, 188–89). Here, then, was a means for administrative integration and policy coordination that Wilson could obtain without the unlikely constitutional changes his cabinet government scheme required. As Clements (1998, 328) suggests, however, Wilson intended to rely on political leadership as the principal vehicle for policy coordination, with structural mechanisms providing at best ancillary support. Indeed, at the height of the struggles over wartime administrative structures and mechanisms, Wilson concluded there was a certain naïve "faith that some people put in machinery . . . , but the machinery does not do the task; particularly it is impossible to do it if new and inexperienced elements are introduced" (Link et al. 1984, 46:104).

Given the conflicting assessments of Wilson's efforts to advance innovations for government economy and efficiency and fiscal coordination, his actions, or lack thereof, may not be a serious blemish on his record of governance in his quest to realize his conception of modern administration. The promotion of economy and efficiency in particular has behind it an odd marriage of an older American political tradition—the recurring practice of "retrenchment" rooted in Jeffersonian and Jacksonian principles that aimed at keeping the national government, and the executive in particular, small and starved for resources—and an administrative orthodoxy that only really solidified after Wilson's service in office. Wilson had little affection for the retrenchment tradition, but he certainly accepted many of the root tenets of this emerging orthodoxy, because they reflected the kinds of methods Wilson expected a new "science" of administration to uncover or devise. Wilson's ideas about administrative structures and practices, however, had a broader, more systemic orientation, which reinforces the relevance of the Lynch and Rahimi analysis.

With respect to reforms for organizational coordination and efficiency, Wilson's ideas centered on eliminating elected administrative offices and concentrating political authority, responsibility, and hierarchical control in those few offices that remained elective. Along with designs for transparency, he intended the reforms to increase citizen interest and involvement and integrate administration across levels of government to enhance efficiency, responsibility, and democratic control but, most importantly, "organic wholeness." Hence it is not Wilson's lackluster efforts in support of special mechanisms for government frugality but his failure to push in a sustained and politically adept way his agenda for administrative reorganization and consolidation at an institutional level that raises serious doubts. Closer scrutiny of his practices concerning intergovernmental relations and his creation of new and diverse administrative entities is required for pursuing these doubts further.

INTERGOVERNMENTAL PROGRAM ASSISTANCE

In March 1911, Governor Wilson vetoed legislation that would have put local governments on the hook to finance park developments within their boundaries whenever the state Board of Park Commissioners called for such development. In his message accompanying the return of the legislation to the New Jersey Senate unsigned, Wilson detailed his objection to the nature of the financing method, which we would today call an unfunded mandate: "I return it without my signature because of my very clear conviction that it is a serious interference with the self-government of communities that mandatory action of this sort should proceed from the Legislature of the State. I feel that we are in danger of drifting away from some of the essential practices of local self government and that the tendency is to have all initiative in matters of expenditure and of exercise of authority proceed from Trenton" (Link et al. 1976, 22:527). On at least two other occasions Wilson vetoed legislation that he saw as violating local autonomy and the spirit of providing cities and towns assistance—but not dictation—in the systematic effort to improve fiscal management (see Link et al. 1976, 22:508; 1977, 23:146). He thus seemed to be conforming, in both rhetoric and action, to the ideas from his lectures on administration about the need to maintain local autonomy and prerogatives in a general system of vertical administrative integration. As with most of Wilson's governance, matters became much more complicated once he moved into the White House.

Policy or Administrative Centralization

Regarding federal fiscal relations with, and programmatic assistance to, state and local governments, Larry Walker found Wilson's practices worthy of high praise. Under Wilson, the flow of financial assistance downward in American federalism increased severalfold and began to take a more systematic shape. In seeming contrast to Wilson's original ideas and his apparently conforming practices as governor, however, Walker particularly emphasized the "*centralizing* character" and "close national-government supervision" of the developing system, which "restricted the ability of generalist state officials to control the federally-supported programs" (Walker 1989, 514, emphasis in original). In an earlier, more detailed treatment of the topic, Walker and coauthor Jeremy Plant found that "national funding of state programs was greatly increased during the Wilson presidency," but "with little disturbance of the broader federal relations of the day. Records of the era indicate that national prescription of policy in aided activities was minimal," with "few reports of state hostility to the new assistance policies." Hence, "the extension of the national government into new areas of domestic policy apparently occurred with little controversy and little immediate centralizing effect on the federal system" (1984, 124). In contrast to such lack of *policy* centralization, however, Walker and Plant found considerable *administrative* centralization and even federal interference through grant-in-aid programs. They determined that federal administrative controls "reduced the scope of policy discretion enjoyed by state officials" (125) and "denied participation to the elected representatives of . . . state publics" in program implementation and adjustment to local conditions (127).

Clements has offered a parallel analysis, although approaching the subject from a slightly different perspective. His focus is on the unintended consequences of Wilson's "attempts to shift power over some programs from Washington to the states," which would seem to have been consistent with Wilson's endorsement, in his lectures on administration, of considerable local autonomy within a system of much greater administrative integration and concentrated political authority. Clements argues that grant-in-aid programs "giving states greater authority over the expenditure of federal funds" ended up "enlarging the size and power of federal bureaucracies." The problem lay with "Congress's expectations of accountability," specifically its "desire for closer supervision of expenditures" (Clements 1998, 329). Like Walker and Plant, Clements recounts the historical progression of federal controls in grant programs, beginning with the Morrill Acts of 1862 and 1890. Of particular importance was the creation of the agriculture extension program in the Smith-Lever Act of 1914, which required federal-state cooperation in planning the use of federal funds. Perhaps even more significant was the Federal Aid Highway Act of 1916, which "for the first time required that state recipients of aid establish a special kind of state agency . . . to administer the program." The Smith-Hughes Act of 1917 did the same for the area of vocational education. The single-state-agency requirement remains a relatively permanent, oft-maligned fixture of federal-state fiscal relations in many policy areas (see, for example, Seidman and Gilmour 1986, ch. 9).

Clements attributes the progression "along the continuum toward greater federal control over state functions" to Wilson's strong tendency to delegate most responsibility for policy execution to his department heads and to his attention to other policy matters, primarily the expanding conflict overseas. Walker and Plant made a similar point, stressing the influence of Secretary of Agriculture David Houston (Walker and Plant 1984, 130–31n3). But both treatments peg Wilson with the responsibility for the deviation from his ideas in this area of administration and management. Clements in particular insists that Wilson should have expected "the development of the grants-in-aid programs" to be shaped by the "evolutionary responses of federal administrators to the demands of Congress for bureaucratic accountability" (1998, 329).

Creeping Bureaucracy and Limits on Leadership

Although both these analyses offer revealing perspectives on the meaning of the Wilson administration's practices with respect to intergovernmental relations, there is more to consider. First, reinforcing the point about the extent to which Wilson delegated executive authority, in the area of agricultural extension Wilson had virtually no involvement in its development other than signing it permanently into law. The legislation hit Wilson's desk only a year into his first term, and, more to the point, if Daniel Carpenter's recent account is to be taken as definitive (see esp. Carpenter 2001, 248–54), the Smith-Lever Act was merely the legislative ratification of a system the USDA already had in place for almost a decade (see, in comparison, Clements 1992, 57–59). The law adopted the department's county-agent model of extension as the centerpiece. Although Wilson "seems to have had quite a clear idea of where he wanted agricultural policy to go" (Clements 1992, 54), he had little time even to try to exert influence on the department's plan before it was enacted—and little *incentive* to try because David Houston was just the sort of administratively expert advisor on which Wilson wanted to rely.

Second, and more remarkably, Houston had a hand in all of the major laws affecting federal assistance to the states that went into force in the Wilson era (Link 1956, 138), insisting in particular on stricter federal standards that states had to meet in their use of federal funds. Thus, although Houston may have reoriented the USDA and its programs along the lines envisioned by Wilson following the advice of his close friend and campaign contributor Walter Hines Page (Clements 1992, 55–56), the much broader endeavor to tighten federal requirements and administrative structures in grants-in-aid to the states is not a policy or administrative innovation directly attributable to Woodrow Wilson's expressed ideas or direction. But Wilson did approve of these innovations—or at least acquiesced in them. How well, then, did they comport with his ideas about administrative structure?

Recall that Wilson favored what he termed the *concentration* of authority, not *centralization*, in a system integrated from the national government all the way down to the municipal level. By this he meant not direct dependence of local officials on central authorities, and thus complete control of the latter over the former, but rather a more unified organizational structure and "prudential" supervision to ensure that local administration was sufficiently consistent with the peculiar life of the democratic state and its interests in national unity and national power. But democratic life involved the forces of distinction and differentiation as well as the developmental drive toward unity. Although these forces needed to be restrained, to take advantage of their benefits local and even state officials would need some autonomy within a well-integrated system that would include several points of concentrated political authority along its vertical span. The system that emerged under Wilson, if the Walker and Plant characterization is accurate, of at best very loose policy uniformity or coordination but strict or even rigid administrative uniformity, would seem to be close to the opposite of what Wilson envisioned in his lectures.

There is enough ambiguity in Wilson's vision, however, to make the consistency or inconsistency of the actual system of intergovernmental fiscal relations Walker and Plant portray difficult to pin down. Trying to do so also distracts attention from the feature of the system that should be of greater import in terms of Wilson's success in translating his ideas into practice. The analyses I have cited seem to agree that the most notable innovation in Wilson's federalism polices and practices was the advent of the "single-state-agency" mandate. This is just the sort of administrative innovation I suspect Wilson would have favored as consistent with a more integrated, unified administrative structure requiring only limited supervision to secure that "nice adjustment of local administration to national aims and conveniences" he imagined in his lectures. Indeed, over the ensuing years the single-state-agency requirements in various statutes "have served to rationalize state administration within prescribed functional areas and have helped to improve the quality of state personnel by introducing professional standards and merit-system principles." Yet this functional administrative integration came "at the cost of professional inbreeding, organizational and administrative rigidity, further impairment of central executive authority, and loss of political responsibility" (Seidman and Gilmour 1986, 202). Such guild-like ramifications came to be termed "picket-fence" federalism (197). It is a phenomenon against which several of Wilson's presidential successors battled, and it would seem to be just the sort of uncontrolled bureaucratization that Wilson took pains to argue would *not* emerge from the introduction of foreign methods and practices under the watchful eye of political leaders steeped in American political values and principles.

One might dismiss this result as a clear case of Wilson's early ideas being far too removed from future political reality to be of much use in guiding practice. Yet in light of the thrust of Kendrick Clements' observation about the likely behavior of administrators, it is surprising that Wilson did not see the possibility of "vertical functional autocracies" (Seidman and Gilmour 1986, 197) emerging from the single-state-agency mandate, especially given his reservations about experts. In addition to his skepticism about the worldview of academics, Wilson often stressed the narrow vision of technical experts. They thus required watching, and citizens and their representatives could not and should not rely on experts as a substitute for self-government. Wilson also argued quite pointedly against Theodore Roosevelt's idea for a commission to regulate monopoly precisely because he feared that "experts in destructive competition" would form an unholy alliance across the public-private divide, leading to a kind of administrative tyranny he sought to assure voters would not emerge with proper constraints and political leadership.

Although Wilson claimed "large powers and unhampered discretion" would serve to induce responsible behavior and thus operate as an important source of internal constraint on administrative irresponsibility and excess, he also emphasized the need for external constraints primarily in the form of effective policy design, concentrated political authority, and interpretive leadership. I suspect that in Wilson's ideal of an integrated administrative system, local officials would have sufficient autonomy and control over their experts, and those experts would have such a strong orientation to their locales that the formation of professional autocracies across the levels of government within functional areas would be unlikely. But Wilson's ideal did not exist, nor did he pursue it as a politically feasible objective. He faced the need to work within a system that he well knew was politically fragmented horizontally and vertically, and thus administratively weak.

The burden of fighting creeping bureaucracy rests, therefore, almost exclusively with national political leadership. As I will argue more fully in the next chapter, if Wilson had put into practice some closer approximation of a cabinet of true national party leaders with experience in both legislation and administration and with recognized authority and political responsibility in their policy domains, national political leadership may have had the time, energy, and incentive to keep irresponsible bureaucratic alliances at bay. By choosing instead to separate responsibility for policy execution from interpretive leadership and place the latter solely in the hands of a president not structurally different from the Framers' problematic design that combined the head of state with the head of government, Wilson left national political leadership without the resources to be vigilant about developments that could undermine political control, conceal responsibility, and threaten administrative legitimacy.

WILSON'S ADMINISTRATIVE EXPANSION:
GENERAL CONSIDERATIONS

"Although the Constitution is almost wholly silent on the subject of executive branch organization, there seems to be little doubt that the framers intended that all executive functions be grouped under a limited number of single-headed executive departments" (Seidman and Gilmour 1986, 250). The complex of Wilson's ideas about administrative structure contains only hints as to what Wilson thought about the number and types of organizations a national administrative system ought to employ. From his emphasis on concentration of political authority and responsibility, on coordination, on broad functional specialization, it seems safe to infer that Wilson was receptive to ideas such as a limited span of control for the president and a compact, departmental structure. Particularly given his emphasis on administrative integration and political coordination, it seems unlikely that Wilson would have supported the proliferation of organizations further removed from direct presidential control and outside the coordinating sphere of the cabinet. Sticking with the departmental structure also would have relieved Wilson of the necessity to develop further attempts to upend constitutional form and tradition.

How, then, to account for the most dramatic departures from key forms and traditions in American political history to that time that took place on Wilson's watch? His political obstetrics in the birth of the Federal Reserve System and his change of mind and subsequent push for the establishment of a trade commission with broad but largely unspecified regulatory powers are only the most prominent instances of Wilson's actions leading to an expansion in the number, type, and distinctive characteristics of national administrative entities. Wilson was not the first president to oversee the creation of agencies outside the direct presidential scope and purview of the departmental system (which includes, it is important to emphasize, unconditional presidential removal power). With the minor exception of Grant's Civil Service Commission, however, Wilson was the first president to seek and preside over the creation of administrative organizations that expanded presidential span of control in such far-reaching and distinctive ways.

The Federal Trade Commission had as a precedent the Interstate Commerce Commission, but the ICC was originally placed as a bureau within the Department of the Interior and only became independent two years after its creation. Scholars disagree about the impetus, although the possibilities—either by congressional initiative as a strategy to distance the commission from presidential control (Rohr 1986, 95) or at the behest of the secretary of the interior (Seidman and Gilmour 1986, 251)—are not mutually exclusive. It is remarkable, in any case, given the ICC's history and Wilson's ideas about administrative integration and the corrosive effects of irresponsible congressional meddling in administration, that he ceded so much control over the FTC to Congress and the courts (see the more extensive assessment of the FTC's creation in the next chapter). He accepted, it would seem, the fragmenting of responsibility against which he had so long campaigned. The Federal Reserve was a different animal entirely, with an unprecedented mix of private business and public authority that also appeared to divide and obscure rather than concentrate political power and responsibility.

A number of explanations for Wilson's departure from what would clearly seem to be his preference for a simple, hierarchical, integrated organizational architecture for the executive branch come to mind. First, although "the concept of an integrated executive branch structure is accepted in principle, it has encountered strong opposition from those seeking independence and autonomy for programs benefiting their interests" (Seidman and Gilmour 1986, 251–52). Thus, much of the structure of the Federal Reserve System reflected the banking industry's scheme for rescuing the nation's monetary system (see Link 1956, 200–202, 206). Major industrial and commercial firms welcomed an interstate trade commission to eliminate patchwork regulation, to rationalize the economy further, and to bring greater certainty to business-government relations (Link 1956, 435; Noble 1985, 371). Wilson originally opposed a trade commission in part because he thought it would legitimate behaviors that threatened competition and entrepreneurship, furthering the trend toward consolidation and monopoly. But Wilson the pragmatist realized that there was a limit to how far he could go in fighting major economic interests, and giving them no quarter was not entirely consistent with the conception of progressivism on which Wilson had settled (Link 1956, 436, 449; Cuff 1978, 241; Skowronek 1982, 271).

A second explanation for Wilson's departure from structural integration, organizational regularity, and close coordination also involves his pragmatism and embrace of a principled expediency in his conception of statesmanship. The social, economic, and political turmoil of the era prompted what Arthur Macmahon nicely termed "innovative zest" in government organization. Further, "there is little evidence of conscious thought and planning in the development of new institutions. The approach generally has been highly pragmatic and eclectic. The process has been more derivative than creative" (Seidman and Gilmour 1986, 258). Wilson must have found the challenge of confronting and the success of resolving real and immediate national problems invigorating. His conception of political leadership and its anchor in a particular idea of a political science pointed toward a reliance on experience and an immersion in the commotion of political thought and interaction, drawing out of it the common denominator around which a majority could form. This is consistent with his rejection of any strict adherence to theoretical perfection and his embrace of a notion of conservatism as careful, progressive adaptation to changing conditions. The synthesis of existing ideas behind the FTC's creation was also consistent with the circumstances—commissions were already a legitimate administrative form associated with progressive policy—and with Wilson's intellectual predispositions (Link 1956, 5–6; Clements 1992, 12–13). Although it is not clear to what extent Wilson himself considered the existing evidence from antitrust administrative experience in leading the development of these policy innovations, certainly the government's frustrating enforcement experience under the Sherman Act was a critical stimulus to the general search for organizational alternatives.

A third and complementary explanation draws again on the point Kendrick Clements advanced about Wilson's preference for presidential leadership over new mechanisms as the way to achieve administrative reform. In short, Wilson may have had such confidence in his rhetorical abilities and his capacity and commitment to unite the nation through interpretive statesmanship that he may not have thought much about the difficulties for coordination under the concentrated, coherent political authority inherent in creating "innovative" administrative entities. The Federal Reserve and the FTC might in fact be considered exceptions to Wilson's otherwise consistent adherence to administration within the established departmental structure. Thus he may not have regarded their addition as adding much to the challenge of binding legislation and execution through his rhetorical leadership while at the same time maintaining the structural integrity and integration of the executive. Wilson expanded national administration significantly, however, especially with respect to government intervention in the economy. He did so implicitly, through the authority he ceded to some of his chief administrators, and explicitly, in response to specific elements of his policy agenda, most dramatically in answer to the need to mobilize vast resources for what eventually became the nation's entry into World War I. Therefore it is worth taking a more extended look at Wilson's expansion of national administration and his thinking behind it for further insights into his governing practices and their implications for modern public management.

WARTIME ADMINISTRATIVE EXPANSION

Extensive reliance on business resources and the private managerial expertise and the coordination efforts of the volunteer "dollar-a-year" men—these were the signature features of government administration during the "Great War." Two factors were central to the shape of this business-government cooperative approach to managing war mobilization and the war itself. First, the national government's administrative capacity was simply too underdeveloped, lacking in sufficient expertise and political and administrative experience to carry most of the burden (see Cuff 1973, 41, 269; 1977, 359). As I have already noted, Skowronek (1982, 195–200, 234–38) placed the lion's share of the responsibility for the enfeebled condition of national administration squarely on Wilson's patronage practices, his drive for party leadership, and the consequent partial shift of control over administration back to Congress. Second, Wilson's embrace of close business-government cooperation for managing the war effort reflected his progressive ideology as well as his concern for the character and legitimacy of administration in the regime—especially his commitment to preventing un-American notions about the state and bureaucratic organization from creeping in with the adoption of "foreign" methods and practices. In particular, Wilson's New Freedom centered on "an appeal to American entrepreneurs to live up to their own standards of liberal capitalism" and to resist the temptation to trade away "creative entrepreneurship" for "security and order, or state-oriented economic forms" (Cuff 1978, 241). Going into the struggle to mobilize America for war, then, Wilson "had already helped to fashion an ideology of liberalism which subsumed both the idea of friendly cooperation between business and government and an ambiguity toward the role of the state" (Cuff 1973, 5; see also Skowronek 1982, 241; Noble 1985, 333).

The result of these two influences was a rather haphazard, chaotic administrative mélange. A host of boards and committees proliferated in an attempt to coordinate various economic sectors in support of the government's effort to build up and then maintain a war-fighting enterprise. Volunteer businessmen filled most of the positions on these boards and commissions, the most prominent being the Council of National Defense, the central entity for coordinating industrial mobilization. Other entities with influence included the War Labor Policies Board, the Committee on Public Information, and the Price-Fixing Committee. Numerous subcomponents of the major boards and committees also came into being. All these entities operated as appendages to the regular executive departments, especially War, Navy, and Treasury. At least that was the idea. The intent behind their creation was to aid in marshalling the nation's industrial and commercial resources for the war effort and to help smooth over various disruptive fluctuations and disparities in prices, production, and distribution.

Cautious Expansion

Wilson and Congress also authorized the creation of a number of independent agencies whose administrators reported directly to the president. These included, most prominently, the Food Administration, headed by Herbert Hoover; the Fuel Administration, headed by Harry Garfield; and the National Railroad Administration, headed by Treasury Secretary William McAdoo; this last agency was created to allow the government to take control of the national railway system when it verged on collapse at the end of 1917. The belated creation of perhaps the most visible of these independent agencies, the War Industries Board, demonstrates especially well the convoluted nature of Wilson's wartime administrative approach and the ideological and pragmatic political maneuvering that shaped it.

The War Industries Board was originally an appendage of the Council of National Defense intended to coordinate industrial production of war supplies, especially munitions. Under constant pressure from Congress and business leaders to improve the coordination and efficiency of government purchasing, Wilson incrementally moved the War Industries Board to a more prominent and autonomous position in the war's administrative structure. In March 1918, Wilson issued an executive order, under the general reorganization authority of the Overman Act, that established the War Industries Board as an independent agency responsible for coordinating purchasing agreements for war resources. The chairman, Bernard Baruch, reported directly to Wilson. Yet Wilson remained concerned about creating an excessively centralized and bureaucratized organization that would resemble too closely "munitions ministries," like those created in England and France for the war. He had consistently opposed the formation of such entities as not workable in the

American system. Wilson kept the authority and reach of the War Industries Board limited, including no grant of price-fixing authority, preserving that to a committee under the chairmanship of Robert Brookings. Furthermore, four of the most prominent administrators in Wilson's wartime structure—Baruch, Brookings, Garfield, and Hoover—were businessmen committed to the idea of volunteerism and close business-government cooperation as a way to avoid centralized, intrusive, coercive state regulation.

Wilson's incrementalism in the planning and development of the structure for the war administration revealed his considerable caution on administrative expansion and centralization, especially when outside the regular, existing administrative structures (Cuff 1973, 67, 104, 244, 269). It was rooted in a preference for "voluntary cooperation over political coercion, and informal agreements among like-minded men over formal, bureaucratic order," personified by the likes of Baruch and Hoover (269; see also Cuff 1977). Wilson's cautious approach was also evident in the rhetorical care he took to stress that the business volunteers served in a clear subordinate capacity to political authority, either through direct responsibility to him or through his principle executive subordinates in the regular departmental structure. Thus Wilson "never relinquished his commitment to regular forms of federal administration, firmly embedded in legal authority" (Cuff 1973, 244). In consolidating purchasing under Baruch in the War Industries Board, for example, Wilson nevertheless stressed that the chairman was to "let alone what is being successfully done and interfere as little as possible with the present normal processes of purchase and delivery in the several Departments" (Link et al. 1984, 46:521). More generally, Wilson emphasized in his State of the Union address after the armistice at the end of 1918 that the special war agencies were experts in "the field of supply, of labour, and of industry" when they "became thoroughly systematized; and they have not been isolated agencies; they have been directed by men which represented the permanent Departments of the Government and so have been the centres of unified and cooperative action" (Link et al. 1986, 53:279).

The temporary, emergency nature (Cuff 1973, 244; 1977, 361) of the ad hoc administrative design was at the heart of Wilson's justification for his approach allowing private sector interests into close and authoritative interaction with the operational organs of the national government. This is best illustrated in his position favoring rapid demobilization after the war. Given Wilson's "commitment to the basic structure and prerogatives of corporate capitalism and an aversion to the growth of an extensive and powerful state bureaucracy" (Cuff 1973, 269), Wilson opposed "those who favoured extensions of bureaucratic forms of capitalism" created for the war effort (Cuff 1978, 243). He made his argument clear in the post-armistice State of the Union address: "Our people . . . do not wait to be coached and led. They know their own business, are quick and resourceful at every readjustment, definite in purpose, and self-reliant in action. Any leading strings we might seek to put them in would speedily become hopelessly tangled because they would pay no attention to them and go their own way." He proposed executive-legislative cooperation "to mediate the process of change here, there, and elsewhere as we may," but he stressed again that no "general scheme of 'reconstruction'" had emerged which he thought "it likely we could force our spirited business men and self-reliant labourers to accept with due pliancy and obedience" (Link et al. 1986, 53:278).

Wilson did not intend a complete free-for-all in peacetime reconversion, however. In addition to government guidance "here, there, and elsewhere," he laid out specific options for the railroads, including having them "go back to the old conditions of private management, unrestricted competition, and multiform regulation by both state and federal authorities" as well as "the opposite extreme" of establishing "complete government control," accompanied, if necessary, by actual government ownership. Wilson strongly implied, however, a preference for the intermediate possibility "of modified private control, under a more unified and affirmative public regulation and under such alterations of the law as will permit wasteful competition to be avoided and a considerable degree of unification of administration to be effected, as, for example, by regional corporations under which the railways of definable areas would be in effect combined in single systems" (284). Wilson's language here is particularly interesting, emphasizing as it does a commitment to regulation that targets only "wasteful" competition and promoting, as he did in his lectures on administration nearly two decades earlier, unified administration that included functional differentiation across and specialization within government levels.

Caution's Problematic Consequences

Wilson may have insisted on the rapid dismantlement of the war effort's administrative machinery for the further reason that in heading off to Paris for the peace negotiations, he would not be around to exercise close presidential supervision over the specially created entities required during the war. Thus for management in the postwar period he was only comfortable placing the prewar administrative structure at the disposal of his regular administrators (Cuff 1978, 243). But Wilson's cautious incrementalism in building an administrative structure for the war proved problematic in a variety of ways. Two are of particular import for the present analysis.

First, in following his incremental, cautious path, Wilson found himself caught in the middle among contending forces, some seeking even less government intervention (Cuff 1977, 364) but most pushing greater centralization and government control, albeit for different reasons. Supporters and even some critics in Congress insisted on more centralized presidential control to ward off uncontrolled bureaucratization. In recalling his earlier unsuccessful attempts to allocate greater reorganization authority to the president, Senator Lee Overman told Wilson, "If something is not done along this line, sooner or later we will have a bureaucracy in this country which is really as bad as an autocracy, in my judgment" (Link et al. 1984, 47:446).

The business establishment also demanded a more centralized, autonomous manager to oversee the government's use of the nation's industrial resources. In a lengthy critique of the Wilson administration's mobilization efforts in late 1917, the U.S. Chamber of Commerce called for the "subordination of all business to the war needs of the Government" through the creation by statute of "a Department of War Supplies for the period of the war. To make effective use in this war of the industrial resources of the country is a great undertaking, which can be accomplished to best advantage by a member of the President's official family" (Link et al. 1984, 45:62, 65). Furthermore, the effort of the "executive-professional coalition" to build up administrative professionalism and competence, especially in the War Department, would be aided by centralization but was threatened by Wilson's introduction of the business volunteer element (Skowronek 1982, 238–39). The upshot of Wilson's careful path seemed to be, again especially with respect to the War Department, "blurred responsibility and lowered . . . standards of business practice at the middle levels of the bureaucracy. Without government providing authority and direction, business became even more susceptible to charges of profiteering and corruption. A strong administrative arm within the government was the key to the success of a cooperative partnership" (237). Thus, although he had long championed the modernization and improvement of administrative organization and methods, Wilson's attention to legitimacy in that endeavor and his related caution about preventing even the perception of the growth of a centralized, bureaucratized national administration seems to have threatened his aims for modernized American administration.

Second, bureaucracy appears, ironically, to have crept in anyway, despite his caution and the worries of other political actors. Wilson's careful approach, his strong resistance to the development of centralized state bureaucracy in the Prussian mode, and the ideology of voluntarism that led to the use of "voluntary expert staff and the private administration of public policy" (Cuff 1973, 269) tended to obscure "how bureaucratic traits invaded the mobilization process despite protestations among administrators to the contrary" (Cuff 1977, 365). Just as disconcerting, the hybrid organization and management design of the likes of Herbert Hoover's Food

Administration "embodied two contradictory trends in the upper reaches of war administration," that is, greater autonomy but also greater integration under higher coordinating authority. Wilson's governing practices, especially during the war, thus left unresolved the "persistent conundrum of how to manage the managers," a problem that Wilson presumably thought he had resolved conceptually years earlier.

THE QUANDARIES OF PUTTING IDEAS INTO PRACTICE

Wilson's management of the war illustrates the kind of puzzle he faced in any effort to maintain some semblance of coherence as he attempted to adhere to his ideas while facing the need to find immediate, practical solutions to unexpected, complex, shifting problems of governance. His structural and rhetorical improvisations aimed at finding the path toward administrative *improvement* while not going so far to threaten administrative *legitimacy* are particularly revealing in this regard. Hoover's Food Administration is exactly the kind of careful but innovative organizational design Wilson preferred to employ to address this dilemma. It operated with an "administrative informality and unitary authority" (Cuff 1977, 362) that ensured focused, transparent responsibility while, in Hoover's estimation at least, preventing the emergence of dictatorial bureaucratic tendencies (361).

What Cuff called contradictory Wilson would have regarded as complementary. Greater autonomy and discretion were possible *because of* greater concentration of authority and responsibility, which led to greater coordination and integration. In the case of the entire administrative system across levels of government, autonomy and discretion within a more integrated system would allow greater sensitivity to local conditions within the unified priorities set by national political authority, ensuring that administration could conform to the local conditions while also supporting national unity and power. In the midst of the furor over fuel administrator Harry Garfield's decision to restrict manufacturer use of fuel during the harsh winter of 1917–18, for instance, Wilson noted that "the local fuel administrators,—I mean the state administrators,—are left a very considerable degree of discretion as to particular instances in which it might seem imperative to grant some sort of relief. Personally, I believe that it would be very dangerous for them to exercise this discretion except in the rarest cases, because cases are very hard to discriminate one from another, but in the very nature of things this is the utmost leeway which is practicable in such circumstances" (Link et al. 1984, 46:36).

If even the real administrative entities close to Wilson's ideal experienced creeping bureaucratization and executives of such agencies tried to establish personal bases of power (Cuff 1977, 363), then the integrity of Wilson's ideas for improving administration while preventing the emergence of elements Americans regarded as illegitimate are placed in considerable doubt. On the other hand, if ideas about governance cannot be made to work in practice, especially by their progenitor, then perhaps the practices are the source of the problem. Wilson's more general governing practices during the war thus raise additional troubling questions about the relationship between his ideas and his practices.

Wilson justified the most expansive elements of his wartime administration as a temporary response to a national emergency. He took the actions he thought were necessary to defend the nation's security by using the constitutional powers and prerogatives of the presidency, especially its Article 2, Section 2 powers as commander in chief and primary agent of the nation's interests in international affairs. He tried to bind this constitutionally traditional understanding of the presidency to his decidedly untraditional notion of interpretive leadership by suggesting in his public statements that he had decided to move the nation from the status of armed neutrality to active engagement on the side of the allied powers based on German aggressions and his reading of public opinion.

It is not that Wilson's attempt to overcome the debilitating effects of the separation of powers had led him to repudiate the presidency's constitutional powers and prerogatives. Early in his reform endeavor he simply downplayed these features of the presidency, concerned as he was for the domestic issues arising from the internal turmoil of a maturing, modernizing democracy experiencing relative peace. He gave those powers and prerogatives greater emphasis in the adjustments to his thinking he made as he saw the issues facing the nation become more international in nature. In his prosecution of the war, however, Wilson set aside fundamental elements of his conception of a reformed American governance system. As I discuss in more detail in the next chapter, he sought little in the way of common counsel and cooperative deliberation with Congress, blocking all efforts to form a joint executive-legislative war cabinet. Inside his administration he shut out the cabinet from much of his war planning and decision-making, creating instead a separate war cabinet that included some regular department heads but also the heads of the key independent war management agencies.

I do not mean to suggest that Wilson should have acceded to congressional demands for more direct legislative involvement and oversight of war administration. Nor do I mean to suggest that Wilson's calls for national unity and national purpose were insincere. Quite the opposite: I believe that Wilson regarded his conduct of the war as the effective combination of interpretive statesmanship and executive power. Action was a core element of Wilson's conception of leadership; in the face of war, such action needed resources like those of the constitutional executive. Wilson also largely succeeded in convincing the American people of the legitimacy of his actions. They accepted that executive command authority should supersede cooperative deliberation in the face of a serious threat to the nation's security, global interests, and commitment to international peace.

Yet the legitimacy of Wilson's actions with respect to the structure and character of his war administration rested solely on a traditional constitutional understanding of the presidency as an independent executive with substantial autonomous powers for representing and defending the nation. That is, Wilson never sought to explain why common counsel was not possible or desirable under war conditions, or why the only linkages of legislation and execution he sought were blanket delegations of authority for the organization and control of the wartime administrative machinery. If he had to abandon central tenets of his reform conception—the need to reconstruct American governance to ensure the close linkage of policy formation and execution that would better harness administrative power for American democracy in the modern age—in the face of war, then just how legitimate or defensible or useful could his reform endeavor be? The question is made even more compelling with the recognition that war is, if anything, close to a pure administrative undertaking. By falling back on the constitutional presidency to legitimate his conduct of the war, Wilson undermined his claims to presidential leadership as the binding force that would tie policy formation and execution together, harness administrative power most effectively, and secure the legitimacy of that power by making sure it operated in consistency with American political values. That he was not able even in his cautious approach to constructing the war's administrative structure to prevent "un-American" elements from cropping up only further undermines his claims about presidential leadership.

My argument here is part of the larger "two presidencies" dilemma (e.g., Stid 1998, 62, 134–35) Wilson faced in putting his reform program into effect. I explore this dilemma further in the next chapter in examining Wilson's efforts as an interpretive leader. I take up first, however, the business regulation side of Wilson's administrative expansion, as well as his use of the cabinet, to portray more completely his governing practices in juxtaposition to his ideas.

CHAPTER SIX

Legal Structure, Cabinet Government, and Interpretive Leadership

Upon taking the oath of office to become governor of New Jersey in 1911, and president of the United States two years later, Woodrow Wilson set about following the guidance for governing he had laid out in books, articles, lectures, and public addresses over the previous quarter century. The evidence pointing to an affinity between Wilson's ideas and his actions is considerable. And indeed, even some of Wilson's notable departures in practice from his established ideas can be seen as reflecting the continued suppleness of his mind and his willingness to evolve his thinking further. The departures also reflect his conception of statesmanship, which carried in it a recognition of expediency as necessary to good leadership in the face of unexpected events and changing conditions (Clements 1992, 45). Nevertheless, a careful examination of his decisions and actions in pursuing some of the key components of his policy agenda and in confronting some of the most demanding political and governmental challenges of his era raises troubling questions about his practices in relation to his ideas and the whole framework of his reform concepts and aims.

I continue my assessment of Wilson's governing practices in this chapter, covering additional areas that have typically received attention in the history and political science literature on Wilson, supplementing existing analyses with my own observations. I begin by looking at Wilson's expansion of national administration with respect to business regulation. I then turn to his attempts to govern with the aid of his cabinet and close with a consideration of his performance as interpretive statesman. Again, my intention is to keep the focus as much as possible on the administrative and managerial facets of Wilson's governance in light of the interpretation of his ideas about democracy and administration I have offered, so that we can develop insights that bear on the challenges the theory and practice of public administration and management confront in the twenty-first century.

DEFINITE LAW

The broad, general grant of authority to root out unfair methods of competition the Federal Trade Commission received in its organic statute in 1914 has a checkered status in some of the primary scholarship on Wilson's practices. It stands alongside Wilson's acceptance of patronage appointments to keep his congressional majority under control as a key strategic reversal of a relatively firm—some would argue naïve—policy or political stance. With respect to the regulation of interstate commerce, evidence and arguments regarding political and administrative feasibility precipitated Wilson's reversal, allowing him to gain major victories for his New Freedom agenda (see, for example, Clements 1992, 47–50; Stid 1998, 109). Traditionalist assessments celebrate Congress's broad delegation of authority to the FTC for the expansion of the federal government into previously unregulated areas it permitted, for the increased versatility of administrative organization it added with the creation of an "independent" agency, and for its modernization of regulation through expert administration rather than regulation through the courts and the common law, which seemed increasingly "anachronistic" (see, for example, Turner 1956, 252–53; Walker 1989, 513–14; the characterization is from Lowi 1979, 96).

Other assessments of the creation of the FTC and its broad regulatory authority are less complimentary. Skowronek praises the act as "Wilson's greatest administrative achievement in his first term" because it "secured administrative discretion in determining the difference between a monopoly and a big business" and thus "deserved public commendation." He notes, however, quoting Herbert Croly, that Wilson had to "sacrifice . . . administrative standards" to revive the Democratic Party through his leadership (1982, 333–34n10). Moreover, the FTC triumph is not enough to overcome Skowronek's assessment that Wilson did not adequately advance the cause of expanding national administrative capacity, with the FTC described as one of the "great institution-building accomplishments of Wilson's first term [that] bore the stamp of the spoilsmen" (195–96).

In Charles Noble's neo-Marxist critique, "Wilson began his first administration by attempting to build the autonomous interventionist state he had envisioned" in the reform ideas of his academic years. Recoiling at the intensity of opposition from bankers, monopolists, and archconservatives aimed at his prime New Freedom proposals, however, Wilson chose to work with "moderate social reformers and corporate liberal capitalists," in the end "undermining the movements that were pressing for the autonomous state he had theorized" (1985, 327). With respect to business regulation in particular, "corporate liberals demanded a strong trade commission to preclude antitrust prosecutions and create a community of interest between the state and industry, not more of Taft's legalisms" (329). Hence Wilson retreated from his own "legalistic" approach embodied by the Clayton Act. He chose to support a trade commission that enjoyed a broad, general grant of authority. Opposition from "conservative capital," however, resulted in statutory constraints that "produced a weak commission with little power." The ambiguity of the FTC Act's directive to prohibit unfair methods of competition left the commission open to conflict "between proponents of business concentration and antitrusters." This consigned the FTC to "negotiate voluntary agreements among firms and to prosecute smaller firms for violating the law rather than regulate industrial concentration." Only later, after "major reforms," did the FTC become "a more effective proponent of a state or public interest in industrial structure" (331).

Although interpreters of Wilson's legacy in business regulation from the traditionalist and administrative orthodox perspectives praise the creation of the FTC with its broad, general grant of authority, the reality of the commission's early operations is much more consistent with the critical analyses of the likes of Skowronek and Noble (see, for example, Eisner 1991, 59–75). The puzzle of these contrasting assessments suggests that it is worth looking more closely at the evolution of Wilson's approach to business regulation, as it will reveal more about the relationship between Wilson's ideas about administration and his actions.

Definite Law through Policy Principle

When Wilson entered the political arena, his ideas about the regulation of business and the control of "destructive" competition focused on three main components: how the administrative mechanism would work, who would be held to account for violations of the law, and what the specific statutory violations would be (the second and third areas constituting "definite law"). Wilson had defended the notion that business regulation through definite law could be, and should be, administered by the courts. He had begun, however, to accept the idea of regulation by administrative commission as he began to engage more fully and formally in electoral politics. His embrace of the progressive agenda in New Jersey thus did not require a major transformation in his thinking. Acknowledging the successful creation of public utility commissions in other states by progressive forces, Wilson willingly endorsed via the 1910 New Jersey Democratic platform the creation of a commission "with ample powers *under explicit rules*" to regulate public utilities (Link et al. 1976, 21:95, emphasis added).

During the ensuing gubernatorial election campaign, Wilson stressed several functions that this administrative mechanism would fulfill. It would hear complaints about rates and seek to set rates that would be fair to customers and to the utilities. More important, it would engage in information revelation—transparency and publicity. Through "fair and judicious inquiry" (196), it would "display to the public . . . full information concerning the affairs and finances of the public utility corporations." On that basis it would, in part, provide guidance and advice to the businesses under its purview. Equally important, it would "rectify abuses," "correct inequalities of service," and "check all those preferences which may be shown to be inequitable to individuals or to localities." It was in light of the information obtained and in the exercise of its regulatory function that it would "establish equitable rates" (496). Investigation and information revelation, guidance and advice to business, including the setting of rates, and identification and correction of violations were the functions Wilson accepted for regulatory commissions. The law under which the commission worked would have to state expressly whether the commission could pursue individuals as responsible for the violations, and it would have to specify just what constituted acceptable or unacceptable practices.

Wilson got what he wanted in the form of a beefed-up public utility commission in 1911, but he did not really confront the implications of his demand for legal specificity in business regulation until the following year. In April 1912, with the state legislature in Republican hands, Wilson vetoed a bill for the elimination of railroad grade crossings. Authority to carry out the law went to the Board of Public Utility Commissioners. Wilson had no objection to the intent of the law. It was a widely accepted public safety objective. He vetoed the bill because of "that portion of the bill which arbitrarily provides that every railroad of the State shall every year eliminate at least one grade crossing on its line for every thirty miles of its whole extent, the commission to determine which crossings shall be dealt with first." Wilson contended that the provision "seeks to accomplish an impossible thing. It is not possible thus to lay down a hard and fast rule, and enforce it without a likelihood of bringing on conditions under which the whole undertaking would break down and result in utter disappointment." Wilson elaborated further by arguing that the "circumstances which surround this problem are not the same for any two railways of the State, but what might be a reasonable enough requirement for one of the railway systems of the State might be a very unreasonable requirement for another, leading to an impossible situation and breakdown of the law, and that is certainly not the purpose of the people of this State. The bill does not forbid the creation of new grade crossings, neither does it attempt any classification of those already in existence" (Link et al. 1977, 24:321–22).

With his veto, Wilson seemed to have repudiated the very specificity—or definite law—he had been advocating. It would appear he was arguing the very point of the inadvisability of detailed specifications in law that would make law far too inflexible for the unexpected conditions that might arise. He seemed to heighten the incongruity, with both his previously expressed position and the attack he would launch on Theodore Roosevelt's trade commission proposal in the upcoming presidential election campaign, when he contended that what was needed was "an adequate enlargement of the powers of the Board of Utility Commissioners. The Board can be empowered, and should be empowered, to push the elimination of such crossings as fast as it is possible to push it without bringing hopeless embarrassment upon the railways." But Wilson then clarified what he would find as an acceptable basis for the further empowerment of the regulators through the law. "The law could easily establish a principle by which it might be determined when it was equitable that the several communities affected should participate in the expense, and to what extent, if any, they should participate. In this way all the results that could possibly be attained by the present bill would be attained without risk and perhaps the discouragement and discredit of attempting a thing, in itself inequitable and impracticable" (322–23).

In urging the establishment of a policy principle, Wilson seems to have been trying to clarify his idea of definite law by distinguishing specification amounting to micromanagement from specification that would be detailed enough to guide administration in its application of the law, and yet general enough to allow the balancing of equity and practicality in case-by-case assessments and determinations. Discretionary authority guided by a principle would be better than an inflexible formula that provided no assistance about the choices that would still be required (e.g., which grade crossings should the commission require it to remove first?). After some subsequent confusion and convoluted maneuvers, the state legislature passed a "revised version of the grade crossing bill, one embodying Wilson's recommendations" (323).

Abandoning Real Definiteness

When he trained his ideas on the national antitrust problem and the inadequacies of the Sherman Act, Wilson found the characteristics of the problem and the political circumstances in which they were embedded rather more daunting than the removal of railroad grade crossings. In particular, existing law "seemed clearly to forbid all conspiracies in restraint of trade. Yet, the burgeoning of multimillion-dollar firms through patents, through growth, and through consolidation at that very time gave the Court and many others second thoughts." Court efforts to draw "distinctions among reasonable and unreasonable restraints" left the definition of a trust "more and more muddied" (Lowi 1979, 100–1). The conditions Lowi described seem to match perfectly Wilson's vision of the situations in which administration could be of greatest value to a modern democratic regime: coordinating the power of applied science and economic enterprise, monitoring changing societal conditions and taking action in response, and, on the basis of this experience, guiding adjustments to law. Could the approach he articulated in the railroad crossing bill veto yield such results with respect to interstate trade? Wilson seems at first to have pursued the possibility.

In December 1913 Wilson called for a new antitrust law "to reduce the areas of that debatable ground" surrounding the Sherman Act "by further and more explicit legislation" (quoted in Clements 1992, 47; see Link et al. 1979, 29:7). What business sought from public policy in this area, he declared in January 1914, was "something more than that the menace of legal process in this matter be made more explicit and intelligible. They desire the advice, the definite guidance and information which can be supplied by an administrative body" (156). Hence, business sought definite law, but also help from administration in understanding and complying with that law—functions he had earlier accepted as legitimate for regulatory commissions. Still trying to distinguish what he was proposing from Theodore Roosevelt's scheme to regulate monopoly, Wilson stressed that public opinion "would not wish to see it empowered to make terms with monopoly or in any sort to assume control of business, as if the Government is made responsible. It demands such a commission only as an indispensable instrument of information and publicity, as a clearinghouse for the facts by which both the public mind and the managers of great business undertakings should be guided, as an instrumentality for doing justice to business." The economic justice that businesses sought was no longer sufficiently available through the market or the courts because "the processes of the courts or the natural forces of correction outside the courts are inadequate to adjust the remedy to the wrong in a way that will meet the equities and circumstances of the case" (156). This was so especially because the principal remedy, "dissolution by ordinary legal process," often involved "financial consequences likely to overwhelm the security market and bring upon it breakdown and confusion." Hence public opinion called for "an administrative commission capable of directing and shaping corrective processes, not only in aid of the courts but also by independent suggestion, if necessary" (157).

The legislation that the new commission would carry out would still contain the two key dimensions of specificity that Wilson sought. He again called for "a further and more explicit legislative definition of the policy and meaning of the existing antitrust law" (quoted in Clements 1992, 47; see Link et al. 1979, 29:156–57). And he sought to direct "penalties and punishments . . . , not upon business itself, to its confusion and interruption, but upon individuals who use the instrumentalities of business to do things which public policy and sound business practice condemn" (157). By the summer of 1914, however, as the legislative process dragged on in part over struggles to incorporate "explicit definition" into the legislation that eventually became the Clayton Act, Wilson had to admit that "the most difficult thing to do is to make a definition which will cover just what you want it to cover, not more, not less" (Link et al. 1979, 30:268). The classes of practices eventually specified in the Clayton Act—price discrimination, exclusive dealing and tying contracts, the purchase of the stock of one company by another (merger or acquisition), and interlocking directorates—all of which an administrative agency would flesh out in detail through specific cases, might have been consistent with the idea of the need for classification, and specification of principles rather than outcomes, expressed in Wilson's veto message on the grade-crossing bill. Unfortunately, Congress and the president left "the problem of developing standards for determining when one of the specified practices . . . would lead to a substantial lessening of competition or tendency to monopoly and when a practice became an unfair method of competition" to the commission and the courts (Miller 1958, 138).

In the end, Wilson accepted a commission with broad and presumably muscular regulatory powers to complement its information-gathering and guidance functions because it was "virtually impossible" to achieve much explicitness in the statutory definition of unfair competition. It seemed at the time to be better to have an administrative agency that, as a result of its greater autonomy, could really concentrate on applying its technical expertise to the task for which it was charged. The commission could combine that expertise with experience from individual cases and "build up precedents" (Clements 1992, 50; see also Miller 1958, 138–39; Eisner 1991, 58). Wilson defended the final policy products as offering "elasticity without real definiteness, so that we may adjust our regulation to actual conditions, local as well as national" (quoted in Clements 1992, 50; see Link et al. 1979, 30:320). To do that, however, it had to take corrective action against specific practices. But there wasn't any specific guidance anchored in law that might help it do this.

Consequences of Policy Design for
Administrative Capacity and Development

Assessing Wilson's contribution to antitrust policy, John Perry Miller concluded nearly half a century ago that the "basic accomplishment of the commission, and one not to be minimized, was the codification of a series of practices illegal under common law or under the Sherman Act and the provision of an administrative mechanism for their eradication." Miller argued that the FTC succeeded against a number of monopoly-related practices. Yet the commission expended considerable effort on many other practices "not particularly germane to the problems of monopoly" and aimed "more often than not [at] the practices of small firms rather than of large." More discomforting, "the commission had been less successful in interpreting conditions under which Clayton Act practices are in violation of the law and in defining new practices which contravene the law" (Miller 1958, 139).

Three observations are central to understanding and evaluating Wilson's practices regarding administrative expansion in the realm of business regulation in light of his ideas about administration and modern democracy. First, drawing on Theodore Lowi's critique of policy without law (Lowi 1979, ch. 5), Wilson succumbed to liberal pressures to allow broad but exceedingly vague delegations of authority to business regulators. This resulted almost exclusively in what Lowi characterized as "bargaining on the case" rather than "bargaining on the rule" (108). It occurred across a broad swath of allegedly unfair methods of competition and restraints of trade. Virtually no meaningful development of explicit, authoritative rules about good and bad corporate behavior has emerged over the ensuing ninety years. More serious for Wilson's ideas, his capitulation let business into a partnership with government of the sort he had seen in Theodore Roosevelt's proposal for monopoly regulation and warned so vehemently against. The result has not exactly been the administrative tyranny Wilson projected had Roosevelt's idea become reality, but it has amounted to the nearly complete absence of the integrity and authority of law Wilson had championed. More serious still, these outcomes raise worrisome questions for Wilson's claims about presidential leadership as the tie that would best bind good policy and good administration, guaranteeing the legitimacy of modern administration by subjecting it to concentrated, visible political authority. In response to intense interest-based pressure and his own desire to get legislation passed that would establish the success of his policy agenda, Wilson failed to use one of the most obvious tools of the presidency—the veto—to insist on good policy design that would in turn have met his standards of good administrative design. He thus missed a chance to secure the kind of collective responsibility that would legitimate more fully administrative discretion by attaching it to demonstrably responsible political authority (on this point, I follow Lowi 1979, 302).

Wilson's 1916 reelection campaign rhetoric suggests that he sensed the leadership-legitimacy-responsibility quandary his policy choices had produced. At the start of the campaign, Wilson characterized the FTC as "a means of inquiry and of accommodation in the field of commerce which ought both to coordinate the enterprises of our traders and manufacturers and to remove the barriers of misunderstanding and of a too technical interpretation of the law" (Link et al. 1982, 38:137–38). Later he stressed the FTC's inquiry function, to "inform the American businessman of every element, big and little, with which it is his duty to deal. Here are created searching eyes of inquiry to do the very thing that it was imperatively necessary and immediately necessary that the country should do—look upon the field of business and know what was going on!" He characterized the accomplishment in creating the FTC as "creating . . . instrumentalities of knowledge, so that the businessmen of this country shall know what the field of the world's business is and deal with that field upon that knowledge" (265–66).

Wilson subsequently described the policy-making process regarding antitrust as "an attempt . . . very properly made to define what was fair and what was unfair competition; to provide tribunals which would distinctly determine what was fair and what was unfair competition." But he then made a very revealing distinction, arguing that the policy supplied to "the business community" encompassed "not merely . . . lawyers in the Department of Justice who could cry, 'Stop!', but . . . men in such tribunals as the Federal Trade Commission, who could say, 'Go on,' who could warn where things were going wrong and assist instead of check" (340–41). Wilson never made any direct reference in the campaign to the FTC's regulatory and enforcement authority to "correct abuses." His distinction between Justice Department lawyers with the authority to say "Stop!" and FTC experts with the task of finding ways to say "Go on" only further highlights his view of the legitimate province of the commission. The locus of the FTC's legitimacy, Wilson's rhetoric signaled, was its work with business to determine appropriate behavior. In light of his previous worries about experts in business and government controlling policy without the authoritative guidance of definite law, it seems a strange kind of legitimacy for Wilson to have promoted.

Second, Wilson's distinction between organizational types and their legitimate roles raises doubts about his dependence on presidential leadership for administrative legitimacy. Without the anchor of definite law, modern administration, with an expanding reach into society and taking on new and innovative structural forms, was completely dependent on presidential leadership for its legitimacy. The FTC's status as an "independent" agency outside the integrating sphere of the regular departmental system left it less secured by the centripetal force of presidential authority. The agency's experience after its creation bears this out: the "FTC received support only when it partially fulfilled its mission. It was rewarded for occupying the middle ground between activism and incompetence, punished for attempting to fulfill its legislative mandate" (Eisner 1991, 62). Even the FTC's information-gathering and reporting functions, although they sometimes helped shaped legislation, were weakened or curtailed to the extent they were linked to regulatory activism. Thus the FTC's vague and general regulatory authority, which stands in contrast to the more vigorous and specific statutory language for its investigative authority (see Eisner 1991, 30), combined with its status as an independent organization outside the president's direct sphere of supervision, served to hamstring the commission more than to empower it through broad administrative discretion. Not being integrated into the regular administrative system of supervising political authority from president and cabinet and thus not enjoying the protection of a political leadership willing and able to defend it, the FTC was vulnerable to control and manipulation by Congress and the courts. This undermined the agency's ability to organize and manage itself internally for competence and efficiency. It also exacerbated policy and administrative fragmentation, reflected particularly in the patronage-like protections from the FTC's "corrections of abuses" some industries were able to win from Congress (Eisner 1991, 60–61).

The development of antitrust enforcement by the Justice Department only reinforces the evidence from the FTC experience. Since the Justice Department had only the vague and general antitrust language of the Sherman Act to enforce, it needed direct support from the president in order to get anything done. When presidents were hostile or indifferent to antitrust aims, the antitrust unit within the department got few resources and showed little success; when presidents were committed to antitrust enforcement, the department mostly got the resources it needed. The first instance of strong presidential support for antitrust enforcement using the Sherman Act was Theodore Roosevelt (Eisner 1991, 50–52). With better law and more sustained presidential commitments, the Justice Department's antitrust effort was "marked by the consciously directed and dramatic expansion of administrative capacity" and by broad, vigorous enforcement activism (76). One might say, then, that Wilson's notion of "large powers and unhampered discretion," especially to the extent that it applies to police-like powers, could only be effective in securing both responsibility and successful policy outcomes within his more sweeping structural idea of a system in which administration is well integrated under secure, concentrated political authority. Absent such an arrangement, broad discretion makes agencies vulnerable to political attack and interference, weakening them and making their supposedly broad authority virtually meaningless.

Third, considering the overall character of Wilson's actions with respect to administrative expansion, the significance of his choices lies in the degree of their departure from existing structures and practices—and from his own ideas—as well as in the qualities of the entities created, rather than in the quantity of organizations placed in various orbits around the presidential sphere. Wilson did set the government and the presidency down the road that led to the Brownlow Committee's plea, "The president needs help." But Wilson's actions posed not so much a problem of span of control as an increasingly complex challenge to his own conception of the president as the primary if not sole source of leadership, energy, and legitimacy in a system based on harnessing administrative power. His idea, again, was to bind legislation and administration together more closely to foster collective responsibility and thus overcome the tendency of the separation of powers to generate fragmented, irresponsible policy formation and its detachment from the needs of effective execution. With respect to administrative legitimacy in particular, the few presidents since Wilson inclined to attend to it have found little time to do so. Most have found little inclination, preferring to exploit the feebleness of administrative legitimacy to serve their own political ambitions. Perhaps Wilson sought greater adherence to his notions of coordination and collective responsibility in his governing practices than my analysis so far gives him credit for, however. A look at his actions with respect to his cabinet is thus in order.

CABINET GOVERNMENT

A difficulty in assessing Wilson's practices with respect to his conception of the composition and use of the cabinet is that he promoted two different models. Wilson's fidelity to his ideas in his practices is easier to confirm with reference to the conception of the cabinet's composition and role he settled on in *Constitutional Government*. In that model, again, members of the cabinet were only executive or administrative advisors to the president. They might serve in a temporary or limited capacity to help coordinate policy development, but the president relied on them primarily if not exclusively to carry most of the actual executive burden of the presidency, to a considerable extent quite on their own, while the president undertook the interpretation and articulation of public opinion and the task of party leadership. Coordination of policy-making and policy administration was one step removed, and it flowed through the president. But how attentive to administration did Wilson intend the president to be?

There are at least two reasons to retain Wilson's original conception of the cabinet in a reformed American republic as a reference point for his practices. First, Wilson developed the original conception much more fully and embraced it for a much longer period of time, including late in his tenure as president and after he departed the presidency. Second, Wilson seemed initially to want to follow this model in the conduct of his presidency, and he continued to cling to it at least rhetorically afterward. He also seems to have embraced it for a short period during World War I, in a slightly different form, with interesting results. The original model, again, envisioned the cabinet as a truly deliberative, consensual body coordinating policy development and policy execution. The president would in some respects only preside over this body of party leaders possessing both legislative and administrative standing and expertise. Absent constitutional changes altering the separation-of-powers barriers, they could not be legislators and administrators simultaneously, but, as Wilson argued in his essay on Grover Cleveland's cabinet, they would still constitute the "natural connecting link" between the president and his party in Congress. In Wilson's original conception of reform, which would have introduced ministerial responsibility into the American system, members of the cabinet would be the true interpretive leaders, reading the popular thought and incorporating it into legislative and administrative action. Even without the preferable constitutional changes, Wilson contended, they might still play something akin to this role.

Glimpses of a Collective Cabinet Role

Although Wilson never made his initial cabinet appointments in strict conformity with the cabinet government model, the evidence of his briefly toying with that conception includes his insistence that "I will not name a Cabinet of college presidents. . . . What I am seeking to get is a *team*" (Link et al. 1978, 27:94, emphasis in original). There is also the oft-repeated recollection of Josephus Daniels, secretary of the Navy, that Wilson initially sought to conduct cabinet business "more like a Quaker meeting" (see Link 1956, 74), where any member could comment on any issue, whether within his purview or not, and the president guided the meeting to a consensus rather than announcing a decision based merely on individual or collective advice. Daniels further described the nature of early cabinet deliberations as having an academic quality. On the matter of President Taft's blanketing fourth-class postmasters into the merit service, "The opinion prevailed that the merit system was not advanced by such use of the civil service regulation. But the virtual decision was that Post Master Burleson should draw up a paper to be presented to the cabinet embodying his views" (160).

The richest early statement characterizing the cabinet and its role in Wilson's plans for collectively responsible governance came in his May 1913 letter to Senator James O'Gorman regarding cabinet advice on appointments. Wilson stated that he did not see "any member of the Cabinet as a subordinate." He regarded them as occupying offices "of the first dignity and consequence." He argued that a presidential administration had to function as a unit. Drawing on his "long experience in cooperative administrative action," Wilson declared, "I know that I must support my colleagues as loyally as they support me and must defer to them in every matter in which I do not disagree with them in principle or upon grounds of large public policy." He accepted that he had "to attach the greatest possible weight to the judgment and preference in respect of their subordinates, especially their chief subordinates" and that following the guidance of his cabinet was essential "if I am to have an efficient and successful administration" (Link et al. 1978, 27:400).

Wilson's characterization here can just as easily be interpreted as describing how he sought to run his administration rather than how he intended to run "the government" in the full parliamentary, cabinet government sense. But something akin to ministerial responsibility may have existed in the Wilson cabinet such that any conflict that led to Wilson overruling a department head resulted in the secretary's resignation (Link 1956, 19, citing the cases of Secretary of State Bryan and Secretary of War Garrison in the first term). In point of fact, however, despite his continued, occasional claims over the course of his presidency to the contrary (see, for example, Link et al. 1980, 34:450), Wilson never really operated as if he were merely presiding over a collective decision-making body. Indeed, he only very intermittently governed with the help of the collective advice of his cabinet.

A Cabinet of Separate Advisors

In most policy and administrative matters Wilson primarily dealt with department heads one on one, often by correspondence (Link 1956, 18). His closest advisor, Col. Edward House, endorsed Wilson's decision to move away from a collaborative, consensual conception of governance, having never supported a group approach to deciding the policies and programs of individual departments in the first place: "The President consulted with the individual members of his Cabinet about their departments, but he did not consult with them on matters affecting their colleagues, and I thought he was right. If he did this, he would soon have every Cabinet officer meddling with the affairs of the others, and there would be general dissatisfaction" (quoted in Macmahon 1958, 114).

Wilson's consultations with department heads were apparently close and extensive—but piecemeal and fragmented rather than collective and integrative; the secretaries often felt isolated and uninformed. Wilson also gave department heads great discretion in both routine organizational and departmental policy matters but reserved coordinating authority largely to himself to avoid conflicts with the administration's policy agenda (Link 1956, 19; see also Clements 1992, 53; Stid 1998, 131). Wilson also kept his use of White House staff to a minimum to avoid "short-circuiting" communications and relations between himself and department heads on the key policy and administrative matters pertinent to their organizations (Macmahon 1958, 115). Yet there were also numerous instances, especially as the European war loomed larger on the agenda, in which Wilson simply refused to talk to department heads, especially if the matter was outside the narrow purview of the secretary seeking an audience.

Opportunities for a more collective governing process existed in the Wilson administration, but they were limited. Early in his decision-making process on any matter, Wilson "was receptive to advice" and "anxious to listen to all sides of an argument, to obtain a complete picture . . . , and to make certain that he lacked no pertinent . . . information" (Fenno 1959, 38). It was at this stage that his cabinet "could . . . be effective as an advisory body . . . where Wilson felt he needed to delineate and document a problem requiring his decision." But from that point until "his announcement of a decision[,] his advisers were not likely to be involved." He might submit "his final conclusions to their discussions," but "his mind usually would be well fixed," and "he would be testing out their reactions or seeking assurances, but not inviting debate" (39).

Especially with respect to foreign affairs, diplomacy, and the conduct of the war, Wilson simply abandoned any pretense of collective governing in favor of an isolated, personal form of governing, reaching "his decisions by himself, after lengthy, painstaking and solitary deliberations. He did not make up his mind in the presence of conflicting voices" (39). In international affairs, especially after he had lost confidence in Secretary of State Bryan and the patronage-heavy State Department, Wilson handled much of the substantive communications and policy negotiations himself. Combined with his leaving much of the day-to-day operations of the government to his department heads and their subordinates, Wilson's overall mode of governing appears to have been consistent with the tendencies in his personality (see, briefly, Clements 1992, 13) and his scholarly habits as well as the approach he developed as president of Princeton and followed as governor of New Jersey (see in particular Fenno 1959, 119–25).

Because Wilson delegated substantial operating authority to his department heads, portrayals of how he managed those relationships deserves some attention. In a letter to a senator midway through his first term, again with respect to administrative appointments, Wilson stressed that "the only possible living program upon which I can go in administering the Government is to trust the men whom I have chosen for the headships of the departments. . . . The only conceivable way of maintaining a right relationship to my colleagues is to trust their judgment if I hold them responsible for the results" (Link et al. 1980, 34:273). In remarks to the National Press Club, Wilson indicated that "when I give a man an office, I watch him carefully to see whether he is swelling or growing. . . . [T]he men who grow, the men who think better a year after they are put in office than they thought when they were put in office, are the balance wheel of the whole thing. They are the ballast that enables the craft to carry sail and to make port in the long run, no matter what the weather is" (Link et al. 1981, 37:51). Wilson suggested in a press interview as the 1916 election campaign neared its end that his approach to governing, including the delegation to and autonomy of department heads, made administration more responsive to public opinion: "I think the whole cabinet has felt the influence of opinion as directly and as sensitively as I have tried to feel it. And I think I can say with confidence that there never has been a time when the executive departments of the government were more immediately responsive to the influences proceeding out of the body of the people themselves than they are now" (Link et al. 1982, 38:569).

Other views of Wilson's management of relations with his principal advisors were not quite as rosy as Wilson's public contemplations. In his diary a month after the 1916 election, Edward House carped, "The trouble is the President does not know what is going on in any of the departments. He does not follow their work and has an idea that every department of the Government is running smoothly and well. As a matter of fact, most of them are, but a few are inefficient. I have complained of this from the beginning of his administration. He could remedy it easily if he would go at it in the right way." House concluded that Wilson "is one of the great men of the world today, but he sadly lacks administrative ability" (Link et al. 1982, 40:239). Continuing a bit later in his diary entry, House reported that Treasury Secretary McAdoo had pushed for Wilson to "revamp his Cabinet and get rid of the weak members. He also feels that the President has no business head, and what the office needs now is someone with that kind of ability" (241).

House returned to the subject following Wilson's second inauguration, apparently having pushed Wilson directly on the matter, perhaps revealing what he had meant with his earlier reference to the "right way": "If he [Wilson] did not get rid of Daniels and Baker, then I thought it was imperative that he make changes in the heads of bureaux. He listened with a kindly and sympathetic attention and while he argued with me upon many of the points, he did it dispassionately" (Link et al. 1983, 41:483). House returned to the subject once more late in the summer of 1917: Mc-Adoo "complained . . . of the President's unwillingness to face any sort of friction or trouble. This trait . . . has grown of late rather than diminished. It is a fact that the President does try to evade issues among his subordinates. I have seen him grow grey in the face when I would suggest the need for action that would entail the facing of a disagreeable situation concerning his official family." But the irony of House's endorsement of Wilson's decision to isolate cabinet members from one another's business and eventually the cabinet as a whole from Wilson's policy and administrative plans, noted above, then emerged: "McAdoo grumbled at the lack of coordination in the Cabinet. He declares the President never consults any of them about critical situations and never makes plans for the Cabinet to work together as a whole" (Link et al. 1983, 43:390–91).

The War Cabinet

House's private observations clearly indicate that Wilson's method—extensive delegation to and heavy reliance upon department heads and other top administrators for day-to-day governance—was not without its pitfalls. Yet Wilson's approach has garnered scholarly praise as one effective method for coping with the heavy, complex pressures the combination of head-of-state and head-of-government roles the Constitution assigns the presidency. The interesting question is, given Wilson's earlier ideas about cabinet government, was it practical to conceive of Wilson having chosen an alternative path? During the war, it appears, Wilson did just that.

The impetus seems to have been a combination of the tendencies shaping Wilson's management approach noted above, along with his refusal to abandon intellectually the idea of cabinet government and the severe administrative and managerial problems brought on by the war. In those circumstances, Wilson restored a somewhat more collective form of governing and connected himself more directly to executive action. He had fought off congressional efforts to create a formal war cabinet that would have included established political leaders, like Theodore Roosevelt, who at the time were not holding any elective office. This group would have been positioned between the president and the regular cabinet departments. Wilson also had deflected demands to create a munitions ministry or a more general "war machine," which even some of his department heads had advocated (see Stid 1998, 131–32).

Despite his success in fending off these efforts to help him manage the war, Wilson did recognize that the complexities and demands of war management far exceeded what any one individual could handle. Add to that the burden of a greatly enlarged span of control with the addition of the "mushroom agencies" (Fenno 1959, 150)—the boards, commissions, and independent agencies he had authorized—and, from the perspectives of both political strategy and management effectiveness, Wilson faced the necessity of doing something to relieve the load. He created "an informal war cabinet that began meeting on March 20, 1918, in lieu of one of the biweekly meetings of the regular cabinet." In addition to Wilson, the primary members were Secretaries Baker, Daniels, and McAdoo as well as the major independent agency heads: Baruch, Garfield, and Hoover. Quite significantly, the meetings involved attempts "to hash out the broader questions of policy and conflicting administrative objectives that arose during the remainder of the war." Equally important, from the perspective of Wilson's ideas and governing practices, the war cabinet took on "questions concerning the basic structure and day-to-day operation of the administration over which [Wilson] was presiding" (Stid 1998, 133).

Reports from those involved suggest that through the war cabinet Wilson returned to something like the "collegiality of academic life" as his governing model, making "management of the war effort . . . essentially a collective enterprise" (Thompson 2002, 168). The labors of the war cabinet were less than permanently serene or universally substantive, of course. "We used the words coordination and cooperation until they were worn out," Herbert Hoover, the champion of autonomous, professional management, recorded in this memoirs. "We surrounded ourselves with coordinators, and we spent hours in endless discussions with no court of appeal" (quoted in Fenno 1959, 150). Furthermore, in all matters concerning diplomatic relations with the belligerents, Wilson "retained firm control" in order to respond "to complex, dramatic, and swiftly changing circumstances in the manner that best promoted his own goals" (Thompson 2002, 168). On the most vital question of the nation's acceptance of Germany's terms for an armistice, the war cabinet had very little involvement or influence (Fenno 1959, 124; Stid 1998, 126–27).

Wilson's "war cabinet" did not quite fulfill Wilson's original vision of cabinet government. The centrifugal forces continuously at work in American politics manifest themselves dramatically in the tendency toward Fenno's "departmentalism" in the cabinet itself. Each cabinet secretary "feels his responsibility—as indeed it is—personally to the President and not to the President in Council, nor to the President and his Cabinet, *and above all not to his Cabinet colleagues* (Fenno 1959, 134, quoting Brownlow 1949, 100; emphasis Fenno's). These same tendencies were at work in Wilson's war cabinet. Yet it is remarkable that the war cabinet took as seriously as it did the need to achieve cooperation and coordination and that it drew Wilson into direct engagement in executive action, into a more prime minister–like role, which stands in contrast to his conception of the presidential role enunciated in *Constitutional Government*. All this took place, of course, under circumstances that were both dire and temporary. It nevertheless suggests the possibility of concentrated political authority and an integrated, coordinated exercise of administrative power alternative to the usual model of extreme president-centeredness. The further irony, as I explore more fully in the next section, is that Wilson found his way to it via a retreat from his ideal of interpretive presidential statesmanship and common counsel and toward the original, constitutional conception of the presidential office.

In hindsight it is hardly surprising that Wilson was unable to overcome the barriers of structure, culture, and practice to make the cabinet a truly collective, deliberative body of statesmen and expert administrators, coordinating and integrating policy-making and policy execution in a comprehensive way that would draw the informed attention and scrutiny of the citizenry, resulting in the responsible wielding of administrative power. It is, as Richard Fenno noted long ago in his valuable study, a matter of context. Cabinet government with collective responsibility requires "the lack of an independent executive, the absence of a separation of powers, the existence of a responsible party system"—all the features Wilson originally imagined in a reconstructed American regime. "In the presence of the separation of powers and the checks and balances wielded by an Independent Chief Executive," however, "the Cabinet's characteristics and behavior are highly derivative" (Fenno 1959, 252). As Fenno went on to note wryly, analysts "of the American Cabinet might be excused for wishing that Walter Bagehot's classic had never been written, for it has predisposed students of American government to view the President's Cabinet as fulfilling its most important function by bridging the legislative-executive gap. There is no reason why the Cabinet might not help in this regard, but to assume that it should hyphenate or buckle together the American system is to ignore its indigenous power-responsibility relationship to the president" (255).

Wilson saw the precarious position of the cabinet fifty years before Fenno's insight. Thus he insisted on placing in the hands of the president the task of bringing the creation and execution of laws within hailing distance of one another, and he diminished the cabinet's potential help in this regard, nearly to the point of ruling it out altogether. If there is value in "bridging the legislative-executive gap" in a system of divided institutions sharing powers, then, as Wilson also concluded, the burden for doing so would seem to fall primarily to the president, even as it raises substantially the weight on the qualities of leadership individual presidents must possess. But this also further reinforces the pressure on presidents to succeed in wielding administrative powers effectively. This in turn yet further reinforces the dependence of administration on presidential leadership for the quality of its contributions to the regime, as well as the long-run legitimacy that follows a recognition of those contributions. If administration's fortune in securing a legitimate place in the American regime is strictly bound to presidential leadership, then Wilson's practices and their consequences suggest that such fortune might remain forever unfulfilled.

INTERPRETIVE LEADERSHIP

As I noted in chapter 5, scholarly recognition of Wilson's executive leadership triumph gives pride of place to his success in realizing his vision of national statesmanship and interpretation of public opinion (also see Milkis and Nelson 1999, 226–29). That vision included, to paraphrase various incarnations of Wilson's description of it, a grounded expediency or principled opportunism. It was a "subtle conception of political leadership," combining "convictions and policies evolved over the years in response to the prevailing sentiments of public opinion, the logic of compelling ideas, and the experience of and responsibility for governing" (Stid 1998, 73–74). This is, moreover, readily consistent with the portrayal of Wilson in the Thompson (2002) analysis. He was not slave to unbending ideals but was guided by ideas that to him remained compelling even if circumstances demanded deviation from the guidance they offered.

Wilson's performance reflecting his conception of leadership began as governor, where, in "responding to public demands for reform" and "pursuing the logic of progressivism," he "emerged as the sort of interpretive statesman he had always esteemed" (Stid 1998, 74). In particular, Wilson offered a "vision of engaged, public, and comprehensive executive leadership" that provided the legislators of the state with both "guidance and political cover." Furthermore, Wilson's political leadership in New Jersey encompassed not just "public pronouncements" and expansive interpretations of "gubernatorial prerogatives" but also "more consensual means"—close interactions with legislators in the search for common ground (75).

Of critical importance, Wilson accepted the "natural history" of the circumstances that enabled his leadership. This clearly reflected Wilson's view that effective political leadership must not be too innovative, must not get too far out ahead of public opinion. The right timing was crucial, both in terms of a particularly adept leader rising to prominence when the public was receptive to the new directions the leader favored, and the subtle efforts of a statesman to bring to mature receptivity, as it were, the minds of the public and their representatives toward policy ideas and projects.

Even more impressive were Wilson's "remarkable acts of interpretive leadership upon taking office" as president. Wilson "undertook his initiatives deliberately, as a symbolic unification of the executive and legislative branches whose separation had long troubled him." Hence, through "his deeds and his words," Wilson exercised "interpretive leadership." In particular, "Wilson delivered . . . concise and resonating messages every few months, as the time grew ripe for each new piece of legislation. They were thus focused upon and widely disseminated in their entirety by the newspapers" (91). In nearly all of these instances, "Wilson was not imposing legislation upon but rather drawing it out of Congress" (92).

Interpretive Leadership: Wilson's Rhetoric

Wilson was often quite direct about what he was doing in attempting to follow his ideas about leadership as interpretation and giving expression to the general interest against various and threatening "private" or "special" interests. In one of several missives expressing distress that the president really "runs the government" and that the presidency is a never-ending job, for example, Wilson wrote, "No one but the President seems to be expected, or to expect himself, to look out for the general interests of the country. Everybody else is special counsel for some locality or some special groups of persons or industries. . . . He alone has the acknowledged duty for studying the pattern of affairs as a whole and of living all the while in his thoughts with the people of the whole country" (Link et al. 1978, 28:107). In October 1913, in an address marking the restoration of Constitution Hall in Philadelphia, Wilson declared that "politics is a business of interpretation, and no men are fit for it who do not see and seek more than their own advantage and interest" (436).

Wilson did not limit his public pronouncements on the interpretive leadership he was pursuing to the first two years of his tenure as president. In an address to the Pan American Scientific Congress in January 1916, he argued that the "mere politician" failed to perceive and understand the vital connections between politics and life. "Statesmanship," in contrast, "begins where these connections, so unhappily lost, are re-established. The statesman stands in the midst of life to interpret life in political action" (Link et al. 1980, 35:443). Wilson also made it a point several times during the 1916 presidential election campaign to emphasize his understanding of leadership as the interpretation of public opinion. And opinion was, to emphasize again Wilson's view, a reflection of life—modern life. In his remarks to the National Press Club that also included his philosophy about administrative appointees cited earlier, Wilson stated pointedly that "I am put here to interpret, to register, to suggest, and, more than that, and much greater than that, to be suggested to" (Link et al. 1981, 37:50). Redeploying ideas from his lecture "Leaders of Men," Wilson told the National American Women Suffrage Association that "when you are working with masses of men and organized bodies of opinion, you have got to carry the organized body along. The whole art and practice of government consists, not in moving individuals, but in moving masses. It is all very well to run ahead and beckon, but, after all, you have got to wait for the body to follow" (Link et al. 1982, 38:163). And in a press interview late in the campaign, Wilson noted, "every man who tried to lead a party or promote a policy must realize, as I have realized, how difficult it is to be sure that he had put the right interpretation upon public opinion" (568).

An interesting facet of Wilson's efforts in the 1916 campaign to make the model of leadership he was following transparent concerned what he regarded as his sources and methods for interpreting public opinion. As Wilson pointed out in a speech in Detroit, a particular method of reading the public thought—reflecting the conception of a science of politics he had first formulated thirty years before—had to accompany interpretive political leadership: "Men are colored and governed by their occupations and their surroundings and their habits. . . . You get a good deal more light on the street than you do in the closet. You get a good deal more light by keeping your ears open among the rank and file of your fellow citizens than you do in any private conference whatever." The guidance and counsel that would allow him to discern the general interest embryonic in mass public opinion was what Wilson claimed to be seeking: "And what I am constantly asking is that men should bring me that counsel, because I am not privileged to determine things independently of this counsel" (Link et al. 1981, 37:391).

The representations of public opinion he depended upon seem, however, to have been somewhat different than what Wilson here suggested. He "ascertained public opinion . . . through his advisers and leaders in Congress, and, above all, by the tremendous volume of organized opinion expressed in the letters, petitions, resolutions, which poured daily into the White House" (Link 1956, 25). This suggests that Wilson's reading of public opinion was based primarily if not solely on elites and organized interests. This would not have been entirely inconsistent with his understanding of modern democracy. But it does raise questions about whether he really operated according to the model of the consummate interpretive leader he promoted: operating at the center and not from above and, at least occasionally, immersed in the talk, and thoughts, of the common folk.

Wilson's solitary mode of decision-making adds to the questions and heightens the incongruity. Not surprisingly, it shows that Wilson had left a number of aspects of his conception of interpretive statesmanship undeveloped, making all the more relevant his contention that a true science of modern democratic leadership needed to be devised. And Wilson certainly tried during his time in office to develop a number of facets of modern American statesmanship. Despite having very uncomfortable relations with much of the press corps, he understood the importance of cultivating a working relationship with the press that would allow a two-way flow of information and views. He maintained a reasonably regular schedule of press conferences (see the compilation in Link et al. 1985, vol. 50), and he accepted the importance of allowing Joseph Tumulty to maintain his own good relationships with reporters as a way to smooth over the rough patches resulting from Wilson's testier interactions (Link 1956, 79–85).

As he did during his 1912 campaign for the presidency, Wilson also sought to articulate the special character and value of administration and management, defending the work of administrators on grounds beyond mere competency, characterizing their contributions as essential to the modernization of the nation and describing the work of administrative entities in terms consistent with his broad ideas about the place of administration in the regime. In addition to his portrayal of the place and value of the FTC, Wilson described the "nonpartisan tariff commission" as "[a]nother eye created to see the facts! And I am hopeful that I can find the men who will see the facts and state them, no matter whose opinion those facts contradict. For an opinion ought always to have a profound respect for a fact. And, when you once get the facts, opinions that are antagonistic to those facts are necessarily defeated." His administration was thus engaged in "creating, one after another, the instrumentalities of knowledge" (Link et al. 1982, 38:266). Wilson also argued that these administrative "instrumentalities of knowledge" found and disseminated the knowledge of others as much as they created it themselves, as in the case of the agricultural extension program: "It is a noteworthy fact that the improved agricultural methods which have been promoted by the agents of the Department of Agriculture have consisted of spreading the processes which those agents learned from the best farmers, rather than those which they carried to the farmers out of their own studies" (569).

Thus, as part of his very self-conscious effort to fulfill his own vision of interpretive statesmanship, Wilson sought to cultivate a national consensus on the legitimacy of a modernized national administration, one greatly expanded in scope, capacity, and structural forms. Yet one dimension of Wilson's conception of the presidency as national interpreter and connecting link between lawmaking and administration that he dramatically magnified in practice raises doubts about the long-term efficacy of his rhetoric regarding the value and legitimacy of administration generally, as well as the peculiar expansions in national administration he oversaw.

Interpretive Leadership and the Constitutional Presidency: Exigency and Reform

Wilson's repositioning of the locus of leadership, interpretation of public opinion, and thus guarantor of the effective and legitimate wielding of administrative power from the cabinet to the presidency was in part an acknowledgment of the durability of the constitution's structure and theory of governance. In seeking to achieve some synthesis between his key ideas and the constitution's structure and developmental history, Wilson accepted the presidency's constitutional construction and conception of its powers and roles. In particular, he accepted the "two presidencies" configuration implied in Article II: a domestic head of government with a general grant of executive power but significant restrictions on overall control of policy and law because of overlapping powers across separate institutions and a head of state, still with shared powers but also with a much freer field of action in relations with other nations and in protecting the security of the nation, especially in time of war (Stid 1998, 62).

Wilson trained his reform aims primarily on the domestic presidency, seeking to bridge the constitutional divides to ensure the visible, coherent, coordinated, and responsible wielding of administrative power to address the imperatives of national growth and the turmoil brought on by modernity. For the president as head of state, Wilson sought much less in the way of modification to bring policy and administration in closer coherence across the institutional divides. Indeed, in this respect, Wilson argued, policy and administration were commingled wholly within the executive realm. As he moved toward his second presidential term and the dangers from the war in Europe grew, Wilson told the journalist Ray Stannard Baker in May 1916, "When foreign affairs intrude the people look to the president. His foreign affairs policy must be his own" (quoted in Stid 1998, 124; see Link et al. 1981, 37:35). Wilson's private musings became public observations in his National Press Club remarks, which followed shortly thereafter. After characterizing his principal presidential job as interpreting, registering, suggesting, and being suggested to, Wilson went on to admit, "Now, that is where the experience that I forecast has differed from the experience that I have had. In domestic matters, I think I can, in most cases, come pretty near a guess where the thought of America is going. But in foreign affairs, the chief element is where action is going on in other quarters of the world, and not where thought is going in the United States."

In admitting that in international relations he would pay less heed to public thought and be less bound by a responsibility to shape, coax, and articulate public opinion, Wilson presaged the path he tried to follow in governance during the war. That path was a departure from his ideal of interpretive leadership and responsible government bridging the separation-of-powers divide and bringing the president, cabinet, and Congress into "common counsel."

Wilson in fact took actions that contradicted his ideas about the necessities of modern democratic statesmanship even before he got to the White House. During his campaign for governor, Wilson had mocked his opponent's pledge to be a "constitutional" governor, promising instead to be an "unconstitutional" governor by spanning the institutional divide between legislature and executive. When Republicans gained control of the legislature for the 1912 session, however, Wilson resorted to the use of the fail-safe mechanisms of the separation of powers to operate independently, if necessary against the policy aims of the legislative majority (Stid 1998, 79). As president, Wilson fulfilled his vision of interpretive leadership in the formation of domestic policy, bridging the divide between the executive and the legislature through rhetoric, symbolic actions, and party leadership to draw out the progressive policies that would, in form and substance, be relatively consistent with what he envisioned. When confronted with divided party government, however, or with the more serious circumstances of domestic emergency and international conflict, Wilson retreated to the relative protection of the Founders' design, in which a stricter separation of governing institutions sharing powers enabled him to operate as an independent, energetic, Hamiltonian executive, acting much less through common counsel with Congress and fending off strong congressional desires to exercise some semblance of oversight and control of administration (see esp. Stid 1998, 62–63, 119–33). As Wilson put it most succinctly in his statement urging passage of the Lever Food Control Act, "it is absolutely necessary that unquestionable powers shall be placed in my hands" (quoted in Turner 1951; see Link et al. 1983, 42:345). His qualification of this pointed claim—"I am confident that the exercise of those powers will be necessary only in the few cases where some small and selfish minority proves unwilling to put the Nation's interests above personal advantage"—shows his continued cautiousness in accepting the expansion of the powers of the independent executive but also his conviction that the president embodied the national interest.

In shifting the locus of national leadership and responsibility for wielding administrative power effectively from the cabinet to the president, Wilson tried to resolve the powerful tensions between his reform aims and the realities, including dramatic changes in the conditions the nation faced, of governing under a constitutional structure that did not easily yield, perhaps did not yield at all, to schemes for major reconstruction. Significant tensions remained, however, especially if it was necessary to distinguish between interpretive statesmanship and common counsel in domestic affairs and Hamiltonian energy and executive autonomy in foreign relations. To a lesser extent the same dynamic might even attend domestic politics manifested in divided party control, reflecting deep-seated and unresolved divisions of opinion in the electorate.

If it was not explicit in his rhetoric explaining his actions, especially in the run-up to and engagement in the war, then certainly implicit in what Wilson said and did was a presumption that he was making reasonable adjustments and accommodations to increasingly extraordinary circumstances with whatever governing resources he had at his disposal. This was certainly in keeping with important aspects of his conception of national leadership, and, the League of Nations ratification failure excepted, his leadership led to national success both domestically and internationally. But further consideration of Wilson's efforts to mesh several distinctive and not wholly compatible ideas in his practices during the war reveals the leadership chimera Wilson produced. This in turn raises serious questions about the efficacy of his solution, centered on the president, as the way to concentrate political authority and coordinate policy and administration to ensure the responsible and legitimate wielding of administrative power.

What Wilson essentially promoted was an "extraordinary times" exception to the reformation of American government he promoted in response to the ailments of the constitutional system he had diagnosed. Accepting the possibility of such an exception would mean accepting that the normal state of administrative centrality in a mature democratic state could be knocked askew, not so much in the sense of the revolutionary overthrow of a political regime but rather in the sense of internal disturbances reflecting unusual dissension among the citizenry or external disturbances such as international conflict. Wilson could still accept the rise of these sorts of conditions as consistent with his general idea of the evolutionary progress of modern democratic states shaped by the buffeting of changing conditions. But if these kinds of conditions arose relatively frequently, when could a modern democratic state ever settle into the "unexciting business" of "peaceful development" Wilson expected in his analysis in *Congressional Government*? Wilson's assessment of the nature of modernity implies that he realized the possibility of much greater flux in societal conditions. This is in part what led him finally to shift the locus of his reform aims from the cabinet to the presidency, especially with respect to fluctuating external conditions. With that conceptual move, however, along with the suggestion that in extraordinary times his reform ideas and practices might no longer apply, Wilson created even more daunting obstacles to the ultimate realization of the object of his reform: responsible government in the form of effective, accountable, and legitimate wielding of administrative power.

In accepting an "extraordinary times" exception to his reform scheme, particularly regarding external threats, Wilson stimulated the flow of power to the executive despite his own efforts to limit it. He was very careful to make clear the temporary, emergency nature of the administrative expansion under the direct control of the president he was obliged to undertake during the war. He was cognizant of both the impracticality of continuing many of the wartime measures after the threat of war had been eliminated and the temporary foundation of legitimacy on which his more extraordinary administrative actions stood. Both elements were also part of Wilson's calculus in insisting on rapid demobilization, especially the quick and nearly complete dismantling of the wartime administrative apparatus. Franklin Roosevelt similarly used temporary administrative devices in response to the emergencies of both the Depression and World War II. With each subsequent event and accompanying invocation of the exception to Wilson's vision of the president orchestrating through interpretive leadership close policy and administrative coordination and common counsel across the legislative-executive divide, however, an increasing accretion of power in the executive has occurred. This is a direct result of the retreat to the constitutional presidency that Wilson felt compelled to accept—even endorse— because of the omnipresent influence on thinking about governance the Constitution exerts in the regime.

Certainly the nation can accomplish great work through the expansion of executive power in a crisis. But at the center of the dynamic of power flow is the presidential temptation to create or perpetuate crises and translate them into what is accepted as "normal" in politics. The temptation is even greater, and the aim accomplished more easily, when the principal political implement presidents deploy is rhetoric and the interpretation of public opinion. This ties power directly to public opinion, with potentially unseemly consequences for efforts to make good public policy and for the integrity of political decision-making (Tulis 1987, 175–81; also see Lowi 1985). Ironically, it also contradicts Wilson's core conception of the nature of modern democracy in which public opinion is one clear step removed from governing.

As I noted in the previous chapter, mobilizing for and fighting a war is in many respects the definitive administrative endeavor. If Wilson saw it as a necessary adjustment to conditions to retreat to the constitutional presidency and the relative protections for autonomous executive actions found in the separation of powers, then it raises serious doubts either about the efficacy of his whole analysis and conception of a remedy to the ills of the constitutional system or about the ability of any president to fulfill the vision of interpretive statesmanship in circumstances where the effective and legitimate wielding of administrative power is most central.

In Wilson's case, the retreat to the constitutional presidency produced the ironic turn I explored in the previous section. As the wartime administrative apparatus grew, he engaged much more fully and directly in executive work. In retreating to some extent from his idea of the president as the great interpreter standing above the executive and legislative institutions and bridging the divide between them with his interpretation of public opinion, Wilson reverted in many respects to a more parliamentary or cabinet government form. Perhaps even more so than during the triumphs of his New Freedom legislative thrust, he operated as prime minister and head of government, much more attentive to the administrative dimension of statutory construction and thus much more immersed in the coordination of policy design, administrative plans, and their execution. Of course, members of the war cabinet remained his clear subordinates, and they did not take on the task of interpretive statesmanship Wilson had envisioned in his original cabinet government conception. He continued to reserve that role and responsibility largely to himself. Nevertheless, he embraced a more collective approach to administrative planning and policy execution through his war cabinet. At least in comparison with results of his effort to be more detached from executive work on the domestic policy side, one could justifiably argue that once Wilson took charge in this way, the mobilization and the war were more effectively administered and the nation was better governed.

There is further irony, then, in the results of the 1918 midterm elections, in which the Republicans regained control of Congress. Wilson had promoted the elections as a referendum on his wartime leadership (Stid 1998, 133–35), but he did not behave like a prime minister in the formal sense by resigning with the defeat of his party in the legislature. In an informal sense, however, he did resign, or at least he retreated from much of his governing duties. He seized on the Paris peace conference negotiations to become primarily if not solely an über-diplomat, leaving most of the postwar reconversion and regular policy development and management to his department heads. When he returned with the League of Nations treaty in hand, he became again the rhetorical president, investing almost all his time and energy in the cause of its ratification, but he seemed to misinterpret public opinion badly on this score; at best he certainly failed to cultivate the mood he sought. Accumulating health problems were much more likely a contributing cause than an effect of the political disaster of the ratification failure that followed his cross-country speaking tour on behalf of the treaty. But his reversion to his conception of the president as the focal point of interpretive leadership combined with his constitutional-presidency under-standing of the control of foreign policy left him with an inflexible model for govern-ing in the face of divided party control.

The evidence, therefore, is compelling. Although "traditionalist" defenders have praised Wilson most highly for redefining presidential leadership and thus restoring the presidency to a place of prominence in national governance and "revisionist" critics of Wilson have attacked his efforts to deviate from a constitutional design that attempts to restrain "presidential leadership of public opinion" (Stid 1998, 5), it was Wilson's attempts to *adhere* to the apparently irresistible force of constitutional form and structure and adjust his ideas about leadership and the legitimate exercise of administrative power accordingly that produced the most problematic aspects of his governing practices and proved most detrimental to his ultimate reform aims with respect to democracy and administration in the United States.

WILSON'S PRACTICES AND PUBLIC MANAGEMENT CHALLENGES

Over the course of the long development of his ideas about modern democracy and administration, Wilson always accepted the need to adjust his reform notions in light of changing societal, economic, and political conditions and in response to the counterforce of constitutional structure and tradition and the deep-rooted political legitimacy it enjoyed. Wilson's acknowledgment of the necessity of change and adjustment was consistent with his understanding of political conservatism, the nature of progress in modern democracies, and the requirements of modern demo-cratic statesmanship. In very important respects, moreover, Wilson's adherence to this principle, about the necessity of equilibrating governing principles with govern-ing realities, produced impressive results.

In the Wilson administration's efforts at administrative capacity-building, one can readily see the embryonic structure of the national executive establishment that came fully into being by the end of World War II and has only grown in complexity and reach since then. It is a combination of executive departments, independent, single-headed agencies under direct presidential control, independent commissions with a more arm's length relationship to the president, and the extensive inter-mingling of public and private organizations and expertise assembled around the achievement of major (usually quite specific) governmental objectives covering the gamut from fighting wars, guarding the peace, and harnessing natural and human resources. Wilson thus led the way toward significant policy and administrative innovation, and he secured a remarkable level of national political legitimacy for the policy and administrative innovations he helped bring about. In addition, in anticipation of the focus of the two chapters that follow, it is important to recognize that, from the perspective of certain central tenets of public management theory and practice, one must consider the most prominent of Wilson's administrative and managerial actions as president a notable triumph. While making clear a concern for consistency with his primary policy agenda, Wilson granted substantial discretion and autonomy to his administrators and managers, allowing them to focus on solving substantive problems as they saw them and developing initiatives grounded in their experience and expertise. Identifiable improvements in national administration and management—in the life of American citizens—ultimately followed.

Although Wilson's policy and administrative advancements were unprecedented, they have nevertheless been subject to harsh criticism, both for failing to secure the autonomy of the national state from the influences of private capital and for not going far enough in providing the modern American state with sufficient administrative capacity and executive power to help the nation cope adequately with the demands, pressures, and threats of modernity. There is much to commend in the caution in Wilson's moves (for which he has been sharply criticized, however), for it was grounded in a concern for maintaining in a precarious political environment the legitimacy any endeavor aimed at state-building and administrative expansion would require to succeed. When it came to administration in particular, Wilson's caution did not reflect so much ambivalence as a recognition of the challenge of achieving a fragile balance between the necessity of adopting modern administrative structures and methods and of keeping those structures and methods subservient to American political values.

Wilson and his advisors, political allies, and even critics all saw it as especially important to avoid establishing a European-style statist bureaucracy (see Clements 1992, 151). Wilson's plan was to create an integrated administrative system that, although only indirectly subject to public opinion, was under a much more concentrated form of political authority and thus much more readily subject to citizen scrutiny, which in turned increased the incentives for citizen engagement in government. This political authority was also in the hands of a political leadership that interpreted and marshaled public opinion. The result of all these elements was increased democratic control—or as Wilson saw it, more and better democracy—especially by preventing excessive private, especially business, influence on government.

It was perhaps one of Wilson's most significant insights to suggest that legislative and judicial processes are primarily conservative forces in democratic regimes, while administration is a progressive force. This is a reflection of Wilson's conception of administration as the leading edge of the state—its experiencing organ. It is thus most in touch with the flux and change in society wrought by the forces of modernity. It must respond and find ways to cope, and its actions in this regard pull legislators and judges toward more permanent adjustments enshrined in laws and constitutional interpretations. Because it is progressive, administration's legitimacy is vital to the health of the modern democratic state. This further reinforces the point about Wilson's caution in approaching administrative expansion and reform. It was not just ideological in the Burkean conservative sense in which he understood change. It was also practical.

American political culture, especially as shaped by the Constitution, was bound to resist the modernization of government through administrative improvement. As Wilson argued—and made clear in practice as well—expanding administration beyond its capacity, especially given the bureaucratization that was bound to creep in despite efforts to avoid it, would alter and undermine what was perhaps administration's chief value to a liberal democratic regime: finding the right line to draw between "*Interference* and *Laissez faire*," between state domination and unrestrained pursuit of private gain, which could give form and definition to a healthy political economy. Excessive administrative expansion would weaken administration itself and the government generally. It would be overly intrusive and tutelary, extending beyond the effective reach of legitimate political authority. It would thus be poorly led and inadequately controlled. This in turn would open administration to chaotic, fragmented, interest-based interference, especially through the legislature. Among citizens and their representatives, respect for and acceptance of administration's constitutive impact could only come by care in limiting its scope and role—tying it to the central purpose of the modern democratic state, which involved finding the right arrangements for fostering equal individual development through society's auspices.

Wilson thus focused his reform enterprise on getting his fellow citizens to recognize the central importance of administrative power to their maturing democratic regime and to accept the use of the administrative forms and methods most likely to ensure the effective use of that power in the face of modern conditions. He sought to achieve these objectives through means that would not threaten them, in particular by avoiding expansion beyond administration's capacity and legitimacy and by avoiding fragmentation that would leave administrative entities vulnerable to irresponsible interference from Congress, interest groups, and even the courts. If one looks back from the present and surveys the landscape of American national government from Wilson's presidency forward, however, what one sees is almost exactly what Wilson sought to avoid. How did this happen?

Wilson's failure was not in his diagnosis nor, in the abstract, was it in his initial remedy centered on cabinet government. Certainly there are deep-rooted questions about how a small body of truly national political leaders can govern successfully by subordinating their ambitions to a collective endeavor while still facing personal accountability for the governing results in their areas of responsibility. I attend to some of these questions in chapter 8. But Wilson's wartime practices and the examples of several other presidents indicate that effective governance, especially coordinated, collectively responsible governance, in the fragmented, competitive, interest-driven system of American politics is possible without the entire burden resting on the shoulders of one person. Wilson's failure, then, was in his decision to vest responsibility for the leadership and legitimacy needed to ensure the effective wielding of administrative power solely in the presidency. It is an impossible task of administrative integration, coordination of policy and administration, and interpretive statesmanship for one official, no matter how well supported by the Constitution or the expression of national sentiment.

Wilson was correct that his aims for the reconstitution of the regime centering on administration required effective national leadership and, through it, the legitimation of the modern power of administration. But his solution to the leadership and legitimacy challenge in practice ultimately left national administration leaderless, fragmented, and largely on its own to gain legitimacy, which it did so piecemeal, reinforcing a trend already well under way when Wilson entered the White House (I explore the consequences further in the next chapter). The aim of countering this trend was at least implicit in Wilson's advocacy of an integrated national system of administration. In placing the leadership and legitimacy burden completely in the president's hands, furthermore, Wilson helped to release Congress from much of its residual institutional responsibility for two central governing tasks: first, coordinating policy and administration in a national, collective fashion, and second, giving policy real legal integrity, which would keep administration from expanding beyond its capacity and legitimate reach.

Unlike most of the presidents after him if not all of them—Wilson undertook a recognizable effort to shape in public thought and national opinion an understanding of what he sought to achieve for the nation through his practices regarding administrative expansion and reform. But the vehicle for leadership and legitimacy on which he chose to center his entire scheme did not provide what he sought for his enterprise. It did not empower the modern democratic citizen of the United States by providing either the incentives or the avenues for reconnecting and reengaging with government by scrutinizing national administration and holding officials accountable for the results of their efforts at wielding administrative power. Despite the claims about the responsibility-concentrating effects of elections that elected officials axiomatically make, political accountability remains elusive and obscure, detached from any real consequences that a doctrine like ministerial responsibility might engender. Both presidents and legislators have thus largely abandoned all but superficial pretexts for providing the leadership and legitimacy administration requires to fulfill its role in the regime. Worse, in avoidance of responsibility and maintenance of power, they have seriously eroded whatever legitimacy administration had enjoyed. The responsibility to provide the leadership and legitimacy administration requires to fulfill its role is now largely in the hands of public administrators and managers, who are largely untrained and ill-prepared for such a burden. The central challenge confronting modern public administration and management today is thus reestablishing the responsible political leadership that provides public administration and public management with its necessary legitimacy. I turn now to further explication of this challenge and to arguments about the direction responses to the challenge ought to take.

PART III

A Wilsonian Perspective
on Governance

CHAPTER SEVEN

The Continuing Relevance of Wilson's Ideas

In his influential treatise *Creating Public Value*, Mark H. Moore recounts the emergence of a "strategic management" orientation toward understanding and improving modern government. He points to a "natural synthesis" combining the traditional public administration focus on organizations as the unit of analysis with the spotlight on policies in the more recently established subfield of public policy studies. The synthesis resulted in a conception of "public organizations as relatively flexible instruments to be used in achieving changing public purposes. The public purposes would develop as a consequence of both changes in political aspirations and demands and shifting problems in the world" (Moore 1995, 8). Further on, Moore explains that creating public value fundamentally means "satisfying the desires of citizens and clients," both for the production of publicly valuable things (clean streets, new recreation areas, low risk of communicable disease) and for the maintenance of "properly ordered and productive public institutions" leading to "a well-ordered society" (53).

More than one hundred years before this intellectual synthesis, Woodrow Wilson observed the dynamic developmental nature of modern democracies. All modern democratic states, Wilson concluded, had the same lineage in the sense of being the product of a transition in the relationship between the state and the individual. This transition reflected a change in the "morals and conscience of government," which led to "new ideas about what constitutes social convenience and advancement." All modern states also shared a general evolutionary ascent toward more mature forms, achieving democratic, and more significantly, liberal-democratic, status only at the most advanced stages of development. Individual democratic regimes matured at different rates, however, depending on the initial conditions and the responses to external pressures and internal stresses. Wilson found that modernity brought with it a pronounced intensification in the complexity and rate of change in social and economic conditions that, in particular, presented new barriers to the aim of individual development and advancement that was now at the center of the state's purposeful existence. Increasing complexity and change in conditions, including problems arising from the interactions among nation-states, generated new demands on liberal democracies to find ways to enable individual development and advancement while preserving the essential autonomy and independent spirit of the individual.

But Wilson also presented a conception of administration as the principal and most frequent point of contact between society and the modern democratic state. The policy-executing and purpose-fulfilling tasks were central to administration's role in a modern, liberal-democratic polity. Wilson further stressed that as part of its executive function—or even beyond it—administration tested the suitability and effectiveness of laws, and tested and monitored public needs and societal conditions. Through its expertise and its experience gained through application of the law to particular cases, administration tried to alter conditions or to make minor adjustments to law and policy on its own in response to new conditions. Equally important, through expertise, experiment, and experience, administration provided guidance to the more extensive responses and adjustments enshrined in statutes and, in the long run, in constitutions. In Wilson's view, none of this could come to fruition except within an integrated system of national administration anchored in the "permanent principles" of popular self-government and individual liberty and presided over by statesmen serving as the binding link between administration and democracy and harnessing administrative power to advance national unity and national purpose.

The linkages and dissimilarities between Wilson's body of ideas and practices and Moore's compendium of current wisdom point toward the main purposes of these final two chapters. First, I aim to show that many of the central tenets of the emphasis on public management and governance that seem to dominate public administration theory and practice now have forebears in Wilsonian ideas and practices. Woodrow Wilson prefigured many of the arguments and insights about administration in the modern American state that advocates of the public management and governance orientations claim as their own. Indeed, I will argue that the current emphasis on public management is, at a minimum, an indirect outgrowth of Wilson's governing actions, particularly his failure to realize in practice central components of his reform enterprise concerning the place and structure of administration in the regime.

Second, I intend to show that the current public management and governance thrust, as rich and valuable as it has become as an analysis of and practical guide for

modern and postmodern American government, has nevertheless failed to acknowledge adequately—and may even be exacerbating—the most serious challenges facing governance in the current age. The central insights Wilson offered about democracy and administration illuminate these challenges. Wilson's insights concern in
particular the formative impact of administrative power and the consequent necessity for a national or regime-level orientation to administrative legitimacy. That is,
the full value of harnessing administrative power can only be realized by situating it
in an integrated structure that is national in scope and tied to long-run national
unity, national purpose, and the deep and permanent principles of the regime
through national political leadership of a peculiar sort. Current public administration and public management theories and practices have yet to understand these
challenges fully or to address them systematically. I present all these arguments in
the current chapter. In the final chapter I build on them by assessing the prospects
for effective systemic and institutional responses to the challenges and by considering the most promising conception of a public administration and administrative
science that can aid in surmounting them.

THE SCHOLARLY DEROGATION OF WILSON'S IDEAS

Two particular efforts at analytical synthesis and appraisal in the public administration field, although published a generation apart, are nevertheless bound together intellectually by their common objective of explicating and addressing a crisis
they claim to have uncovered in the theoretical foundations of American public
administration. They also find common cause in identifying Wilson and his ideas as
the primary—if not the exclusive—source of the crises they illuminate.

The Crisis of Centralized Bureaucratic Hegemony

Vincent Ostrom's analysis, first published in 1973, focused on exposing the incongruity between the conception of administration Woodrow Wilson sought to
introduce, establish, and legitimate and the kind of administrative system that would
naturally follow the characteristics given to the American political regime at the
country's founding. Ostrom argued that Wilson, reflecting the continental sources
on which he relied, sought to establish the legitimacy of a theoretical view that
accepted the existence of a single center of power in the American system. From this
premise followed Wilson's advocacy of the politics-administration dichotomy, one
rule of good administration and one science of administration applicable to all
democratic regimes, and a highly centralized, hierarchically ordered administrative

system. This became the core, Ostrom contended, of what emerged as the dominant orthodoxy in American public administration theory. Although accepting in the second edition of his critique that the formulators of this orthodox administrative theory did not "consciously" follow in Wilson's "footsteps" (Ostrom 1989, 20), Ostrom nonetheless continued to insist that the central trouble with American administrative theory was its reliance on a paradigm of power and governmental structure best represented by Wilson's ideas, which were, again in his analysis, focused on centralized authority and the efficiency of hierarchical ordering. In short, this was bureaucracy in the Weberian ideal type. This paradigm was not only intellectually vulnerable, Ostrom argued; it also produced governance dominated by centralized bureaucracy and the aggrandizement of executive power, a combination that led to serious pathologies. These are the characteristic features of the crisis in public administration theory and practice that Ostrom sought to reveal. (For one illuminating critique of Ostrom's characterization of Wilson through a comparison with Weber's thought, see Cuff 1978.)

To escape the crisis in which American public administration found itself, Ostrom advocated an alternative model, a more "democratic administration" rooted in the theory of the Founders. In place of a "fully integrated structure of command," this alternative model exhibited "substantial dispersion of authority with many different structures of command." It did not sanction any monopoly over the "legitimate means of coercion . . . by a single authority structure." At its core, in other words, democratic administration was polycentric, not monocentric (71). Ostrom further called on "practitioners and students of public administration . . . to rethink both the theory and the practice of their science of administration" by preparing "to advance and serve the interests of the individual persons who form their relevant public," serving them in particular "as users or consumers of public goods and services" rather than serving, as under orthodox theory, "political masters." Ostrom called for "a new theory of democratic administration" not grounded in the ideas of Wilson or his contemporaries and intellectual descendants but in the ideas of Madison and Hamilton, as well as Tocqueville, Dewey, and the progenitors of public choice theory (114).

The students and practitioners of public administration who were the intended target of Ostrom's entreaties seemed to have listened carefully: "The field of public management rejects the politics-administration dichotomy and much of the empirical (structural) focus of the past" (Khademian 2000, 41). And: "The new public management and reinventing government grew . . . more from ad hoc experimentation than from the more coherent philosophy that shaped the Progressive influence" (Kettl 2002, 95). Indeed, proponents of public choice theory, as well as a consumer or customer-service orientation in the New Public Management (NPM), did not just establish an intellectual beachhead; one can fairly say that they conquered the field of study and practice in public administration (for a brief account, see Garvey 1993, 25–35; more generally, see Kettl 2002, ch. 4; Frederickson and Smith 2003, esp. chs. 2–4, 7–8). Much of this intellectual transition was well under way by the time Ostrom published the second edition of his critique. It is thus particularly interesting to find another call of very recent vintage for attention to the continuing crisis of theory and practice in public administration or, to be more precise, the crisis *between* theory and practice.

The Crisis of Theory Disconnected from Reality

In his book *The Transformation of Governance*, Donald Kettl points specifically to the divergence between administrative theory and administrative work, between the structure of government, which remains based primarily on orthodox theory, and the structure of governance, "the way government gets its job done" (Kettl 2002, xi). Although Kettl does not acknowledge this, the latter looks a lot like what Ostrom advocated. Kettl does argue that many of the new ideas shaping how government gets its work done are the result of a widely dispersed, pragmatic, bottom-up process of public managers faced with many social, economic, and political changes and having to find ways to cope with the increasingly complex, even idiosyncratic, demands imposed on them from multiple directions. In terms of Ostrom's argument, the power of action seems widely dispersed and responsive to the problems and demands of citizens as consumers of public goods. This dynamic has actually been global in its scale and reach, and until recently managers and other public officials in several other nations have led the way in innovative, systematic responses, with the United States lagging behind (see more generally Kettl 2000).

Kettl repeatedly presses his point about the mismatch between the orthodox theory of government organization and the structures of actual administrative practice that have proliferated in the past three decades. His real concerns, however, are first, that public administration theory in the United States is failing to keep up with the nature of practice so as to provide helpful guidance to managers and policy makers in dealing with the problems they must confront, and second, that public administration theory has yet to develop responses to the "challenges to democratic accountability" posed by the new structures and methods of governing that have proliferated without theoretical anchors (Kettl 2002, ix).

In contrast to Ostrom, Kettl finds one source of the problems of orthodox public administration theory, and the structure of government that reflects that theory, in the perspectives of the Founders, specifically Jefferson, Hamilton, and Madison. Kettl portrays key ideas from each of these Founders as forming three distinct traditions offering various value emphases and normative arguments about government and governing, and thus public administration. They have intermingled and recombined over the course of the development of American government, politics, and administration. It was only later that a fourth tradition emerged with the Progressives, as epitomized by Woodrow Wilson's ideas. Kettl takes great care in his analysis to show that the problems of existing public administration theory, especially the barriers to its progression beyond its current state of relative helplessness, are rooted in the dilemmas posed by various combinations of all four of the traditions he explicates. Like Ostrom, however, he finds the problematic core of current theory to lie with the Progressive recombination of values and ideas as embodied in Wilson's thinking, and his description and critique of Wilson's ideas are virtually the same as those offered by Ostrom.

Traditional thinking about "government management" views it "as a matter of framing decisions, delegating responsibility to administrators, and holding government administrators accountable for the results" (23). Wilson supplied the method, which was "to concentrate administrative power in hierarchically structured organizations" (29). Thus Wilson's thinking, although "it did not broadly shape the Progressive tradition, . . . certainly captured its most important administrative ideas." Wilson's ideas and the orthodoxy that troubles Kettl are thus one and the same, embodying these central admonitions: "focus on the process and structure of government organizations; explore strategies to make them more efficient; keep them separate from political institutions to ensure their effectiveness; but ultimately hold them accountable to elected officials for their exercise of power" (41).

Unlike Ostrom, Kettl does not call for the complete abandonment of the traditions that have shaped American thinking about public administration and continue to prevent theory from advancing in helpful and essential ways. He finds enduring value in those various traditions, including the focus on hierarchy and centralized authority that he so closely associates with Wilson's ideas. Thus Kettl offers ten principles that "suggest how to build . . . bridges" between existing theory and what managers and policy-makers need so that they can cope with the transformation of governance (168). His principles include fitting hierarchy and authority better to the coordination needs public managers face, adjusting and harnessing hierarchies to manage the increasingly complex intergovernmental and public-private networks that have proliferated as well as shifting from structure to process in the management of networks, thus relying less on authority and more on interpersonal and interorganizational relations.

The representations and explicit or implied critiques of Wilson's thinking Ostrom and Kettl offer generally reflect the treatment of Wilson's ideas in the arena of public administration in the United States for at least two generations, even among those not seeking to discredit Wilson. That treatment, obsessed as it remains with boiling Wilson's thinking down to the politics-administration dichotomy and strict hierarchical ordering, has thus proceeded to dismiss Wilson's ideas as lacking a "strong and consistent empirical warrant" (Frederickson and Smith 2003, 21) and, even worse, a normatively naïve obstacle to fixing accountability for the exercise of discretion (Kettl 2002, 42; but see Lynn 2001 for a critical dissection of the mythic rise of the "bureaucratic paradigm").

Recovering Wilson

Critiques from wise and sophisticated scholars like Ostrom and Kettl are bound to capture many of the important elements in Wilson's thinking. Ostrom was right that Wilson sought an integrated system of political authority and administrative structure. Consistent with some of Ostrom's "basic propositions" in the "Wilsonian paradigm," Wilson did insist that the "more power is divided the more irresponsible it becomes," and he did seek the "perfection," or at least the significant refinement, "of 'good' administration as . . . a necessary condition for modernity in human civilization and for the advancement of human welfare" (Ostrom 1989, 24–25). Neither of these ideas are revolutionary departures from founding ideas, however, as a rereading of *The Federalist* would readily reveal, particularly the essays penned by Alexander Hamilton. I more vigorously question Ostrom's claim that a strict separation between politics and administration along with a "hierarchical ordering of a professionally trained public service" wholly and exclusively defined Wilson's notion of good administration. Similarly, Kettl captures well the general sequence in Wilson's thinking and the forces that led him to a focus on administration in his efforts at system reform (Kettl 2002, 42), especially the centrality of the forces of modernity and of administrative power in precipitating the need for that reform (81). But Wilson did not, at least initially, locate concentrated authority in "the executive," and he did, contrary to Kettl's suggestion, come to the "issue of effective administrative power" with a prime "commitment to *national* power" (43, emphasis in original).

My purpose here is not to debate the finer points of alternative interpretations of Wilson's ideas and practices. It is, instead, to suggest that in narrowly focusing on Wilson's initial enunciation of his thoughts about administration, even some top scholars have missed the richness and variety in Wilson's ideas and actions, which have remarkable parallels to prominent theories and practices today. Scholars, critics, and practitioners have projected what they saw in orthodox theory back onto a reading of Wilson. They presumed that, if what they saw at the center of the theory (which they were finding increasingly wanting) also appeared as recognizable elements in the few samples of Wilson's thinking to which they had easy access, then Wilson must have wanted that particular frame of ideas and practices to come about. This treatment of Wilson is much like the error that Ostrom accused Wilson, and other realists, of committing: "Though purporting to address themselves to reality, the administrative, legal, and political realists allowed themselves . . . to be informed by presuppositions about that reality . . . and make their general assessments of reality with reference to models . . . as ideal types" (1989, 142).

I do not propose to argue that Wilson intended or foresaw the emergence of something like a "new public management" or a vast edifice of networked governance. But Wilson had some thoughts about, and experience with, notable precursors to today's governing realities and prominent ideas. It is foolish for scholars and practicing public managers not to consider the insights that may lie in Wilson's ideas and practices as they confront their own realities and seek to devise new conceptual and practical responses.

WILSON, THE NEW PUBLIC MANAGEMENT, AND THE NEW GOVERNANCE

As a starting point, consider three of the principles Kettl promotes as a way to revamp administrative thinking to match the new practices and the newly complex problems of a post-orthodox age. The first of these, transparency, Kettl characterizes as "the foundation for trust and confidence in government operations" (2002, 169). Second, Kettl also calls for "new strategies and tactics for popular participation in public administration." Third, Kettl points to the need for "new constitutional strategies for the management of conflict," which would not entail fundamental constitutional change but rather "fresh strategies" based on the existing constitutional arrangements (170), although he does not delineate what sorts of strategies he has in mind. I hope that the reader by now can recognize in these principles compatibilities with key elements I have highlighted in Wilson's reform enterprise and framework of ideas about democracy and administration.

Transparency, for instance, was at the heart of Wilson's successive reform proposals aimed at exorcising "hide-and-seek" politics from congressional anterooms by altering the distribution of elective and appointive offices, regulating corporate behavior, or improving the design of statutes. Also, Wilson's idea of an integrated administrative system included a thorough reconception of municipal government aimed precisely at providing a new avenue for popular participation in administration. And finally, conflict, both among sectional and economic interests and between the executive and the legislature across the federal structure of American constitutionalism, was the point of departure for Wilson's recurring call for systemic reform, first by constitutional reconstruction but later by less structural and more strategic means, which would smooth the way for the emergence of strengthened national unity and national power.

Even more forcefully, I believe the evidence justifies arguing that Wilson attempted to offer precisely what Kettl contends is "so essential" to overcoming the gap between existing theory and governing reality, namely "a theory of administration that is a theory of politics, and a theory of politics that is informed by administration" (48–49). Kettl even seems to concede as much when he notes that "at the dawn of the twentieth century . . . public administration underwent a major transformation, driven by the Wilsonian tradition" (153). While I must be careful not to stretch the parallels beyond reason, there is value in considering the situational and conceptual linkages between the ideas and actions of Wilson and the theory and practice of administration today. This, I hope to show, can lead to a greater understanding of the political development of American public administration and to insights that may bear on the challenges to the theory and practice of democratic governance, challenges with which scholars and practicing public administrators, citizens and their elected representatives, continue to struggle.

Comparable Conditions

Across such areas as the dominant social values; the relations among generations; the size, growth rate, and ethnic and racial composition of the population; the available information and communications technologies; the scope and velocity of commerce and trade; and the knowledge, skill, and technical capacities of public administrators at all levels of government, there are vast differences between the era in which Woodrow Wilson sought to change the way the United States was governed and the current era, with its own multiplicitous efforts to foment transformations in governance. The two eras do, however, have their similarities, ranging across the social, economic, and political conditions impinging on government and spurring reform efforts, the aims of the reform efforts, the content of the prominent ideas promoted and subject to recurrent tinkering, and the practices employed and tested (and replicated and discarded). With respect to Wilson's era and his ideas and practices, there are several distinct parallels with the current era of agitation for change in governance.

Every generation, it seems, comes to see itself as living in the most complex, confounding, and challenging of times. There must be some truth to this, at least in terms of the increases in the sheer numbers of people alive at a given time, and thus the increasing challenges emanating from more people living with and relating to one another within a fixed space and with relatively inelastic resource boundaries. But does that make the governing problems any greater? In denouncing apologies for Congress's failure to design statutes with "legal integrity," apologies that rest on claims about how much more complex the modern legislator's job is, Theodore Lowi has argued, "In fact, to the state legislators of the 1840s, society must have seemed immeasurably more complex than ours seems today. They were, after all, living in the midst of the Industrial Revolution; there was not yet any established economic theory of capitalism, no clear grasp of fractional reserve banking or insurance. . . . Meanwhile, there was less continuity among legislators and less education. They had fewer staff members and a smaller budget with which to buy expertise and research" (Lowi 1993b, 167; see, more fully, Lowi 1991, 10–12).

I would not venture to argue that the conditions of Wilson's time were more complex or difficult than conditions prevailing today, but there are a number of striking similarities. The dawn of the twentieth century brought with it the emergence and consolidation of new, large, and powerful economic entities promising great economic benefits but also seeming to threaten social stability and the balance of governing forces. Interconnections and relations between nations were expanding significantly in commercial, social, and political terms, especially for the United States. Several waves of human migration were washing across the globe and onto American shores. The old ruling edifice in Europe was crumbling, and new ideas about governance, very menacing to some, seemed ascendant. New technologies for communications and for obtaining information with increasing rapidity emerged in succession, first the telegraph, then the telephone, and eventually the first version of wireless transmission of text, voice, and music. Within the United States, the pressures of increasing immigration, urbanization, industrialization, and the opportunities and risks involved in creating wealth generated increasing uncertainty for both citizens and public officials about the stability of society, the resources available to attend to societal problems, and the prospects for improved economic conditions. Amidst all this, there was also growing dissatisfaction with government, the appropriateness of its structural arrangements and modes of operation, and the extent of its capacity to cope with the burgeoning changes in social, economic, and political life.

There were also many new and sometimes competing ideas about what to do per-colating up from scholarly *and* popular sources and circulating widely. And it is especially important to note that the progressive theoretical consolidation and even-tual ascendance in support of an administrative state did not firmly take root until after Wilson's presidency. Indeed, Wilson pointedly warned against establishing a science of politics based on a natural science orthodoxy and a science of administra-tion based on the authority of expertise.

Conceptual and Practical Antecedents

Beyond the comparabilities in conditions, one can quite effectively argue, as Don Kettl has, that in general the Progressives were engaged in a theoretical and practical reform effort very much like that of the public management and network governance proponents of today (for a similar tack, see Stivers 1998, esp. 269–70). There are, however, several quite distinct similarities between what Wilson specifically tried to do and the efforts of the current generation of practitioner and scholarly reformers generally associated with the focus on public management.

There was, for example, a strong comparative and international orientation to Wilson's endeavor and a recognition that one could, and should, borrow ideas and practices developed in other nations. The NPM movement has had that same orien-tation from the very beginning, tied in part to what has come to be called "globaliza-tion" (Kettl 2002, 93–96, 130–38). Wilson encouraged a search for the commonal-ities in administrative structures and practices to find the universally applicable technologies and approaches. Similarly, NPM proponents have focused on a com-mon set of problems—overcoming the rigidities of orthodox structures and manage-ment philosophies—and have promoted a common stable of reform approaches centered on such devices as flattened hierarchies, internal government markets, and a variety of incentive arrangements. An important dimension of this parallel is the heavy emphasis on learning from private business, under the presumption that business is better at devising means to satisfy core administrative values such as efficiency.

Yet Wilson not only acknowledged but also emphasized that even modern states that were the same by virtue of being democratic differed in fundamental ways relating to the peculiarities of their historical development and key political values, to which commonly accepted structures and practices had to be adapted. There appears to be general acceptance in NPM circles of the need to adapt the new tools and techniques to the peculiarities of a given regime, although there has been plenty of criticism of its failure to do so adequately (e.g., Frederickson and Smith 2003, 109–

14; Hood and Jackson 1991; Mazouz and Tremblay 2006), leading one to suspect that the new "gospel of efficiency" (see Hays 1959), grounded as it is in ideology (see below), has become as dogmatic as the previous governance and management doctrine it has sought to supplant (see Lynn 2001, 155).

In his search for a science of administration, Wilson downplayed the importance of theory and stressed the value of experiment and experience in developing and refining structures and practices, adapting them to the peculiarities of a given regime. In the past two or three decades, public managers in the United States and many other advanced industrial nations have faced new problems and demands, have had to experiment with new techniques, and have had to refine their existing approaches, sometimes through trial and error. Kettl laments this because the lack of academic theory to guide public managers left them with no "intellectual or moral support" (2002, 21). This portrayal is somewhat misleading, because as Kettl himself and other scholars have shown, the new reformers were particularly influenced by theory—not established public administration theory but the emergence of public choice (Kettl 2002, 85–96; Frederickson and Smith, ch. 8).

To the extent that experiment and experience have driven the current ferment in theory and practice as well as the development of new theory, Wilson would have found reason to applaud the new developments. It is inescapably clear, however, that the "global public management revolution" (Kettl 2000) has been driven by the revolution in political philosophy, especially neo-liberalism, that preceded it. Or, to be more precise, neo-liberalism created the political conditions—downsizing, devolution, shrinking budgets—to which pragmatic public managers had to respond. And they were encouraged to draw from a generic toolbox grounded in public choice theory and its ingrained ideology (see Terry 1998, 1999). To the extent that it has been theory and ideology shaping the new structures and practices relatively unleavened by experiment and experience, Wilson may have been more reluctant to embrace them even as he welcomed continued efforts to develop the science of administration, especially through comparative analysis and the diffusion of innovation in the form of ideas hardened through practical application and tied to the actual lives, and problems, of citizens.

Wilson's orientation was also comprehensive, however. He sought a new science of politics as well as a new science of administration, and his focus on modern conditions and administrative power was not the end but the impetus for a systemic reconception and reconstruction of government and governance. Wilson's aim in all this was to harness administrative power to sustain, and improve, modern democratic government—to make it more capable, more democratic. The push for a more comprehensive framework of theory informed by practice has similarly become evident in some of the most recent work in public management scholarship, especially the work pushing a refocusing on governance (e.g., Lynn 1996; Lynn et al. 2001; Frederickson and Smith 2003, ch. 9). The New Public Management is essentially about the development of new tools of modern public management, then, while the thrust in the direction of governance concerns the deployment of those tools in a context linking results to public purposes. Yet proponents of thinking about governance rarely identify what those purposes might be. There are some references, mostly in passing, to the core aspirations of a democratic polity—"to both respect individual rights and promote collective justice" (Heinrich, Hill, and Lynn 2004, 17)—but there seems to be very little in the way of systematic discussion of what all this theoretical development, even the extensive experiment and fashioning of new structures and techniques of practice, is for—what purposes it is intended to serve— other than the immediate demands to do more with the same or fewer resources. This hardly sounds much different, again, than the obsession with efficiency for which the orthodox public administrationists stand accused (see Lynn 2001, 154–55).

Wilson's Comprehensive, Forward-Looking Ideas and Practices

What I find most surprising, however, are the specific links between a number of the currently predominant approaches and Wilson's ideas that current scholars, and their students engaging in practice, have simply failed to notice. For example, Wilson did not try to "break through" bureaucracy (Barzelay 1992), but he certainly saw his effort, both in conception and in practice, as trying to fend it off. Of course, Wilson had a somewhat broader understanding of bureaucracy than the structural imperatives of the Weberian ideal type. Many of these structural features—hierarchy and chain of command, division of labor, professionalism and expertise, and the blocking of partisan interference with administrative work—Wilson regarded as "good" business practices to be commonly, if not universally, applied. But in his view, the structures and practices, and those who occupied and used them, had to be set in a context informed by the prevailing values of a given political regime. Bureaucracy, for Wilson, was the absence of regime values in administrative structure and practice such that the structures and practices became the end, with administrators cut off from liberal-democratic aspirations; bureaucrats, with their professional worldview and expertise would come to assume they knew what was best for citizens and would then seek to care for them on that basis. Bureaucracy thus was an approach to governance—a way of political life or even a state of political existence—

that was tutelary and oppressive—"unfree" in a most insidious sense. (This is precisely the future state of democracy that Ostrom accuses Wilson of promoting, against the warnings of Tocqueville; see Ostrom 1989, 84–85.)

Wilson simply was not doctrinaire about the features of structure and operations —not in theory, and certainly not in practice. Although he expected that his department heads would employ the "best practices" of good public business, Wilson did not saddle them with any demands for the use of particular structures or methods. In the especially dire circumstances of the war, he essentially encouraged managerial experiment by leaving it up to the heads of the special agencies how they would order their tasks. This allowed the likes of Herbert Hoover to pursue his anti-bureaucracy, anti-hierarchy, open, "professional" approach to organizing and managing the Food Administration. Indeed, Wilson's own management of the varied organizations created to marshal the home front and prosecute the war did not reflect at all a rigid hierarchical ordering of relationships with these agencies or a strict separation of policy and administration. Wilson not only accepted that these administrators were making policy decisions, but he also allowed those decisions to shape to some extent what was by necessity continuously evolving national policy.

Certainly Wilson also sought an administrative system grounded in concentrated political authority and national in scope, both horizontally and vertically. This would seem to imply an absence of structural flexibility and absence of responsiveness to localized variations in conditions and citizen views. This is precisely the opposite of what Wilson envisioned, however. The integration of the system was meant to align local variations and a diversity of views and interests with the imperatives of national unity, national power, and national purpose. The policy and administrative judgments of national officials were not to supplant local decisions but to guide them as a way to move toward the organic wholeness that was the true measure of the health of the state. Concentration of political authority aimed to focus political responsibility on those whose job it was to link policy and administration and who were most directly connected to citizen scrutiny and control, as well as to opinion and public judgment, through elective office. Thus conceptually it seems unlikely that Wilson would have been an unbending opponent of such notions as devolution, performance management, or accountability for results. He would, however, have asked how such notions served the overall health of the body politic, and whether accountability was fixed where it most belonged. He would have sought to expose instances in which those who most declaimed allegiance to the will of the people found ways to elude responsibility for policy outcomes by deflecting it through devolution or other mechanisms onto policy implementers, demanding that transparency and accountability be placed on those principally responsible for policy design.

In practice as well as in conception, then, Wilson seems to have pursued matters of public administration and management in ways not wholly unlike some of the prominent efforts promoted today. Kettl's analysis, based on his identification of four administrative traditions, in fact points to a number of today's conceptual and practical currents—principal-agent theory, the new public management, and reinventing government—as reflecting the synthesis of the "Wilsonian tradition" with Hamiltonian and Jeffersonian views (Kettl 2002, 80–98, 108–10, 116). Again, however, Wilson did not insist, especially in practice, on adherence to any particular administrative doctrine that required synthesis with other "traditions" to make it more pliable. By predilection and necessity he encouraged experiment with new administrative forms and approaches. As I have already noted, Wilson gave agency executives and managers wide latitude to structure and operate their organizations. This provided them with at least the potential to pursue both programmatic and managerial innovations, which a number of them did. He also sought policy designs and organizational structures that fixed personal responsibility for outcomes (although it is unclear to what extent Wilson actually held his administrators and managers to account for programmatic failures or lapses in managerial judgment). Both of these practices seem very much in line with the sorts of changes in public management structures and methods proponents of more entrepreneurship in the public sector have had in mind. But beyond these general predilections, Wilson laid the groundwork for at least two specific characteristics of administration and management largely associated with the much more recently identified "transformation in governance."

Kettl argues that in "the last third of the twentieth century, . . . government began relying on new tools, especially grants, contracts, and loans, which undermined Wilson's theory." Yet it was by Wilson's initiative, or at least his acquiescence, and certainly during his watch, that such "new tools" gained a permanent foothold in federal policy, thereafter to grow pervasively throughout the American system of federalism. As I have already shown, one can detect both consistencies and inconsistencies between Wilson's ideas and his practices in the establishment, development, and remarkable expansion in the use of intergovernmental and public-private fiscal instruments. But this merely reinforces the point that Wilson's "theory" of administration, if it can be called that, was wider in scope and more multifaceted than suggested by the stress on hierarchy and the notion that he could only envision or accept "direct delivery of services by government bureaucracies" (51).

The more striking of the two characteristics is the least noted and analyzed aspect of Wilson's administrative ideas and practices, but it provides perhaps the firmest linkage between the governance and public management present and the Wilsonian past. "In the last decades of the twentieth century," Kettl has noted, "[m]ore of what government—especially the federal government—did no longer fit the hierarchical model of authority-driven government." Hence, "government needed close and active partnerships with nongovernmental partners to accomplish its purposes" (2002, 24). Faced with an international conflict that was becoming global in scope and effect—and thus also faced with the need to mobilize the nation's industrial, transportation, and human resources—Wilson was driven by expediency toward a complex of public-private interconnections in order to get the job done. The expediency was necessitated by the absence of a well-established, well-resourced, and experienced public administrative apparatus. The current fiscal and human resource strains on public administration—particularly the continuing "brain drain" and loss of experienced managers—offer a remarkable parallel. As I have already noted, Wilson was also determined, despite the dire circumstances, not to allow the elements of a European-style statist bureaucracy to take root. The result was considerable administrative chaos and managerial stumbling. Yet Wilson's wide-ranging "adhocracy" included not only substantial government regulation and outright government control but also extensive private management of public functions, especially in the coordination of resources. In short, Wilson's management of the war effort epitomized the manifestation of "fuzzy boundaries" between public and private that Kettl finds so ubiquitous in the environment of governance today (2002, 59–76).

Wilson's governance during the war and its parallels with the governing conditions and burgeoning structures and practices so evident today reinforces the insights in Wilson's conception of administration's place, function, and role in a democratic political regime. Wilson certainly did hold that there were certain functions that belonged exclusively to the government and the democratic state (on "inherently governmental functions," see Guttman 2004). At a minimum, these were his "constituent functions." But the more important question for him from a governing—that is, a policy and administration—point of view was where the line between "*Interference* and *Laissez faire*" lay. Wilson viewed administration as arrayed all along that line, engaged in probing that line continuously by applying the law to particular cases, using its expertise and experience to make minor choices about shifting the line, and communicating with and guiding policymakers—legislators specifically—about the need to reestablish the line more clearly through statute. The larger reality from Wilson's standpoint, however, is that the line-drawing enterprise is highly contingent and developmental in the sense of being connected to the continuing advancement of the liberal-democratic state. It is also a progressive enterprise in the conservative sense, as Wilson understood the term. It concerns making adjustments to changing conditions and societal developments and thus finding successive approximations of the proper balance between interference and laissez-faire according to prevailing conditions, public thought, and "deep and permanent principles." Thanks to a peculiar scholarly counter-orthodoxy, the current generation of public management scholars and practitioners have had to rediscover for themselves the conceptual and practical insights in this regard that Wilson had already realized. One challenge for current theory and practice is to see if a reconsideration of Wilson's thinking can yield refinements to those newly rediscovered insights about the fuzzy boundaries between public and private, between state and society.

THE DEVELOPMENTAL LEGACY OF
WILSON'S GOVERNING PRACTICES

The parallels and similarities in conditions, ideas, and practical initiatives associated with public administration and management between Wilson's era and the present is a heretofore hidden legacy that can be uncovered. To date, understanding and assessing American public administration and management in World War I has been the almost exclusive province of historians. It would behoove public administration and management scholars and practitioners with a particularly strong sense of history to examine anew Wilson's war management for whatever lessons may be drawn that are relevant for coping with a governing reality characterized by increasing fuzziness in public work. The point would not be to explain further how Wilson's efforts prefigured the developmental path that followed, although that would be valuable in its own right. The focus, instead, should be on understanding how members of the Wilson administration understood the administrative and managerial problems they faced, what questions they asked, how they conceived of the responses they chose, and what the experiential results were. As I have argued elsewhere (Cook 1998, 229), this could be part of a larger endeavor to mine prominent cases of innovative institutional and organizational design and managerial practice—successes and failures alike—in the political development of the United States and other liberal democracies for insights that might enrich current theory and practice.

The much more significant legacy of Woodrow Wilson's ideas and practices, however, is the strong linkage that can be traced from his decisions and actions as president to the effects they had on developments in governing and then to the emergence of a public management orientation in theory and practice. The latter follows the former such that the current prominence of a public management focus and the rise of a new, or renewed, focus on governance in public administration theory and practice are the inevitable outcome of Woodrow Wilson's ideas and actions, particularly his choices in conception and practice, to concentrate the political authority over administration, and the responsibility for interpreting public opinion to guide that political authority, almost wholly within the presidency.

In shifting the locus of leadership in his scheme from a cabinet of public executives and responsible ministers to the president and in defining presidential leadership primarily in rhetorical terms, Wilson disconnected the interpretive leadership component of his reform design from the other key interlocking elements. In his original conception, interpretive statesmen were to be both legislators and executives, and they were to have intimate knowledge of, direct involvement in, and responsibility for policy designs, administrative plans, and their successful execution. Policy both more clearly and more definitely designed, and thus more effectively executed, was to be the result. It was also this package of interconnected elements that was to provide the systemic or global legitimacy for the "large powers and unhampered discretion" that administrators were to exercise and for the purpose-creating actions that were inevitably to follow. Wilson in fact envisioned the package of elements as essential to anchoring the way in which a modern, national democracy could take advantage of the purpose-refining feature of administrative power.

By redefining as exclusively a task of presidential rhetoric and public opinion interpretation the pursuit of national unity, power, and purpose that he thought so vital to the continued progression of the American democratic state and by reinforcing this redefinition through his own governing practice, Wilson clearly thought that he could better sustain the drive for national unity by placing its facilitation in the hands of one central administrator-legislator and interpretive leader. By also decoupling almost completely the presidency from the executive dimension of administration, Wilson set in motion the severing of administrative structure and the work of public administrators, at all levels in the national system but especially at the national level, from the integrated regime development enterprise aimed at unified national progress. As I noted in my general critique of Wilson's practices at the conclusion of chapter 6, this left a vacuum of responsible political leadership for administration that would properly constrain its introduction of new methods and structures, providing a more secure regime-level legitimacy. Several further consequences bearing on both the conception and practice of American national governance, and public management in particular, are evident.

First, the heads of major administrative departments—those individuals who, operating within a cabinet, Wilson originally envisioned as being responsible for the political concentration and administrative integration across the American federal system—became completely dependent on, personally identified with, and exclusively responsible to the president. This dependency cannot solely be placed on

Wilson's doorstep, of course. Despite direct grants of programmatic authority in statutes, because of both basic constitutional structure and a long train of political and legal precedent, heads of departments depend on the president for most of the real power they enjoy. Yet Wilson's reconception of the locus of interpretive leadership and his reinforcing practice further ensured that administrators at the apex of the American system would define their public responsibilities almost wholly in terms of allegiance to the president's program and not in terms of fidelity to their own interpretations of public opinion and judgments about what might best serve power and purpose in the polity.

Some presidents have been receptive to independent thought and action and even respectful dissent on the part of their department heads. Yet it is remarkable how much department heads censor their own public rhetoric and restrict the sphere of their actions in order to signal conformity with a conception of their public responsibilities that places devotion to a president and his program on an equal plane with, say, fidelity to the law. It is nearly impossible to detect among the nation's premier administrators any sense of individual or collective responsibility for improving the integration of policy planning and execution and for encouraging good management within the federal government and certainly not for the American system of government in its entirety. The intent behind the creation of the Bureau of the Budget—but more importantly its move into the Executive Office of the President and its later rechristening as the Office of Management and Budget—was to provide some general focus on policy coordination and management improvement. But the existence of this organization merely reinforces the point. It is separated from those top officials actually responsible for policy management, and it focuses primarily on fidelity to a president's program through the budget process (see Wamsley 2004, 213–19).

A second consequence of Wilson's failure in conception and practice has been to undermine the central pillar of his reform aims: the development of a secure institutional home for the cultivation of national leadership. Recall that Wilson sought congressional reform precisely because the organization and operation of Congress under the distorting influence of the separation of powers did not lend itself to cultivating national leaders. The establishment of the cabinet as the institutional bridge between policy planning and execution would create incentives for men to come to the fore who possessed talents and energies different than those that dominated Congress, particularly rhetoric and parliamentary debating skills, especially with respect to scrutiny of policy design and administrative effectiveness and the nurturing of a public attentive to these concerns. In shifting the institutional correlate for his conception of leadership from Congress to the presidency, thus defining national political leadership almost exclusively in terms of presidential leadership, Wilson contributed substantially to the absence of an institutional proving ground for democratic statesmanship. If, as I have argued, Wilson did indeed envision the president as overseeing both the legislative and administrative processes and binding them together through interpretation of public opinion, then short of the presidency itself, there could be no other public institution where men and women could develop their talents and capacities to fill the role. Wilson further ensured this, in his thought and action, by relegating the cabinet to a purely executive role.

The third and perhaps most worrisome consequence of Wilson's reconception of the locus of political leadership and his governing practices that conformed to that reconception is the normatively, conceptually, nearly entirely complete dependency of public administration as an institution on the president for its general system legitimacy and the specific legitimacy of its formative impact on law and policy. In cementing the disconnection between the tasks of interpretive leadership and administrative integration and in setting the precedent of promoting a program as the prime presidential role for most of his successors, Wilson abandoned the establishment of the systemic or global legitimacy for the purpose-creating aspects of administration that was the prime insight and intellectual innovation of his academic years. Wilson, and some of the presidents who followed him, have sought to instruct public thinking about the legitimacy of administration and the work of public agencies and agency leaders (for a thought-provoking example from the New Deal, see Eden 1989, 55–61). Most, if not all, such efforts have attempted to secure administrative legitimacy by linking it to a presidential program, however.

In the absence of an effort by presidents or top administrator-politicians with an independent sense of political responsibility to legitimate administration by implicating it in the general progressive development of the regime, the trend already under way in Wilson's time became much more deeply rooted. The administrative system has thus remained fragmented, with individual agencies forced to develop independent bases of power and a parochial or, more accurately, a *programmatic* legitimacy based on reputation and a political support network anchored in both group interests and professional specializations (Carpenter 2001, 14–15, 30–33). Franklin Roosevelt, the Wilson protégé even more politically successful than Wilson himself, further reinforced the particularistic legitimacy of administration by bringing many more groups into political engagement and tying them to administrative agencies, all under the umbrella of presidential programmatic aims (again, see Eden 1989; also Milkis 1993).

In hindsight, one can see that the current public management orientation toward public administration theory and practice emerged as an obvious and essential extension of this continued fragmentation in the endeavor to legitimate modern administrative power that emerged in the wake of Wilson's failure to achieve more of his original vision of reform in the political-administrative system. Although it includes considerable emphasis on the identification and development of universally applicable tools, techniques, and organizational structures and incentives, the current public management approach retains a notable agency-specific focus, stressing the development of organizational leadership strategies, organizational structures and practices, and methods for delivering results to establish a public organization's reputation for efficacy in meeting its goals and mission. This in turn sustains an agency's special legitimacy, protecting its political autonomy and organizational integrity (see esp. Heymann 1987; Moore 1995).

Out of the recognition that agencies do not operate in isolation, but rather in elaborate, embedded networks of connections among elected officials, executives, managers, front-line workers, contractors, clients, and organized interests, there has emerged a perspective on public administration and management that scholars have come to call *governance*. This development has to date been almost wholly descriptive and analytical, aimed at understanding the newly central dynamics of public administration and management. The effort does exhibit a prescriptive strain, however, mainly with an eye on developing theory that will guide the work of public executives and managers, thus helping to "explain and address the rapidly changing relationship between state and society" (Frederickson and Smith 2003, 225). In other words, the new patterns of administration—governance, if you will—require advances in the science of administration, in both explanatory and prescriptive theory, so that practicing public administrators can understand the working milieu in which they find themselves and have at the ready strategies that will allow them to cope and to succeed. Success, again, primarily means meeting programmatic objectives—realizing desired policy outcomes—and doing so with greater efficiency.

From a historical perspective, the focus on networks and governance may be revealing further advances in the development of the American democratic state, in which "state bureaucracies" are reconnecting "with the very civic organizations and social networks in which they once flourished" (Carpenter 2001, 367). Or perhaps it is more accurate to say that *new* civic organizations and social networks have emerged with the participation, and even the principal impetus, of public agencies and entrepreneurial public managers (O'Toole 2000; Schneider et al. 2003). A fragmented, dispersed, networked system of governance in which power and authority are decentralized and in some cases are not even in the hands of formal governmental actors and in which the purpose of network activity is determined by "professional concepts of the public interest and an obligation among public servants to represent an inchoate public outside of a particular jurisdiction" (Frederickson and Smith 2003, 224) does, however, raise all sorts of troubling normative questions. Such questions reflect concerns about the costs and resource demands generated by the imperatives for coordination, about the responsiveness of the system to democratic control, and thus about the locus of responsibility and accountability—and, ultimately, legitimacy. It is encouraging to hear that public managers may be thinking in terms of a public interest that is not bound by jurisdiction or group orientation. But are American citizens then simply to trust that "professional concepts of the public interest and an obligation among public servants to represent an inchoate public outside of a particular jurisdiction" will adequately serve their foundational and long-run aspirations as a polity? If so, then what role do a national legislature, elected executive, and judiciary have in this new age of decentralized, networked, public-private governance?

If networks of professional managers and private contractors, organized interests and clientele, do not fully express or serve the collective, liberal-democratic aspirations of the American people, that is, their aspirations as a *nation,* then questions of political responsibility and accountability, political legitimacy, and thus political leadership remain fundamentally relevant to matters of governance, and those questions pose a serious challenge to the new scholarship and the new practice in public management. The problem of national political leadership, more than any other dimension, was at the very heart of Woodrow Wilson's reform enterprise. It was Wilson's aim to encourage, and even to accelerate, what he saw in his time as the emerging tendency of his fellow citizens to think nationally and thus to aid the American political regime in overcoming the interest- and section-based divisions and fragmentation that had prevented the United States from reaching what Wilson regarded as the highest stage of development for a democratic state—his "constitutional state." Without this full transformation in public thought, the new and reformed administration and management needed to cope with modernity would be impossible to realize, or at best it would prove to be very weak. Wilson believed that a new kind of statesmanship was necessary to guide the completion of the nationalization of the polity and the establishment of a strong, legitimate national administration. Through a combination of some of his developed ideas and actions in practice, however, Wilson did not fully achieve the reforms and transformations vital to his aim of a more democratic regime that was more capable of coping with modernity.

Certainly in significant respects the United States is much more unified internally and powerful internationally than when Wilson took office. The concentration of interpretive leadership and political responsibility in the presidency has served the nation well in many ways, through Wilson himself and several of his successors. Yet

Wilson could not prevent, and in significant respects he augmented, ongoing internal division, fragmentation, and atomization, which have left national power bereft of unified purpose. Public managers are in many respects the principal heirs to this legacy. Their orientation to leadership, legitimacy, and purpose perfectly reflects, however, the fragmented, divided, "niche-ified" character of American public life overlaid with its superficial veneer of unity. If American citizens agree that the great work of public executives and managers must be connected to Norton Long's idea of power and purpose in the polity, then some restoration or reconception of national political leadership tied to the responsible administration of the nation's affairs is imperative. This is even more forcefully so in the light, again, of Wilson's most profound insight: the formative, purpose-shaping, constitutive qualities of public administration. It is only by understanding and properly placing and legitimating this dimension of administration, Wilson realized, that a modern liberal democracy can gain the full benefits of modern administrative power. To close out the book, I now turn to an exploration of some of the possibilities for meeting this imperative and highlighting the value of Wilson's ideas in the further development of public administration and public management theory and practice.

CHAPTER EIGHT

Public Management, Representative Government, and the Continuation of Wilson's Quest

My reference at the conclusion of the previous chapter to "the full benefits of modern administrative power" may strike many readers as particularly odd. Can it be that innovations in administration and management, especially with respect to organizational designs, managerial practices, and information technologies, are not finding their way into the public realm to make American government more competent and to serve American citizens more effectively? The answer must surely be "no." To the extent that a gap exists between the ideas, tools, and techniques of management and administration that are available to be exploited and those that are actually deployed in public organizations, it is much narrower today than it was in previous generations. Because of the heightened emphasis on improving public management, new practices and new technologies find their way into public organizations with considerable speed and success, the occasional well-documented glitch notwithstanding. The full benefits of the modern power of administration go beyond continuous improvements in public managerial competence, however. As Wilson argued, the benefits also concern contributions to the improved health and resilience of American democracy itself, especially the core institutions of the political regime, and to the continued refinement of the long-run aspirations of Americans as a national polity. To secure these ultimate benefits requires a complex interplay between the emergence of integrating, legitimating political leadership and the extension of theory and practice in public administration beyond the managerial to the political. That is, it requires thinking constitutionally about public management.

In this final chapter, I explore the possibilities for establishing the institutional home of the sort of statesmanship Wilson envisioned. Again, this was a statesmanship that would integrate modern administration fully into the modern liberal-democratic state and secure the legitimacy, and full benefits, of modern administrative power. I reject the cabinet, the presidency, and pubic administration itself as likely sources and settings for the emergence of this distinctive political leadership, although this analysis does yield some suggestions for new, or renewed, focal points for scholarship and political practice. Despite the seemingly overwhelming contradictory evidence, I turn to the most obvious alternative institutional home for Wilson's integrating statesmanship: the legislature. I consider the requisite changes in conceptions of Congress as a representative institution necessary to make it hospitable to the cultivation of such leadership. It is here that public management theory and practice can make its signal contribution. Notwithstanding the great and impressive work now under way to transform the study and practice of public administration and management into something approximating an advanced science of democratic governance, I suggest that if such an enterprise is to realize the aspirations for securing it firmly to American liberal democracy, the architects must broaden the range of their analysis. Albeit in only a very preliminary manner, I try to show them how.

LEADERSHIP POSSIBILITIES:
PRESIDENTS, CABINETS, OR PUBLIC MANAGERS

Statesmanship that recognizes the centrality of administrative power in the governance of a modern, mature liberal democracy, that seeks to bind policy design and its execution more closely together, and that consequently furnishes the legitimacy for administration's inevitable influence on policy designs and public purposes—such statesmanship is rather difficult to find or cultivate in American politics. The obvious source remains the presidency. There are serious constraints on the presidency in this regard, however. Hence I consider first the possibilities of resurrecting something akin to Wilson's idea of cabinet government, and, after assessing the presidency's potential, I examine the possibility that this peculiar kind of statesmanship might best be found among public administrators themselves.

Prospects for Cabinet Government

Nearly a half-century after its publication, Richard Fenno's *The President's Cabinet* (1959) remains a valuable and enlightening study of the political role and governing potential of the cabinet. Although its coverage extends only through the Eisenhower administration, it is still rich in detail about varying presidential relations with and treatment of the cabinet and broad in perspective on the context of the cabinet's prospects as a governing body, given the distinctive character of American national politics. Fenno's principal findings remain remarkably trenchant.

Fenno's primary findings centered on the two main forces that have kept the cabinet from becoming cohesive enough to constitute a viable, independent political actor. The first force is the cabinet's complete dependence on the president. Most cabinet department heads individually have the executive authority granted to them by Congress through statutes. As a collective body, however, the cabinet is completely dependent for any role it may have in policy-making or administration on the authority solely vested in the president by the Constitution, statutes, and American political traditions. The second force is what Fenno calls "departmentalism." It is the centrifugal energy grounded in American pluralism that pulls cabinet secretaries toward the particular interests and concerns of the departments they oversee and the networks of career professionals, interest groups, and congressional supporters in which the departments are embedded. Departmentalism thus tends to pull cabinet department heads away from any sense of commitment to the cabinet as a collective entity with collective political responsibility.

Although the two forces work to undermine any significant role or potential for the cabinet as a distinct and influential political actor, they also work at cross-purposes to one another. The cabinet's dependence on the president means that a president might work to make the cabinet a collective decision-making body, especially with respect to tighter linkages between the legislative and executive components of government. Yet, Fenno observed, any such presidential efforts must push against the force of departmentalism: "The President cannot shape the Cabinet completely in his own image in spite of the basic power-responsibility relationship." Fenno also concluded that "considering the impact of departmentalism, it may be as great a cause for wonderment that Presidents use the Cabinet as much as they do, as it is that they use it so seldom" (Fenno 1959, 141). Hence, Fenno found that, depending on their individual skills and predilections, presidents can make the cabinet useful as a collective entity, at least in a limited way. From Fenno's careful and revealing analysis onward, Dwight Eisenhower's organization and management of his presidency and his use of his cabinet in a collective planning and decision-making fashion, has remained the model for this important but limited potential. Ronald Reagan's selection, organization, and use of his cabinet tends to stand as a more current example (see, for instance, Campbell 1986, 35–37, 54–55). But even Eisenhower and Reagan were severely constrained in their efforts by departmentalism (for a particularly lucid and concise treatment, see Pfiffner 2005, 120–26).

Jeffrey Cohen (1988) concluded that one might best understand the cabinet as a distinctively representative institution in the executive branch, which is otherwise heavily action-oriented. Although one may discern a representative dimension to Woodrow Wilson's conception of the cabinet, his idea of cabinet government rested squarely on the cabinet acting as a policy-making body and as bearer of political responsibility in the national government. And Fenno was particularly harsh in his judgment of Wilson's reform ideas and efforts for the cabinet in this regard as he was of the other designs for cabinet government that followed, whether far-reaching or modest. Fenno argued that Wilson was confused about his aims for the cabinet. As a result, Wilson missed the "paradox of his radical reformist position," namely that because the status of the cabinet was so derivative of the power, authority, and responsibility vested in the president by the Constitution and the American political system, the cabinet itself could never be the vehicle to bring about cabinet government. Fenno also concluded that Wilson "underestimated the potentialities of the Presidency and hence tended to overestimate the relative importance of the Cabinet as a potentially autonomous force in American politics" (Fenno 1959, 252). Thus, "Wilson's Cabinet Government was a halfway house which rested on his own misconceptions of the strength of the presidential pull on the Cabinet and of the nature of the centrifugal forces in the political system which tend to debilitate it as an institution" (253–54).

In defense of Wilson, one might argue that Fenno's critique was insufficiently sensitive to historical context. The political dynamics of the presidency, especially with respect to president-cabinet relations, were in flux when Wilson took up his cause. The centrality of the president in the system that underlies Fenno's finding of the power-responsibility relationship between president and cabinet, although it may have been latent in the constitutional design of the presidency, was only becoming manifest—and legitimate—as Wilson was moving away from his more "radical" cabinet government ideas. Indeed, it is quite reasonable to argue that Wilson's ideas and actions contributed directly to the emergence and legitimation of the president-cabinet dynamic that Fenno claims Wilson misunderstood.

Fenno was, however, equally dismissive of several subsequent efforts to reform American national government centered on the cabinet and the bridging of the separation of powers from scholars who should have been fully versed in the nature of the modern presidency. He concluded that modest advances in coordination and integration of legislation and administration achievable through the cabinet as a collective entity could be realized under current institutional arrangements and the talents and aims of individual presidents. This potential obviated the need for more far-reaching structural changes, such as members of the cabinet holding seats or at least debate privileges in Congress. In a more current and thorough review of the ideas Fenno examined along with a spate of both modestly new and retreaded reform proposals, James Sundquist reached much the same conclusion. Although far more open to considering cabinet government–like ideas, Sundquist noted that when "the two branches are disposed to cooperate, formal arrangements are not needed. But when they are not so disposed, any formal requirement for collaboration is likely to be ignored or negated" (1992, 241). Sundquist further pointed out that when "the political mood calls for collaborative effort, information flows freely between the branches. . . . Even when relations between a president and congressional majorities of his own party become strained . . . , harmonious collaboration will continue in many areas of governmental activity, and nothing in the institutional structure stands in the way" (242). Sundquist also stressed that executive branch officials already hold a privileged position with respect to access to Congress and influence over its deliberations despite the complete lack of formal standing within the institution.

Many of the reform proposals that both Fenno and Sundquist examined were precipitated by concerns about the effects of divided government, especially the phenomenon of legislative "gridlock." It is thus important to stress that this was not Wilson's principal aim in pursuing cabinet government. Wilson sought a robust way to span "the legislative-executive gap" (Fenno 1959, 255) as a means to bring transparency and accountability to American politics, qualities he concluded had been undermined by the separation of powers. All this was necessary, in turn, because the divided, particularistic nature of American politics facilitated and reinforced by the separation of powers put control of administrative power in the hands of private interests rather than national leaders who could harness it to serve national unity and national purpose, particularly adjustments in response to the increasing demands in the modern world for international engagement. This would also legitimate administrative power with respect to the inevitable changes in American character and purposes its exercise would engender. In this respect, Wilson's and Fenno's concerns and aims turn out to be remarkably similar. In closing out his study, Fenno emphasized "the relative difficulty of promoting unity in the face of the basic pluralism of the American political system" (271). Also like the Wilson of the *Constitutional Government* analysis, Fenno put his money on the presidency as the primary engine of unity against diversity and division—so reforms that value and foster "strong presidential leadership" are much to be preferred. Any efforts to raise the cabinet to the status of a collective entity and autonomous political actor, whether radical or more modest, in Fenno's view threaten to diminish presidential political strength and thus the primary force for unity in the regime.

Perhaps the best the American people can hope for is the emergence of presidential candidates and presidents-elect who seek to assemble cabinets composed of men and women of real distinction. Their distinction will in particular lie in their having considerable experience as both legislators and administrators and in having succeeded in both roles. Their distinctiveness will also lie in their capacity to steel themselves against the centrifugal political forces swirling around them and to commit to the cabinet as a collective body that supports the president in his decision-making capacity and responsibility. But even beyond that commitment to the president, the members of the cabinet must collectively be dedicated to sustaining the health of the polity and the effectiveness of governance in the system as a whole. As intelligent, ambitious women and men, they will of course have varying views about what it takes to sustain the polity and realize holistically effective governance. Their principal task is not to have any individual view prevail but to successfully mesh the divergent views and to promote and take responsibility for the synthesis. Mistakes in judgment will inevitably occur. Should an error be significant enough—the pervasive manipulation of analysis to support preordained policy decisions, for instance— resignation of the cabinet *en masse* must remain a viable, legitimate, and responsible answer.

Presidents, for their part, must be willing to use the cabinet as a collective body and to find creative ways to do so, especially with respect to policy and administrative planning such that legislative design and policy execution may be tied more closely together. Presidents will carry the burden, at least initially during their time in office, for creating a sense of collective responsibility. Presidents must give department heads considerable leeway in the day-to-day management of their policy and programmatic domains while not becoming completely detached from what is happening in any department. This means that presidents will inevitably reinforce the particularistic forces of departmentalism. But presidents can also insist that cabinet members bring to the cabinet's deliberations more than their specific departmental orientations. In exchange, presidents must be prepared to entertain collective cabinet objections and critiques of policy directions they seek to pursue or constitutional interpretations of controversial policy issues they seek to promote.

Although the pressures and conflicts emanating from the problems of day-to-day governing will make it extremely difficult, commitment to sustaining and enhancing the character of the regime and its fundamental principles must pervade president-cabinet relations. Even incremental steps in this direction can help stimulate administration's reconnection to political authority more conscious of its responsibilities to the regime, ameliorating some of the harsher effects of the consequences that followed Wilson's failure to realize his reform aims. Imagine, for example, the modest alternative of presidents ceding to heads of cabinet agencies responsibility for announcing legislative agendas in their respective policy areas, working with members of Congress and, if necessary, debating them in public about the development of the legislation and then overseeing the implementation of the legislation and developing proposals for how it might be refined over time on the basis of implementation experience. By forcing department heads to take collective responsibility for the coordination of the various policy agendas through the mechanism of the cabinet, a bold and confident president might stimulate the development of national leadership practiced in the vital task of integrating politics and administration, which can serve the advancement of national purpose and national power.

If today one still takes Richard Fenno's analysis as definitive, then it is clear that cabinet government is a subspecies of presidential leadership, and reforms in the direction of cabinet government represent one possible subset of reforms within the general effort to strengthen presidential leadership. A closer look at the possibilities for presidential leadership, especially with respect to administration, is thus in order.

Presidential Leadership Constraints

There is no dearth of attention to leadership in analyses and commentary on the current state of the modern presidency. Two features of the more general scholarly treatments of the presidency and presidential leadership deserve particular attention in considering whether the presidency can serve the purposes Woodrow Wilson envisioned: to link policy design and policy execution more tightly together and to provide administrative power, especially its constitutive dimension, with a secure legitimacy at the level of the regime.

The first relevant feature is that a substantial share of presidential leadership studies, both classroom texts and scholarly monographs, seem fixed on the constraints presidents face in trying to exercise national leadership and the inability of most recent presidents to transcend the structural and cultural limitations on presidential leadership (for a strongly contrasting analysis, see Warshaw 2005). In his polemic on the presidential leadership dilemma, for instance, Michael Genovese (2003) pegs all the presidents of the past three decades, up through Bill Clinton, as leadership failures to one degree or another. Despite Genovese's semi-comical disdain for the ethical, administrative, or visionary Lilliputians he finds to have recently occupied the office, the core of his analysis rests on the structural and cultural fetters presidents cannot escape: "*All* presidents have presided over a system that put leaders in chains. But there *are* some newer elements to add to the leadership aversion system that inhibits presidents" (170, emphasis in original). The dilemma that Genovese highlights is that these obstacles to presidential leadership exist even though the modern presidency is the essential engine for forward progress in American self-government (see also Cronin and Genovese 1998, ch. 11, wherein the emphasis lies on the *necessity* of the obstacles and constraints).

Along similar lines, George Edwards and Stephen Wayne's *Presidential Leadership: Politics and Policy Making* (2006) focuses its analysis on the growth of expectations for national political leadership from presidents at the same time that constraints have expanded. Presidents are immersed in "a set of critical relationships" (23) that constrain what they can do and even seek to do. Thus it may often be better to understand a president less as "a director of change" (19) and more as "a facilitator of change" (20). As Edwards's (1989) own research has suggested, presidents may function more at the margins than at the center of policy-making and administration, and it is rarely possible to attribute governance failures simply to failures in presidential leadership.

Beyond the analytical perspectives that portray presidential leadership as essential but constrained or as only one important component in a complex, competitively pluralist system are suggestions that presidential leadership, at least of a particular sort, may not even be wise. Reflecting on the benefits and risks of vesting national political leadership in the presidency, Sidney Milkis and Michael Nelson (1999, 394) wonder whether "it may be unreasonable, even dangerous, to rely heavily on presidents to determine the contours of political action. . . . [T]he presidency now operates in a political arena that is seldom congenial to substantive debate and that frequently deflects attention from painful but necessary struggles about the relative merits of contemporary liberalism and conservatism. . . . [P]residents have resorted to rhetoric and administration, tools with which they have sought to forge new, more personal ties with the public. But . . . this form of 'populist' presidential politics can all too easily degenerate into rank opportunism." Along similar lines, George Edwards (2006) has found that attempts at presidential leadership of public opinion have most often had virtually no effect—worse, the political tactics employed in such efforts are corrosive of approaches to democratic governance that are proven in their effectiveness or at least in their tendency to promote collaboration and cooperation rather than division and discord.

A second notable and relevant feature of current presidency scholarship is that leadership is rarely defined explicitly. A prominent conception, if not the leading scholarly paradigm and mode of practice, however, presents presidential leadership in heavily managerial terms (Cronin and Genovese 1998, 121). Perhaps this tendency is rooted in the dilemma of the presidency in the Constitution. At the root of the label *president* is the verb *to preside*, which connotes more the notions of management, supervision, and officiating over the understanding of leadership as a forward-thinking, visionary, action-oriented endeavor in which popular energies are harnessed toward some larger collective aim or purpose. To the Constitution's framers, the latter understanding carried too much of the risk of demagoguery to which they thought democracies were susceptible (see, for example, Tulis 1987, 27–33). Is the American president to be a manager or a leader, a facilitator or a director of change? It may be possible to be both, perhaps in alternating fashion depending on the circumstances. But again, the idea of constraints, constitutional and political, enters the picture. The effect of the quite reasonable endeavor to take account of constraints, especially on the potential of presidents to be directors of change, seems to have been to amplify managerial notions of presidential leadership implicit in the office, and it is remarkable how much the resultant characterizations of presidential leadership look and sound like the conception of leadership that pervades current public management thinking and practice.

It is helpful to turn again to Edwards and Wayne for effective illustrations of presidential managerialism. In the context of the tension between dramatically heightened public expectations of presidential leadership and the extensive systemic and conditional constraints that are operative, Edwards and Wayne make the "exercise of influence . . . central to our concept of leadership." Specifically, they "want to know whether the president can influence the actions and attitudes of others and affect the outputs of government." They arrive at the position that "Presidential leadership typically involves obtaining or maintaining the support of other political actors for the chief executive's political and policy stances" (2006, 19). Further, in both the director-of-change and facilitator-of-change perspectives they offer as guides to their analysis, the authors emphasize mostly a managerial understanding focusing on particular policy aims and the opportunities, constraints, and resources available to satisfy particular constituency demands.

Much of what Edwards and Wayne portray in the conception of presidential leadership they offer falls within the rubric of "transactional" leadership—the ordering, encouragement, and manipulation of discrete transactions (bargaining and compromise) among interested actors that will serve their interests; if positive-sum outcomes can be secured, all the better. In many respects, this is quintessentially a bureaucratic politics understanding of leadership. As Erwin Hargrove has also pointed out, transactional politics is perhaps the dominant understanding of presidential leadership, closely associated as it is with the work of Richard Neustadt, and it reflects the reality that "American politics is transactional much of the time, and rightly so" (1998, 177). But as Tulis demonstrated, presidential rhetoric was not always directed primarily toward the particular merits of discrete policy initiatives (1987, chs. 2–3). Presidential rhetoric could not be completely devoid of policy content because of the constitutional requirement for a State of the Union address and the recommendation of "such measures" as the president "shall judge necessary and expedient" (Article II, Section 3). But presidential rhetoric intended as direct appeals to the citizenry was to be both restrained and confirming of the constituent elements of the regime. Transactional presidential leadership must, therefore, be counted as anchored less in constitutional prescriptions, implicit or explicit, and more in the programmatic orientation of the modern rhetorical presidency as it developed after Wilson. Presidents since have engaged primarily in the tasks of assembling resources, cajoling, persuading, threatening, and creating incentives or disincentives to get others to do what presidents cannot do alone, all with the aim of achieving particular policy or programmatic objectives. Presidents have agendas, which are composed of specific policy action items, and they are subject to evaluation primarily on the basis of how many items they are able to check off their agendas as having been accomplished, mostly in terms of new legislation or the repeal of predecessors' programs.

All modern presidents, even the most pragmatic and programmatic presidents lacking the "vision thing," as George H. W. Bush put it, are notoriously worried about their historical legacies, however. They want posterity to recognize the mark they placed on the developmental path of the nation. Thus all presidents also embrace, to a greater or lesser extent, a notion of *transformational* leadership in the presidency: "'Transforming' leaders articulate and reinterpret the historical situations in times of uncertainty and, as they do so, appeal to revised versions of fundamental moral and political beliefs and values" (Hargrove 1998, 30). Edwards and Wayne capture a sense of transformational leadership in both their perspectives on leaders as agents of change. The director of change creates a constituency and "shapes the contours of the political landscape to pave the way for change." In the more mundane perspective, the mere facilitator of change "uses available resources to achieve his constituency's aspirations" (2006, 20).

More transformational conceptions of leadership are available in studies of the American presidency, of course. In one especially original analysis, Stephen Skowronek has argued that the opportunities available to presidents to engage in transformational politics are constrained by "political time." Skowronek finds something of a recurring oscillation in American political development and political change. New political "regimes"—orderings of "state-society relations" or the "political and institutional infrastructure" of "new governmental" arrangements have arisen, have stayed in place for a while even as their influence waxes and wanes over several election cycles, and then have dissolved as their political energies dissipated, paving the way for the rise of a newly dominant conception of the organization of state-society relations (2003, 112, 114). Although these changes in political orderings have strong partisan elements, they precipitate significant adjustments in constituent elements of the polity even as they remain anchored to, and pledge allegiance to, core components of the regime of the Constitution (see Tulis 1987, 17 for the superb metaphor of a "layered text"). What is particularly significant about Skowronek's thesis is that the confluence of leadership attributes *and* political timing allows only a few presidents to practice transformational politics and thus establish new political and governmental orders. Many more presidents, whatever their personal leadership attributes, will be managers of existing regimes, including some who may belong to the political party that opposed the progenitor of the regime adjustment. And still other presidents, again more numerous than those who would establish a new political order, will be fighting rear-guard actions to sustain an existing order that is unraveling (for a more comprehensive analysis, see Skowronek 1997.)

In a more impressionistic treatment anchored in the political theories of Aristotle and Machiavelli and drawing from his scholarship covering distinctive contributions to studies of the presidency and of public administration and public management, Erwin Hargrove has considered what is necessary in order to qualify presidents as true national statesmen—leaders of the American polity. Much like Woodrow Wilson's own central concerns about achieving national unity in the midst of social, economic, and political diversity and fragmentation, Hargrove begins by arguing that the challenge of *political* leadership is the central task of politics generally, "the search for unity, on matters at hand, within the diversity of society" (1998, 2–3). "The task of good government, then, is to find moral unity in a diverse society," and politics is the Aristotelian invention for achieving such a good society—one that exhibits unity within diversity (5). In the context of the modern American polity, Hargrove introduces the idea of "cultural leadership," which is predicated on the assumption that "politics is animated by understanding, perhaps in limited and partial ways, of a national purpose or purposes toward which we grope" (22). For Hargrove, true national political leadership of the sort presidents might be able to practice requires skill at both transactional and transformational leadership. The former keeps leadership anchored in reality, the latter links that politics to purpose. Hence, "the primary responsibility of political leadership [is] to combine purpose and politics" (39).

Hargrove assesses the leadership performances of three twentieth-century presidents: Franklin Roosevelt, Lyndon Johnson, and Ronald Reagan. He finds some elements of success in meeting his leadership standards in all three cases but exposes flaws and serious shortcomings in the latter two. FDR was not without his own shortcomings either, and his capacities and ambitions needed the restraining force of the separation of powers. Although all three presidents Hargrove considers exhibit elements of the capacities and skills requisite to true democratic leadership, only

FDR rises to the level of exemplar. "The good leaders of a democratic polity must combine moral vision and practical intelligence," Hargrove concludes (187). Further, the "healthiest politics, in the long run, is that of affirmation of the strongest ideals of the American polity" (190). The wellspring of these ideals is the American founding, of course. Early in his study, Hargrove points to Abraham Lincoln's leadership as having "taught us 'the spirit of the constitution'" (24). In a similar vein, Skowronek finds in the episodic patterns of political time that carve out "the potential reach and practical limits of the presidency as a position of national political leadership . . . , a commentary on the Constitution itself" (Skowronek 2003, 155).

As significant as the principles and values articulated in founding documents— and still too often honored only in the breach—is the phenomenon to which the documents give concrete expression: the forging of a new polity, the shaping of a citizenry with a peculiar character, the cementing of general contours in state-society relations, and the articulation of a set of national purposes that will never be fully realized but that serve as a motivation for refinements that lead to successively closer approximations of the ideals. Perhaps the most powerful American cultural value, then, is acceptance of the legitimacy of remaking, reforming, reconstituting— of oneself, one's group, one's society, and one's nation. This makes all the more perplexing the ready American willingness to relegate politics, and especially administration, to mere instrumental functions and incremental problem solving. Even Hargrove succumbs to this at one point, remarking that the "chief task of political leadership is to present effective and politically appealing remedies for public problems" (Hargrove 1998, 38).

Similar to the duality in Hargrove's reflections on the nature of leadership in the presidency, I view political leadership—statesmanship—to consist, in important respects, of a balanced appreciation for the constitutive and instrumental in politics and in the nature of political institutions. Attending to the constitutive requires maintaining the link in the minds of governmental officials and ordinary citizens to the constituent elements of the regime. The constituent elements of the regime are not static but dynamic, however, thus requiring the articulation of new policy goals in the face of changing circumstances as well as the periodic refinement of broad public purposes and the reformation of citizen-institution-government relations. The instrumental dimension of leadership, meanwhile, means having to contend with day-to-day management of the government, administering law and executing public policy to produce results consistent with stated aims. The greatest challenge of democratic statesmanship is to keep both the instrumental and constitutive dimensions of politics in a state of complementarity such that a grand synthesis of norms, values, practices, and outcomes may be possible.

Presidential leadership studies of the sort represented by Skowronek and Hargrove are remarkably circumspect about the actual potential for transformational presidential leadership, finding, in concert with the more dominant managerial orientation, severe constraints on the likelihood of transformational statesmen frequenting the office of the presidency. Hargrove in particular finds "a mutual disenchantment of publics and politicians" in the contemporary American polity. He suggests as causes "the remoteness of government, the distortions of politics by the media, and the intractability of many policy problems." Most serious, however, is that "the political incentives of the main players do not, when taken in total, necessarily permit the resolution of conflict according to an understanding of a common good" (1998, 190). Without the capacity to articulate a broadly appealing conception of the common good and the commitment to make it the centering reference for resolving societal conflict, however, presidents and presidential candidates will pursue as a substitute discrete problems and policy solutions ever more starkly aligned with a particular ideology and its interest patrons, exacerbating existing lines of cleavage.

The many scholarly assessments of presidential leadership prospects convince me that political leadership of the sort that in Hargrove's conception affirms cultural values and, from the conception that I have offered, enables the constitutive as well as the instrumental in politics, is sensitive to the need for strong linkages between policy design and policy execution, and thus provides a general legitimacy for the place and practice of administration in the regime—such leadership is increasingly unlikely to appear in those occupying the Oval Office. Hargrove himself seems to have detected this possibility in an observation sounding more like a wish, one that stands out starkly against his appeal to presidents to meet the standards of statesmanship he offers. Reflecting on the "atypical" leadership example of Abraham Lincoln, Hargrove wonders if it might actually occur "in many small ways throughout the American polity, in the acts of citizens as well as political leaders. Perhaps the search for collective purposes is the business of all Americans" (24). If concentration of interpretive leadership and political authority over administration in the presidency following Wilson has produced the troubling consequences I have enumerated, perhaps the nation can benefit from the smaller ways of presidential leadership. As I mentioned in the previous section, one possibility is the selection of department heads and the use of the cabinet as a collective body for integrating policy and administration. Presidents can also reinforce such efforts by not following Wilson's example in the case of business regulation. They can instead veto "a congressional enactment whenever Congress has not been clear enough about what should be executed, and how" (Lowi 1979, 301). As Lowi stressed, not only does the presidential veto used in this way reinforce the necessity of formulating policy with the needs of, and with proper limitations on, administration discretion carefully considered, but it also creates a form of collective responsibility for law and its administration that spans the separation-of-powers divide.

In the Wilsonian view, administration is the "organ" of government most directly and constantly connected to, even immersed in, the conditions of society. It thus reads those conditions and is the democratic state's front line of response to the flux and change that pose obstacles to the realization of national purposes. Law is administration's guide in this, but in the process administration tests the law's suitability and efficacy. In so doing, it may uncover, or design and disseminate, the many small ways of leadership throughout the polity that Hargrove imagines residing beyond the immediate presidential sphere. With its potential for formulating guidance for adjustments to law and even, eventually, to constitutions, administration might accumulate these small ways of leadership, synthesize them, and introduce them into national politics. Perhaps, then, a more promising place to look for the political leadership that public administration needs to cement its systemic legitimacy and fully realize its value to the regime is within public administration itself.

Regime Leadership in Public Management

Ideas about leadership in public administration and management generally fall within one of two conceptual frameworks. The first such framework is inheritor of the mainline public administration school of thought. Larry Terry's concept of the public administrator as "conservator" exemplifies well this thinking. In his attempt to develop a "normative theory of bureaucratic leadership" (Terry 1995, 16), Terry explains that a conservator "is a guardian, someone who conserves or preserves from injury, violation, or infraction." An administrative conservator approaches the public organization she leads as a social institution that deserves "strengthening" and preservation because of the "desired social function" it fulfills. Reflecting the Burkean roots that form part of the foundation of his framework, however, Terry also stresses that administrative conservatorship recognizes that "controlled adaptation to changing circumstances is . . . an ongoing necessity" (25).

Drawing most heavily on the work of Philip Selznick and John Rohr, Terry, like Hargrove in his exploration of presidential leadership potential, stresses the preservation and transmission of cultural values: "The cultural values and moral commitments of a society are implanted in its institutions" (26). Governmental institutions, including large public bureaucracies, especially at the national level, "must be preserved especially because the strength of cultural values is contingent on the capacity of primary institutions to transmit them without serious distortion." Administrative conservators, acting in their capacity as leaders of vital social institutions, thus practice "a type of statesmanship" (29).

Terry worries about entrepreneurial conceptions of leadership in public bureaucracies (31, 41; see also Terry 1998, 197–98) because the idea, derived as it is from business management and the model of the business leader as one who can radically change a tired, poorly structured, underperforming enterprise and make it profitable again, is a threat to the notion of preserving critical social institutions and the cultural values they embody, protect, and transmit. Yet the entrepreneurial or strategic management conception of bureaucratic leadership stands as the prime competing framework for leadership theory and practice in public administration and management—indeed, it dominates thinking of the sort represented by Terry's framework, because it comports so well with the instrumental, problem-solving orientation to politics and political leadership that began to emerge a generation ago. Every president from Jimmy Carter forward, especially the two Bushes and Clinton, has embraced this orientation in his conception of his presidency, especially in how he directed the complex of administrative organizations over which he exercised general authority.

What is most interesting about the entrepreneurial or strategic management orientation, however, is the extent to which some proponents have sought to portray the leadership exhibited by public executives and managers engaged in entrepreneurship and strategic management as a kind of statesmanship. Although it is not appropriate to place them entirely within the entrepreneurial management camp, there are a number of analyses of the work of executives and managers in public organizations that find them engaged in the preservation, enhancement, and careful alteration of their organizations as valuable governmental and social assets even as they propose new policy opportunities. The emergence in American political development of this way of thinking among appointees and careerists in federal administrative agencies is essentially the tale Carpenter (2001) tells. It is prominent in Heymann's (1987) case-based analysis, and in James Q. Wilson's (1989) interpretation of what executives and managers do in public organizations. It is an endeavor aimed at both internal (organizational) and external (political) matters; that is, the management of both "production" and "politics" (see Kelman 1987) or, as Mark Moore (1995) has presented it, management that looks downward and inward, but more importantly upward and outward.

If proponents of strategic management insist that public executives and managers must take great care to preserve valuable elements of the institutionalized entities they lead even as they seek out new opportunities or otherwise make prudent adjustments in the face of "shifting problems in the world" (Moore 1995, 8), then the contrast between a focus on organizations and institutions on the one hand, and policies and outcomes on the other—between the old public administration approach and the newer public management approach—is not necessarily as sharp as proponents of either often portray it. But is this claim defensible? Doesn't public entrepreneurship go substantially beyond the preservation and careful adjustment of public organizations in response to shifting problems, demands, and aspirations to promote what in some instances might even be radical change? Doesn't the baby get thrown out with the bathwater, so to speak, in the pursuit of innovation for its own sake or in response to unrelenting demands for short-term fiscal and political gains?

Mark Moore's portrayal of public managers seeking opportunities for "creating public value" clearly offers a vision of public executives and managers undertaking risky policy pursuits and, in some cases, substantially altering their organizations in the process—and not always with results that are clear-cut gains for even modest conceptions of the public interest or without unintended consequences. Moore defends the extent of the changes in policies, organizations, and institutions public entrepreneurs bring about on moral grounds and by invoking fidelity to the essential regime value of democratic accountability. He promotes a vision of the public entrepreneur, the strategic manager, as an explorer—clearly an image that has quite noble, even heroic, connotations in Western culture, especially the United States. This "way of thinking" ties the "role of the public sector executive . . . much more closely to the reality of modern governance but [it is] geared to preserving, even enhancing, the ideals of democratic accountability." Society, Moore argues, commissions these public manager explorers "to search for public value." They can preserve and even enhance democratic accountability by fulfilling their "ethical responsibility . . . to undertake the search for public value conscientiously." Public entrepreneurs are conscientious when they are "willing to openly state their views about what is valuable, and to subject those views both to political commentary and to operational tests of effectiveness" (1995, 299).

Moore argues that public managers dutifully responding to and using that political commentary "to revise their efforts to define and produce value" (300) cement their accountability for the use of the substantial discretion they must have in order to do their exploring in service to the public good. But in a version of the adage that it is easier to seek forgiveness than permission, Moore urges strongly that the accountability be secured after the fact, because "it may be easier for managers to learn what is both possible and desirable by producing it first and seeing how people respond rather than by trying to get them to say what they want in the first place" (300–301). Moore also contends that asking permission is the source of much of the sluggishness and delay public organizations seem to exhibit when responding to public problems (393–94n21). For Moore, then, the model of public entrepreneurs who have "a coherent strategic vision" (301) that is centered on seeking out public value in the form of policy goals and the means to achieve them and on subjecting the effort to a *post hoc* public acceptance and evaluation of effectiveness—this satisfies standards of morality and practicality, upholds democratic consent, and in some instances even functions as a better alternative to democratic deliberation that simply is not feasible for every possible public problem and decision. Seeming to respond even to one of Woodrow Wilson's chief worries, Moore suggests that the model placing the initiative in public manager hands will clarify personal responsibility for policy decisions and outcomes (302).

Combining the two models of administrative leadership, exemplified by Terry's administrative conservator and Moore's strategic manager, appears to present an ironclad case that public administration is itself the best place to find the kind of national political leadership necessary to articulate national purposes that are both responsive to changing conditions yet anchored in regime values, that effectively link policy design and policy execution, and that in turn provide a stable, general foundation for the legitimacy of administration and the formative influence it will inevitably have on public purposes and national character. The case is actually quite robust. Through their education and training, public executives and managers are, or at least have the potential to be, more deeply steeped in the tenets of constitutional governance and the peculiar political requirements and expectations of the regime of the U.S. Constitution than are most elected executives and legislators and even most judges. Indeed, there is a great deal of implicit public pressure for this kind of indoctrination, out of fear of the susceptibility of public administrators to the abuse of discretion and out of a mistaken notion that elections somehow inoculate elected officials from distorting constitutional values. To the extent that they receive advanced education and training specifically in administration and management, public managers receive more exposure to thinking ethically, as well as politically, about the problems and decisions they confront. Granted, elected officials are often confronted with ethically difficult decisions in the course of fulfilling the duties of their offices, but so are public administrators. The ethical obligations of unelected public servants, however, are more fully codified, more vigorously enforced, and more strongly reinforced by professional training.

Because public administrators must interact on an extended and often intense basis with all the major branches of government, they may know better the inner workings of all these institutions and how to find ways to satisfy their competing demands. Public managers are also more deeply and extensively immersed in the real nature of governance, which takes place through dense and widely varying networks of public and private actors, and thus they have a better sense of the real potentialities and limitations of this mode of governance, in contrast to the artificiality and distortions of the political environment that emanate from the rhetorical posturing, the narrow representation of the lobbying class, and the manufactured electorates elected officials experience.

Public executives and managers are certainly no more beholden than elected officials to particular interests for sustaining their hold on authority and power and may be less so by virtue of not being subject to periodic election in a system dominated by moneyed interests. There is no easily identifiable reason to suspect that appointed and career administrative officials are more susceptible than elected officials to serving their own self-interest rather than the public interest or that the call to public service would somehow be weaker among the former in comparison to the latter. Indeed, nearly the opposite would seem to be the case, since the political culture condones self-interested behavior in elected officials and condemns it in appointed and career executives and managers.

If the models offered by Terry and Moore are real, or realizable, then public executives and managers have more realistic, battle-hardened, and extensive training in political leadership than the vast majority of elected officials. Public managers are more likely to recognize and have experience in the need to reconcile the instrumental and the constitutive in policy-making and policy implementation because they are constantly confronted with that tension. The pressure on public managers, especially during the past two decades, to be more entrepreneurial, to find ways to do more things and new things with fewer resources, to be nimble in response to fluctuating problems and demands, has been acute. Given this pressure, along with the accelerating global transformations and the increasing rigidity and ineffectiveness of responses rooted in models of state sovereignty (see, for example, the assessment offered by Friedman 2005) within which most elected officials still operate because of the relatively unchanged methods by which they obtain their positions of authority and power, it is only administrators who have the understanding from experience about the nature of dislocation and change in postindustrial society and the practiced dexterity to find ways to adjust to change while preserving recognizable links to the deep and permanent principles of the regime.

The case, in sum, is simple and straightforward. Public executives and managers are stronger students and practitioners of postmodern democratic politics and governance and offer a much deeper and richer reservoir of potential national leadership than members of Congress, presidents, and other elected officials—or, for that matter, judges or private executives.

Notwithstanding the apparent strength of this argument, one can readily advance several initial rejoinders to the notion that public executives and managers are the most promising source of national political leadership of the sort Woodrow Wilson thought essential to cementing the utility and legitimacy of modern administrative power for the American regime facing a world altogether new. First, most public administrators are simply managers or, more narrowly, technicians. They manage fairly limited technical or process domains, and many, if not most, have their training in a technical or scientific specialty. That democratic governments have a large cadre of technical and scientific experts is crucial for coping with modernity, but proficiencies of this type do not by themselves make such people good managers or leaders. In fact it may mean just the opposite if advancement into positions of organizational authority and leadership is based on technical prowess rather than general management skill and success. The characteristics and background of federal managers and executives have been changing in recent decades as more of these men and women enter federal service with general management education and training or obtain it while on the job. The senior executive service was, of course, intended to create a general corps of federal managers and executives, with rewards and advancement based on general management acuity. But from the beginning, successive Congresses and presidents have failed to support the effort fully, and most SES personnel remain with their original agencies and operate mostly within their technical specialties (see Wamsley 2004, 220–22; Ingraham 1995, 84–86).

The largely single-agency orientation of SES personnel reflects a second point of rejoinder to the case for the "bureaucracy" as the source of the national political leadership that can harness the full benefits of national administrative power. The leadership orientation of public executives and mangers is organizational. Bureaucratic leaders may build up institutions that are valuable and vital, but they do so within a relatively narrow policy domain and programmatic orientation. Whether from the perspective of an administrative conservator or a strategic manager, the emphasis is on leadership engaged in the preservation, enhancement, and, if necessary, careful change of a specific agency—preserving, attaining, and sometimes extending its mission. Even though federal executives and managers engage in cooperation and coordination both horizontally and vertically within the American federal system, few of them exercise cross-cutting or systemic leadership in this context. That is in many respects what they turn to the president to provide.

A third rejoinder, more powerful than the first two, draws on Wilson's views on the essentials of national political leadership. As I noted in chapter 3, Wilson saw political authority and leadership as anchored primarily in emotions rather than reason. Wilson argued that reason was subsequent to emotions, and leaders first had to appeal to the people on an emotional level before reasoning with them. Unfortunately, public managers operate almost exclusively in the realm of reason. Their positions and the expectations about their duties demand it. Appeals to emotion by bureaucratic leaders, while they may appear strategically necessary, rarely receive public support and are most often denounced, except when they are expressions of sympathy for victims who have had some tragedy befall them, including as the result of government action. And even then, except in the rarest of circumstances, such as the terrorist attacks of September 11, 2001, citizens tend to regard administrators' public expressions of sympathy with suspicion and cynicism. Although public managers have a variety of ways available through which they can interact with the general public, nearly all of these avenues are formalized and restrictive, requiring the administrator to play the role of rational decision-maker. Thus public managers have very little opportunity to experience the political leadership dynamic Wilson conceptualized. That dynamic can really only be accessed, and mastered, through engagement in electoral campaigns and elections, constituency service, and the many little, often local, ceremonies in which elected officials participate.

These obstacles to tapping the national political leadership potential of public managers and executives are serious but not insurmountable. Although the political activity of federal administrators is restricted by law, many still engage in electoral politics and gain valuable experience, including standing for election themselves. They may thus be able to see how to bridge the divide between emotion and reason in politics and political leadership, and how to ensure that both have a place that lends strength to democratic politics. In this respect also, state and local executives whose positions are filled by elections may serve as a valuable example of the possibility of combining electoral experience and administrative leadership—how to connect experience at balancing the instrumental and constitutive to the dynamics of democratic leadership. Similarly, renewal of operational fidelity to the original intent of the senior executive service can produce leadership experience and perspectives at the top of the federal executive establishment that cut across technical specialties, organizations, and levels of government. This may increase the chances that individuals will emerge who possess all the advantages of administrative leadership with respect to preserving and enhancing valued institutions, fidelity to basic regime values, and agility in response to changing social, economic, technical, and political conditions—but with the breadth of experience and vision to qualify as statesmen.

All these possibilities may be for naught, however, because of two impediments that appear fatal to any notion that the nation might make a deliberate and wholesale turn toward reliance on public executives and managers as the principal source of the kind of political leadership Wilson thought a modern American administrative state required, leadership that can meet the daunting governance challenges the twenty-first century seems likely to present. First, despite the strong cases for the leadership qualities of administrators offered by the likes of Larry Terry and Mark Moore, as well as the broader claims from a variety of scholars about the constitutional legitimacy of politically active public administrators (e.g., Rohr 1986) and despite Wilson's own intriguing argument about the democratic foundation of expert administration, the notion that the nation might deliberately rely on its administrative cadre as a significant source of national political leaders is anathema to American political culture. In general, the American public readily perceives it as a direct threat to the principles and practices of representative democracy. Attempts to neutralize this anxiety, such as John Rohr's notion of constitutionally subordinate but politically engaged public administrators variably choosing which constitutional master—presidents, courts, or Congress—they will side with across varying policy struggles (1986, 181–86) or Mark Moore's portrayal of public managers subject to the control and accountability of political engagement as they try to steer politics in the policy direction they wish to go, can only exacerbate the sense of danger by the subversiveness of administrator political action their visions imply. In the view of those most "disturbed" (see Lowi 1993a) by the prospect, turning to public managers as a prime source of national political leadership would stamp out the last "memory trace of representative government against the triumph of bureaucracy" (Lowi 1995, 249–50).

The second impediment is closely related to the first, if not an extension of it. The polity's deliberate reliance on public managers and executives for the leadership that will link legislation and administration more closely and provide general legitimacy for the harnessing of administrative power will bring with it the managerial orientation of administrative leaders. By this I specifically mean the embrace of broad discretionary power relatively unrestrained by statutory particulars. This is more closely aligned with the strategic management school of thought, but even Larry Terry promotes "broad discretionary power" as critical to the work of administrative conservators and "reserves them a seat at the table of governance" (1995, xix).

Such thinking makes champions of liberal democracy and constitutional self-government nervous or, again with Theodore Lowi as their spokesman, downright hostile. Lowi does not accept the argument that broad delegations of power and subsequent power checking by competing institutional actors is the essence of constitutionalism and the first line of defense for liberty. Lowi's first line of defense is the rule of law, meaning precision in the definition of behavioral standards in statutes and the successive refinement of those standards through experience in administering the law. Lowi accepts that some discretion is inevitable and necessary, but he insists that legislatures should strictly limit it, which is the equivalent of limiting their own authority. This in turn increases the chances that discretionary power will serve law, and ultimately liberty and democracy, rather than patronage. For Lowi, patronage is the most insidious threat to liberty because it is the threat that liberal democracy poses to itself. The argument, running at least from Tocqueville, finding its way through Wilson, showing up dramatically in Hayek, and surfacing again with Lowi, is that patronage leads to tutelage and then to tyranny. And it all happens without a shot ever being fired or a coup staged. It is, nevertheless, the very contradiction of *self*-government.

CULTIVATING NATIONAL POLITICAL LEADERSHIP IN THE LEGISLATURE

Of the institutional foundations I have considered for the national political leadership Wilson insisted was necessary for integrating administration into the regime to help build a mature, organically whole democratic state and to legitimate the wielding of administrative power, all three are tainted. The cabinet is a nonentity without the commitment of presidential power. Along with a constrained notion, in theory and practice, of presidential leadership, the presidency is infected with the embrace of broad delegations of legislative authority to the executive that some see as a threat to liberal democracy. Legislators have happily given up their lawmaking authority in order to create the conditions of patronage that keep their principal constituents satisfied, who in turn protect and maintain their careers in government. They only retain a "meddlesome" control over administration so as to reinforce the patronage-inducing and career-sustaining effects of their broad delegations of authority. And public administrators themselves cannot be the source of national political leadership because of the insoluble fear of a future in which bureaucracy in its literal sense comes to pass, that is, rule by bureaus, rule by the bureaucrats.

My analysis of the weaknesses in all three institutions with respect to the cultivation of democratic statesmanship of the sort Wilson envisioned does suggest some future directions for the development of public administration and public management scholarship and practice. I enumerate and briefly explore these suggestions in this final section. The principal challenge facing public administration and management theory and practice today, however, remains the one bequeathed by Woodrow Wilson's ideas and his failure to fulfill them in practice. It is the challenge of developing a conception of national political leadership, which through its exercise will legitimate a politics dominated by the exercise of administrative power by connecting it to the deep and permanent principles of the regime and preserve and strengthen representative government. It is also the challenge of finding an institutional home for that leadership conception that is constitutionally practical and defensible. In congruence with Wilson's initial analytical insight and despite the obstacles noted in the preceding analysis, the most promising course for surmounting this challenge runs not through the executive but through the legislature.

Public Administration's Legislative Core

In a distinctively valuable contribution to public administration and management theory and practice, David Rosenbloom has recounted the rise of what he calls a "legislative-centered public administration" (2000). This major characteristic of contemporary American national governance reflects Congress's concerted effort since the middle of the twentieth century to reclaim its primacy in the constitutional system in the wake of the emergence of the modern administrative state, especially in the guise of the New Deal. A legislative-centered public administration also reflects Congress's insistence that administration in both design and operation should be consonant with a legislative understanding of representative government, rather than the orthodox understanding that administration should embody primarily if not exclusively executive values such as efficiency and unity of command.

Rosenbloom identifies seven major tenets of legislative-centered public administration (2000, 133–38), which I reduce here to four major interrelated claims: (1) administration encompasses legislative functions, agencies are to a significant degree extensions of Congress, and Congress can thus exercise broad supervision over federal administrative entities; (2) administrative agencies make political decisions and therefore must adhere to "democratic-constitutional" values, which include an understanding of representation that endorses representatives interceding in administration in support of constituency interests; (3) the role of the president and his appointees is restricted to implementation, coordination, "day-to-day" management, and the exercise of discretion "in pursuing the public interest when Congress has not provided specific direction"; (4) judicial involvement in administration is restricted to "review of agency actions" in light of "the terms and conditions established by Congress" (137). In his extended analysis of congressional responses to the administrative state and in his distillation of that analysis into his major tenets, Rosenbloom does not shy away from defending it as both an incontrovertible fact and as an eminently reasonable approach to national politics and government. He finds it practical because it accepts that agencies are "a center of political power in the administrative state" (138), coherent as a solution to Congress's constitutional problem with the administrative state, and legitimate as a constitutionally and politically settled set of concepts, structures, and practices.

In relegating Woodrow Wilson to the status of merely one progenitor among many of the orthodox theory of public administration Congress reacted against in developing its edifice of legislative-centered administration, Rosenbloom fails to see some notable parallels between the thinking that went into Congress's effort and Wilson's own. Most prominent is Congress's embrace of the notion that "administration is not confined to executive functions" and that it is "by no means solely an executive matter or responsibility" (134, 135). This thinking reflects in part the long-standing acceptance that administrative agencies exercise "quasi-" legislative and judicial functions. Although from a congressional perspective it appears that administrative agencies are exercising legislative functions, overall the idea Rosenbloom portrays is very much in tune with Wilson's arguments that administration goes beyond mere execution to active planning and, more significantly, that much of the work of legislatures and courts is actually administration. That is, it involves the management of settled "constituent" functions, such as the regulation of private property, and the maintenance and sometimes expansion of "ministrant" functions.

Another notable parallel between legislative-centered public administration and Wilsonian thinking is the stress of both on close and frequent scrutiny of administration as the heart of the legislative enterprise in the modern democratic state in which the exercise of administrative power predominates. As Wilson originally conceived it, the scrutiny was to be centered on the substance of administration—the plans and programs, structures and outcomes—conceived and executed under the leadership of his new public executives, who were both legislative and administrative leaders. Under legislative-centered public administration, Congress stresses more the scrutiny of procedure. Since it has delegated much of its policy-making authority and responsibility to administrative agencies, Congress is keen to ensure that agencies exercise this authority and responsibility in accord with a legislative understanding of the values of representative government. Hence it has put in place a number of safeguards, like the Administrative Procedure Act, or more recently the Government Performance and Results Act, and monitors agency adherence to their requirements, which include open, public decision-making, demonstration of results, fair representation of interests, and protection of rights.

That Rosenbloom missed these and other parallels between the current legislative-centered public administration and Wilsonian ideas and practices does not diminish the convincing account and defense he offers. Especially powerful is his point that not only is the congressional orientation to the modern administrative state well-rooted and resilient, albeit not immutable, but that it is also a direct challenge to the rise of new, executive-centered administrative orthodoxies like "reinventing government." Rosenbloom also acknowledges several criticisms to which legislative-centered public administration as currently conceived and practiced might be vulnerable. The first two, that it "promotes usurpation of executive powers" (139) and that it "elevates the wrong values" to which administration ought to adhere, Rosenbloom dispatches with little exertion. The constitutionality of Congress's intrusion has been repeatedly affirmed, and Congress's choices with respect to value emphases are legitimate unless proven "obviously and egregiously wrong" (140). The third criticism is, however, much more significant, and it points out the central problems with legislative-centered public administration that still prevent Congress from becoming the institutional home for the integrating, legitimating national leadership that Wilson envisioned and that public administration and management still needs so that administrative power can assume its proper place and fulfill its role in the regime.

Rosenbloom admits that legislative-centered public administration "contains no self-regulating mechanism. It can promote both excessive and self-serving legislative involvement in public administration" (140–41). Thus the long-recognized problem plaguing Congress as a powerful, autonomous legislative body undisciplined by well-organized programmatic parties—which also animated Wilson's own reform endeavor—remains. Rosenbloom tries valiantly to neutralize this criticism, insisting that "the presidency and the courts [can] play a role in checking" the potential for excess "as ultimately can the electorate" and that "Congress has some capacity for self-imposed discipline" (141). With respect to self-imposed discipline, he references the budget process and the military base closure process. As any attentive citizen knows, however, Congress rarely meets its budget targets without cynical gimmicks, relies heavily on continuing resolutions because it cannot finalize appropriations bills on time, and riddles the budget with exceptions and earmarks. With respect to base closures, the process is much less a self-regulating mechanism and much more an additional device by which Congress has delegated its legislative authority to public administrators in an effort to avoid the painful decisions about public resource allocations and their impact on constituents. It casts citizens adrift, giving them no avenue for effective representation on these consequential decisions except through a highly complicated administrative mechanism, but it then allows individual representatives or groups of elected officials to ride to the rescue or at least to claim credit for trying (see, for example, Goren 2003).

Rosenbloom's entire normative and empirical case for the rise of legislative-centered public administration also effectively negates the claims for effectual presidential and judicial checks. Both presidents and courts have thoroughly acquiesced in the central tenets, particularly the broad delegations of policy-making authority to agencies and the close scrutiny of adherence to its procedural mandates that goes with it, no matter how much it might interfere with the president's constitutional obligations for effective management and policy execution, or how much the question of statutory constitutionality has been deflected into questions about agency adherence to procedural requirements. And one look at incumbent reelection rates, especially the inability of challengers to compete financially (see Abramowitz, Alexander, and Gunning 2005), quickly neutralizes the argument that the electorate can exercise an effective check on the potential for self-serving and excessive legislator behavior with respect to their scrutiny of and intrusion into the administrative process. Constituent opportunity, interest, and incentives derived from the structure of legislative-centered public administration flow in precisely the opposite direction. The problems of a legislative-centered public administration are simply that Congress cannot discipline its own behavior with respect to its assertion of primacy over administration, and that in the embrace of the framework it has, in Theodore Lowi's harsh assessment, headed down the path of "legiscide" (1991, 19), that is, the loss of the characteristics of a genuine legislature, namely "deliberation and true collective decision making" (20).

Congress, Definite Law, and Administration

The way to bring something akin to a self-regulatory mechanism to Congress's legislative-centered approach to structuring and controlling public administration is to impose the discipline of policy *with* law, that is, to heed Lowi's call to return to a system centered on the rule of law or, in Wilsonian terms, "definite law." Adherence to notions of the rule of law or definite law requires specificity in legislative drafting and policy design. The objects of a given policy must be clearly identified, or identifiable, preferably in the form of entities with which policy-makers and citizens have real-world experience. Further, the rules of conduct to which the regulated entities must adhere should as much as possible be spelled out in advance, and the consequences for failure to adhere to the rules should be delineated. Responsible behavior is thus more likely to be secured. All public policy, in a significant way, would look more like criminal law.

Administrative discretion will still be necessary—prosecutorial discretion is a well-established doctrine—and essential for good governance, because legislators drafting new policy cannot know all they need to know about a problem they seek to address or what responses will work or not work. Thus administrative experimentation and testing of the suitability of a law is inevitable. Administrative experience can also inform initial policy-making, as can technical expertise in a host of forms. But the rule of law requires that the authority and responsibility for hard decisions about what the problem is and what the rules of behavior required in response should be cannot be turned over wholesale to experts. The boundaries surrounding proper and improper, responsible and irresponsible, conduct will also always be subject to some fuzziness for which discrete decisions on individual cases must be made. As Wilson argued in his veto of the grade-crossing bill in New Jersey, however, the discretion— the experimentation and testing, the judgment on individual cases—can be guided by expressed priorities and specific decision rules rather than open-ended admonitions to regulate "in the public interest" or to "protect public health with an adequate margin of safety." The opposite extreme of mandating unrealistic formulae or unachievable deadlines that only breed cynicism and manipulative behavior must also be avoided. Greater care in legislative construction also puts administration as an institution in the much more comfortable and legitimate role of supporting the further development and refinement of law rather than having to act on shaky legitimacy grounds as a substitute for lawmaking in the legislature.

Two especially significant consequences flow from grounding policy-making more soundly in rule-of-law or definite law notions. First, American politics and governance will reconnect more firmly to modern liberal ideas of constitutionalism and limited government. Second, Congress will move toward becoming (or becoming again) a "legislature of the first kind" (Lowi 1991).

In the mid-1990s Lowi stated much more starkly than in his original interest-group liberal thesis that liberal government, properly conceived, is likely to be smaller government. For Lowi this is a much more legitimate basis for smaller government than the "mere ideologically based negation of representative government itself" (1995, 251) that he sees as the preference of post-Reagan conservatives (see 1995, chs. 4, 5). It is also not a threat but a confirmation of properly liberal-*democratic* government. "Rule of law definitely puts a cap on democracy. But every constitutional provision does that. The whole point of a constitution is to make some rules for the proper conduct of government and then to permit alteration only by extraordinary, supramajoritarian means. . . . Thus what we have here is not a question of whether but *what kind* of caps are placed on democracy. Rule of law is one, the one least observed. Moreover, this cap is reasonable. It is reasonable to deny government the authority to act when it refuses to say in advance how it wants to act" (253).

From the perspective of a study of Wilson's ideas and governing practices, smaller government is hardly anathema to Wilson's precepts or predilections. It is in fact consistent with a host of Wilson's most prominent ideas. In addition, however, note how comportment with a rule-of-law doctrine leading to smaller government is consonant with Wilson's insight about the development of the American citizenry in

Constitutional Government. Recall that Wilson advanced a view of American citizens in his Blumenthal lectures that contrasted with his *Congressional Government*
analysis. Heavily burdened by modern life, especially the pressure to make economic headway, citizens had little time to spend on scrutinizing debates in Congress
about the design and operational success of policy and administration. Instead, they
were more intent on pressuring government to help them fulfill their material wants
and needs. Hence a more limited, smaller government, in which policy and administration are more restrained and well-ordered, less sprawling and vague in intent and
effect, is a more manageable object of limited citizen scrutiny. Although national
public policy and administration will have a somewhat less sweeping impact on the
everyday life of citizens under the rule of law, those consequences that do arise will
be sharper and more readily understandable, and they will be based on knowledge
citizens will find more accessible and thus better able to appreciate.

As Lowi has pointed out, more sharply defined policy with clear consequences
that follow from it will engender opposition in the citizenry, which is in part precisely what leads to smaller government (and, one must admit, to the maneuvering
by legislators to hide from the wrath of constituents). But it also means a citizenry
more motivated toward scrutiny of and engagement in policy-making and administration. It is not all that different from the renewed citizen interest in and scrutiny of
national politics Wilson envisioned arising from contests over policy principles and
national administrative plans. It is certainly not the case, as it was not in Wilson's
time, that a continuous grinding out of a politics of relative interest advantage and
distribution of policy benefits (mostly behind the scenes) draws anything like sustained citizen engagement in national politics. Hence adherence to the rule of law
and the smaller government that might follow is consistent with Wilson's *Congressional Government* aim of reengaging the citizenry in their own governance, rightly
understood, and it is consistent with his *Constitutional Government* insight about
what will most likely reengage a citizenry leading a modern way of life.

For students of administration more generally, adherence to the rule of law and
the smaller government that might follow means much less burden on public administration and public management to take on the whole enterprise of governing
with little but vague and often conflicting instructions or otherwise marginal engagement on policy substance from the constitutional branches. This easing of the
governing burden on administration will also lessen the perpetual suspicions of its
legitimacy, whether stemming from doubts about competence, expertise, authority,
or constitutionality. Policy more clearly defined with respect to rules of conduct and
consequences means policy more effectively carried out. It means administration
not pushed beyond its capacity and a legitimacy rooted in the law—law that spells out

rules of conduct and consequences for not meeting them—and not in claims about special knowledge and expertise with respect to systems and universalities.

There is of course a serious problem with an approach to policy-making and administration that adheres to the rule of law and thus makes for smaller government. It flies in the face of the one tenet that links both old public administration orthodoxy and new public management orthodoxy, both an executive-centered and a legislative-centered public administration. This tenet is the broad delegation of authority to administrative agencies with little statutory specificity. I earlier argued that Wilson came to see the "large powers and unhampered discretion" he championed as effective and legitimate only when tethered to "definite law." Most students of public administration and public policy—indeed, most students of American politics—see the two as incompatible, not complementary. As Rosenbloom argues, Congress chooses to delegate for a variety of reasons: "to alleviate its workload; to avoid a particularly nettlesome political issue; to focus highly specialized administrative expertise on a particular problem; for convenience; or simply because agencies do not face the constraints of a legislature that is reconstituted every two years" (2000, 134). The principal rationale, however, in theory as well as in practice, is that society has gotten so complex that the best Congress can do is identify a problem and direct the bureaucracy to develop the details of a solution and then carry it out. Rosenbloom finds this rationale to be one of the key arguments of supporters of the Administrative Procedure Act (34). As Lowi has pointed out, this rationale requires the designated agency to do lots of extra study in connection with a policy issue Congress has handed off to it, delaying substantive action. This delay often leads the affected parties to pursue judicial or legislative remedies in the form of having the courts or Congress declare a policy goal a protected civil right (1991, 27). It is, to use Wilsonian terminology, the transformation of a ministrant function into a constituent function, which not only fundamentally alters the politics surrounding the matter, as Lowi stresses, but changes drastically the administration and management implications as well.

Social Complexity, Knowledge in the Legislature, and National Leadership

This same idea about social complexity underlies the discovery in the public management and governance literature of what Kettl calls "fuzzy boundaries" (Kettl 2002, 59–60). Increasingly complex social problems require a network of public and private actors to attend to them when the old, constitutionally grounded hierarchical ordering for policy and administration fails. These networks, however, blur the line between public and private. The discovery or creation of fuzzy boundaries also reinforces the argument that policy specificity, with respect to legislated rules of conduct and the identification of who is responsible and accountable for what, is impossible. Again following Lowi, what underlies this thinking is a particular epistemology and related conception of the work of a legislature. Understanding the nature of knowledge and its connection to legislative work helps to reveal how the social complexity–fuzzy boundary dynamic can be altered by grounding policymaking more soundly in the rule of law or definite law.

Lowi distinguishes between two kinds of knowledge: "The first kind is amateur knowledge, knowledge arising from sensory experience. The second is professional knowledge, based on formal agreement about experience" (1991, 12). Amateur knowledge is in important respects the lifeblood of a legislature. It connects representatives not just to "people and their opinions and demands" but also to "conflicts . . . that result from differing expressions of fundamental needs, of injuries, of sources of injury, and of widespread inconveniences." Amateur knowledge is "direct and reactive." In contrast, professional knowledge works with generalities and probabilities, and it filters sensory experience through instruments, including agreed-upon conceptual and operational definitions of phenomena. It thus "virtually replaces concrete connections with statistical associations." Professional knowledge is also, Lowi argues, most compatible with bureaucracy (14).

Different kinds of knowledge bases lead to different kinds of law. The first kind is "law that governs people" and is "composed of rules . . . backed by sanctions, that impose obligations on conduct." It is law as "traditionally understood," and Lowi implies that citizens understand it better and respect it more. The second kind is "law that governs nature or the universe; it is concerned with physical laws. This kind of law is a hypothesis about the way nature works" or about how systems of individuals, groups, or organizations behave (25). The danger arises when a legislature adopts "law of the second kind . . . as if it were the same as law of the first" (26). A legislature that adopts professional knowledge—the attempt to understand whole systems—as the primary basis of public policy produces, in Lowi's view, mostly policy without law. Vestiges of their reliance on amateur knowledge and direct connection to the lives of their constituents remain for most legislators, however. The best they can offer their constituents who seek government help in coping with societal problems are statutes with often highly detailed expressions of goals, often initially expressed or later designated as rights, and extensive delegations of authority to administrative entities to clarify the objects and establish the means to fulfill them. Strict procedural requirements accompany those delegations, of course. The effect over time, in Lowi's view, is to take more and more of policy-making out of the "ordinary politics of representative government" (31).

To adopt or return to a rule-of-law or definite-law conception of policy-making would pull Congress back to its foundations in amateur knowledge and the ordinary politics of representative government, and especially to the original founding conception of the organization and character of a representative assembly (17). A rule-of-law foundation for policy-making in turn positions administration more appropriately to apply its expertise to complex social problem solving via support of the lawmaking process. Congress would still have to be conversant with professional knowledge so that it could scrutinize what administrative agencies do in response to substantive policy directives and so that it could make sense of the policy recommendations emanating from administration. Indeed, professional knowledge, or perhaps more accurately social science knowledge in the form of tests of theories about what works or doesn't work in response to particular societal conditions, might be the basis of the specific rules of conduct that are part of good public policy—that is, policy with law. But Congress would evaluate administration and the policy guidance offered by administration in terms of amateur knowledge and the ordinary politics of representative government. It would, in short, focus much more centrally on policy substance and policy outcomes rather than on the fidelity of the bureaucracy to mandated procedures. It could do so because it would produce policies with real legal substance within the institution that embraces legislative values by its very nature rather than in the institution that must have those values imposed and then monitored for compliance from the outside. Secured to legal substance rather than a legal vacuum, large powers and unhampered discretion can then be more trusted and more useful.

Most important of all, a Congress that operates on the basis of a rule-of-law or definite-law conception of policy will see a different kind of leadership emerge. It will be a leadership not "based on analytic, budgetary, or procedural skill" but leadership "based on skill in legislative drafting" (Lowi 1995, 251). This skill in legislative drafting does not mean merely the skill involved in writing a bill. It also means the ability to articulate specific objects of policy and the accompanying explicit rules and sanctions in a way that can garner majority support and in a form that can be refined through experience toward successively better approximations of the problem and the appropriately practical responses. It will take time before citizens rally to such leadership because it will take time for citizens to realize that this leadership is the source of laws they can more readily understand, obey, and respect. But they will reach that realization because such laws do not offer sweeping promises to get to the heart of complex societal problems or eliminate them entirely. Rather, policy with law offers limited, concrete responses to conditions, which can help citizens make increasingly harmonious, practical, and comprehensible adjustments over time.

The implications of the emergence of this kind of legislative leadership for public administration and public management are enormous. As I have already noted, it can link administration to the more limited but still centrally vital and noble purpose of helping society cope with modernity by guiding the refinement and improvement of public law. It can thus replace the predominant image of administration in American political culture as the wholesale substitute for lawmaking, a substitute needing extraordinary arguments in defense of its legitimacy and extraordinary procedural fetters to keep it from endangering democracy. A new kind of national leadership springing from the legislature can tie legislation and administration more closely together without the need for an unconstitutional breach of the separation of powers. It can lead to citizens embracing administration's legitimacy on the basis of the help it provides them in coping with a tumultuous world. Most important, it presents a challenge that proponents of the new developments in the theory and practice of public administration and management may find consistent with their grandest intellectual and practical aims.

A SCIENCE OF GOVERNANCE AND ADMINISTRATION'S ROLE IN THE REGIME

The burgeoning acceptance of the concept of governance may be the most significant development in the study and practice of public administration and management since the consolidation of progressive orthodoxy in the early decades of the twentieth century. Two predominant and distinct but interconnected uses of the term *governance* appear to have recently emerged in scholarship. The first closely associates new thinking about governance with renewed efforts toward greater civic engagement in government processes, especially greater direct citizen deliberation about, participation in, and even control of public decision-making (see, for example, Cooper 2005 and the accompanying articles, especially Boyte 2005). The second predominant use of the term *governance* is focused more particularly on efforts "to frame the ongoing discourse on public management reform" (Hill and Lynn 2005, 173). The two uses intersect in a focus on administration because the civic engagement thrust is extensively, although not entirely, concerned with the sorts of on-the-ground government processes that have the most immediate impact on citizens and that they can most easily access. As I noted in chapter 4, there are also, therefore, notable parallels with this local civic engagement perspective in Wilson's ideas about local administration.

My focus in what follows is on the second of the two developing conceptions of governance, which has emerged from public management scholarship and practice and seeks to expand and transform it. Although its proponents are circumspect about what they have developed thus far, their agenda seems increasingly ambitious in pushing what they now usually refer to as the "art" of governance (Ingraham and Lynn 2004) toward what they are reluctant to admit openly—but clearly seem to want, namely, a *science* of governance. I mean by "science" two distinct senses of the term that appear to be manifest in this growing scholarly enterprise. First, the promoters of a governance approach to the study and practice of public administration and public management seek to use the tools of modern social science to analyze and generalize about what governments are doing—what conceptual tools, methods, organizational structures, and interrelationships among actors are in operation to deliver public goods and services to citizens. This is largely a descriptive endeavor, but it is also partly explanatory; researchers are seeking to isolate the factors that explain the recurring appearance of particular tools, methods, structures, or interactions. Second, however, students of the new governance seek to learn from their analyses and generalizations what is working and what is not working, to identify which management factors produce particular policy results, and thus ultimately to offer guidance that can improve governance. In this second sense, then, the new study of governance is not much different than the "orthodox" conception of an administrative science and is well in keeping with the classic conception of political science as understood by the American framers and by Woodrow Wilson: the accumulation and systematic organization of governing experiment and experience, combined with theory that is well grounded in that experiment and experience, to inform and ultimately improve self-government.

Working on the assumption that scholars and practitioners of this version of the new governance will not wholly dissent from my characterization of their endeavor, I bring this book to a close by challenging them to think further about what might be required to constitute a true science of governance. Should they deem my challenge worthy of their attention, they will have to consider what additional dimensions they must add to their current conception of the study of governance to produce something akin to the science of government the Founders and Woodrow Wilson had in mind. I suggest three that will aid not only the study and practice of public management itself but also the long-run prospects for a liberal-democratic state that is well administered in Wilson's most expansive sense.

First, the new governance—both what it is currently in practice and how it is conceived in developing conceptions—raises serious normative questions. What makes a *political* science distinctive is that it incorporates both empirical and normative questions. It asks, and attempts to answer, not only what is and what works or fails to work in governing arrangements and why, but also what *ought to be used* consistent with particular purposes and aspirations for good governance and the good society. The normative questions the new governance raises concern especially matters of accountability and responsibility as well as problems of ordinary citizen access, influence, and control. The leaders in the effort to develop a governance framework for study and practice acknowledge that these questions exist, but, with the particular exception of Behn (2001), they have not done much to address them. The normative questions are, however, central to understanding what is happening in the newest stage of development of the modern democratic state. Acceptable answers to them must be an integral part of whatever good governance guidance may arise from the efforts to develop a new science of governance.

Second, it is notable that perhaps the most determined effort at systematic study of the new forms and facets of public administration and management attempts to combine recognition of the vertical "logic of governance" (e.g., Heinrich, Hill, and Lynn 2004, 6–7; more generally Lynn, Heinrich, and Hill 2001) of the American constitutional system with the burgeoning horizontal and cross-boundary networking of the new administration and management. As I argued in the previous chapter, the conception of politics and government underlying this effort is almost wholly instrumental, however. This is understandable since the object of the research is administration and management, which is primarily an instrumental undertaking. But if one of the working assumptions is that administration and management is *political*, then it is necessary to take account of the reality that politics is also *constitutive*. It is not just about matching means to ends; it is also about determining what those ends will be. It is about determining the character of institutions and the interactions among individuals and groups they foster. At its broadest, politics is about constituting a particular kind of political regime. To borrow Wilson's approach, it requires thinking about state and society organically, about its healthful balance and active life as an organic whole.

To take account of this understanding of politics in a new science of governance requires emulating the likes of James Madison and, again, Woodrow Wilson. In particular, it requires that one think constitutionally: "Madison teaches us how to think constitutionally. He is a theorist, not of a piece of paper, but of a working political regime, with all the various interconnections that increase the likelihood that it will operate in the appropriate manner (Elkin 1995, 11). The point is not necessarily to follow Madison's particular designs and prescriptions but to get a sense of the character of the whole regime, especially how the various parts are constituted and how the parts constitute the whole. As I noted in chapter 2 about Wilson's conceptions of the proper study of politics, he wanted it to provide a way of seeing how "things fall into their places . . . , no longer confused, disordered, scattered abroad without plan or action" (Link et al. 1976, 22:270). A proper study of politics would capture the "passion and feel the pulse" of men's lives, and, as Wilson portrayed it, provide an accurate interpretation of life as a whole, shaping the public law and policy that reflected the whole of life. Wilson's constitutional thinking was also fully on display in his enterprise to find the proper place and role for modern administration in the American regime and to secure its legitimacy.

Thinking constitutionally, scholars of the new governance (and practitioners too) will be forced to ask how the new developments in public administration and management fit into the character of the whole regime and its purposes and aspirations, first given expression at the founding of the country. They will have to ask how the new developments are reinforcing, improving, or even substantially altering the character of the regime with respect to the core purposes and aspirations. Going beyond taking account of the existence of a hierarchical "logic of governance" in their analytical framework, mostly manifested as one or more sets of independent variables, scholars of the new governance will ask how the new developments, and any guidance or prescriptions that may emanate from their research, may affect the interconnections in the various parts and the relationship of the parts to the whole (see Hill and Lynn 2005 for a report on research that treats the upper-level components in the hierarchy as dependent variables). Thinking constitutionally about the new governance, in short, means thinking about how the new developments in governance, and the guidance that may arise from analysis of their successes and failures, gives "concrete meaning to the public interest" (Elkin 1995, 12) or, in Wilson's words, serves "the good of ordinary people" (Link et al. 1968, 5:399).

Thinking constitutionally about public administration and management leads to one final point that proponents of the new study of governance may wish to consider as they develop their endeavor further. The constitutiveness of public administration and management can be captured analytically by treating, again in terms of the hierarchical logic of governance framework, manifestations of "discretionary organization, management, and administration" as independent variables shaping interactions and outcomes at other levels of collective action. But this independent, or constitutive, influence of public administration and management invariably raises fundamental questions about the character and composition of a regime of limited government and thus about the legitimacy of administration within that regime and how best to secure it. Indeed, to label the new and seemingly far-reaching developments in public administration and management of the past two or three decades a new kind of governance implies a sweeping reconception of politics and government in a regime predicated on the idea of popular rule through representative institutions.

Wilson's own sweeping conception of administration in a modern liberal-democratic regime—that popular sovereignty is never fully expressed, and national purposes never fully realized, without administration completing its vital tasks of carrying out public law, broadly understood, and continually refining the law's shape and substance—does not require that public management be a mere subordinate agent of the legislature. It does require, however, that administration and management have a close and intimate link to this primary institution of representative government. This includes providing a certain supportive, energizing, and even corrective stimulus—a "check," if you will, broadly understood. This link is all the more necessary because, in spite of Wilson's own powerful brief in favor of presidential leadership, the interpretive statesmanship that can integrate and legitimate, and thus most effectively harness, the far-reaching power of administration has the best chance of emerging from the national legislature, properly conceived.

What I am suggesting poses the most extraordinary challenge to current public administration and management theory and practice in the guise of the new study of governance. It is to see what Wilson saw, namely, that administration extends beyond artificial institutional boundaries, in particular that administration and management begin with the substance and content of policy design. Political scientists already understand this connection, and there are many studies of how statutory structure affects, and often hinders, policy design and the realization of policy intents. Although there is enormous scholarly energy devoted to identifying the tools, techniques, and structures that will enable administrative entities to increase their chances to realize implementation success, there is very little evidence I can find of scholars asking what changes in the legislature might produce policy designs more likely to be administered and managed well. Political scientists are more than happy to tell public managers what they ought to do to improve their performance. It is the ultimate challenge of the study, and practice, of public management as a science of governance to return the favor by following the trail blazed by that young professor of politics over a century ago, turning its sights on the legislature and the requisites of good policy design that are the essential first step toward good administration.

Woodrow Wilson's ideas and practices and their aftermath have left Americans with an ambiguous legacy, and modern pubic administration and management with a number of daunting challenges. But Wilson's ideas and the lessons of his efforts to put those ideas into effect can also arm political leaders and citizens and, especially, public management thinkers and practitioners with insights to guide them toward better understanding the place and role of administration and management in a modern, dynamically evolving liberal democracy. Distilling and applying such insights is an endeavor worthy of the new scholarly ambition.

References

Aberbach, Joel D., and Bert A. Rockman. 2000. *In the Web of Politics: Three Decades of the U.S. Federal Executive*. Washington, D.C.: Brookings Institution.

Abramowitz, Alan I., Brad Alexander, and Matthew Gunning. 2005. "Incumbency, Redistricting, and the Decline of Competition in U.S. House Elections." Paper delivered at the annual meeting of the Southern Political Science Association, Intercontinental Hotel, New Orleans, Louisiana, January 6–8.

Arnold, Peri E. 1998. *Making the Managerial Presidency: Comprehensive Reorganization Planning, 1905–1996*, 2nd ed., revised. Lawrence: University Press of Kansas.

Barzelay, Michael. 1992. *Breaking through Bureaucracy: A New Vision for Managing in Government*. Berkeley: University of California Press.

Behn, Robert D. 1997. "Branch Rickey as a Public Manager: Fulfilling the Eight Responsibilities of Public Management." *Journal of Public Administration Theory and Research* 7 (January): 1–33.

Behn, Robert D. 2001. *Rethinking Democratic Accountability*. Washington, D.C.: Brookings Institution.

Boyte, Harry C. 2005. "Reframing Democracy: Governance, Civic Agency, and Politics." *Public Administration Review* 65 (September-October): 536–46.

Brownlow, Louis. 1949. *The President and the Presidency*. Chicago: Public Administration Service.

Brudney, Jeffrey L., Laurence J. O'Toole Jr., and Hal G. Rainey, eds. 2000. *Advancing Public Management: New Developments in Theory, Methods, and Practice*. Washington, D.C.: Georgetown University Press.

Caiden, Gerald E. 1984. "In Search of an Apolitical Science of American Public Administration." In Jack Rabin and James S. Bowman, eds., *Politics and Administration: Woodrow Wilson and American Public Administration*. New York: Marcel Dekker.

Campbell, Colin. 1986. *Managing the Presidency*. Pittsburgh: University of Pittsburgh Press.

Carpenter, Daniel P. 2001. *The Forging of Bureaucratic Autonomy: Reputations, Networks, and Policy Innovation in Executive Agencies, 1862–1928*. Princeton: Princeton University Press.

Cawley, R. McGreggor. 1998. "We May Help to Make Up the General Mind: Reuniting Wilson, Taylor, and Pinchot." *Administrative Theory and Praxis* 20 (March): 55–67.

Clements, Kendrick A. 1992. *The Presidency of Woodrow Wilson*. Lawrence: University Press of Kansas.

Clements, Kendrick A. 1998. "Woodrow Wilson and Administrative Reform." *Presidential Studies Quarterly* 28 (Spring): 320–36.

Cohen, Jeffrey E. 1988. *The Politics of the U.S. Cabinet: Representation in the Executive Branch, 1798–1984*. Pittsburgh: University of Pittsburgh Press.

Cook, Brian J. 1996. *Bureaucracy and Self-Government: Reconsidering the Role of Public Administration in American Politics*. Baltimore: Johns Hopkins University Press.

Cook, Brian J. 1998. "Efficiency, Responsibility, and Law: Public Administration in the Early Political Rhetoric of Woodrow Wilson." *Administrative Theory and Praxis* 20 (March): 43–54.

Cooper, Terry L. 2005. "Civic Engagement in the Twenty-First Century: Toward a Scholarly and Practical Agenda." *Public Administration Review* 65 (September-October): 534–35.

Cronin, Thomas E., and Michael A. Genovese. 1998. *The Paradoxes of the American Presidency*. New York: Oxford University Press.

Cuff, Robert D. 1973. *The War Industries Board: Business-Government Relations During World War I*. Baltimore: Johns Hopkins University Press.

Cuff, Robert D. 1977. "Herbert Hoover, the Ideology of Voluntarism, and War Organization during the Great War." *Journal of American History* 64 (September): 358–77.

Cuff, Robert D. 1978. "Wilson and Weber: Bourgeois Critics in an Organized Age." *Public Administration Review* 38 (May-June): 240–44.

Eden, Robert. 1989. "Dealing Democratic Honor Out: Reform and the Decline of Consensus Politics." In Richard A. Harris and Sidney M. Milkis, eds., *Remaking American Politics*. Boulder, CO: Westview Press.

Eden, Robert. 1996. "The Rhetorical Presidency and the Eclipse of Executive Power: Woodrow Wilson's *Constitutional Government in the United States*." *Polity* 18 (Spring): 357–78.

Edwards, George C., III. 1989. *At the Margins: Presidential Leadership of Congress*. New Haven: Yale University Press.

Edwards, George C., III. 2006. "The Limits of the Bully Pulpit." In George C. Edwards III, ed., *Readings in Presidential Politics*. Belmont, CA: Thomson/Wadsworth.

Edwards, George C., III, and Stephen J. Wayne. 2006. *Presidential Leadership: Politics and Policy Making*, 7th ed. Belmont, CA: Thomson/Wadsworth.

Eisner, Marc Allen. 1991. *Antitrust and the Triumph of Economics: Institutions, Expertise, and Policy Change*. Chapel Hill: University of North Carolina Press.

Elkin, Stephen L. 1985. "Pluralism in Its Place: State and Regime in Liberal Democracy." In Roger Benjamin and Stephen L. Elkin, eds., *The Democratic State*. Lawrence: University Press of Kansas.

Elkin, Stephen L. 1995. "Pegs and Wholes." *The Good Society* 5 (Winter): 11–13.

Ely, Richard T. 1938. *Ground under Our Feet: An Autobiography*. New York: Macmillan.

Fenno, Richard F., Jr. 1959. *The President's Cabinet: An Analysis in the Period from Wilson to Eisenhower*. Cambridge, MA: Harvard University Press.

Frederickson, H. George, and Kevin B. Smith. 2003. *The Public Administration Theory Primer*. Boulder, CO: Westview Press.

Friedman, Thomas L. 2005. *The World Is Flat: A Brief History of the Twenty-First Century*. New York: Farrar, Straus and Giroux.

Garvey, Gerald. 1993. *Facing the Bureaucracy: Living and Dying in a Public Agency*. San Francisco: Jossey-Bass Publishers.

Genovese, Michael A. 2003. *The Presidential Leadership Dilemma: Leadership in the American System*, 2nd ed. New York: Pearson-Longman.

Ginsberg, Benjamin, and Martin Shefter. 1990. *Politics by Other Means: Politicians, Prosecutors, and the Press from Watergate to Whitewater*. Rev. ed. New York: W.W. Norton.

Goren, Lily J. 2003. *Politics of Military Base Closings: Not in My District*. New York: Peter Land Publishing.

Guttman, Dan. 2004. "Inherently Governmental Functions and the New Millennium: The Legacy of Twentieth-Century Reform." In Thomas H. Stanton and Benjamin Ginsberg, eds., *Making Government Manageable: Executive Organization and Management in the Twenty-First Century*. Baltimore: Johns Hopkins University Press.

Hargrove, Erwin C. 1998. *The President as a Leader: Appealing to the Better Angels of our Nature*. Lawrence: University Press of Kansas.

Hays, Samuel P. 1959. *Conservation and the Gospel of Efficiency: The Progressive Conservation Movement, 1890–1920*. Cambridge, MA: Harvard University Press.

Heckscher, August. 1991. *Woodrow Wilson*. New York: Charles Scribner and Sons.

Heinrich, Carolyn J., Carolyn J. Hill, and Laurence E. Lynn Jr. 2004. "Governance as an Organizing Theme for Empirical Research." In Patricia W. Ingraham and Laurence E. Lynn Jr., eds., *The Art of Governance: Analyzing Management and Administration*. Washington, D.C.: Georgetown University Press.

Heymann, Philip B. 1987. *The Politics of Public Management*. New Haven: Yale University Press.

Hill, Carolyn J., and Laurence E. Lynn Jr. 2005. "Is Hierarchical Governance in Decline? Evidence from Empirical Research." *Journal of Public Administration Research and Theory* 15(2): 173–95.

Hood, Christopher, and Michael Jackson. 1991. "Is There a New Public Management? Keys and Locks in Administrative Argument." Paper delivered at the annual meeting of the American Political Science Association, Washington, D.C., September.

Ingraham, Patricia Wallace. 1995. *The Foundation of Merit: Public Service in American Democracy*. Baltimore: Johns Hopkins University Press.

Ingraham, Patricia W., and Amy E. Kneedler. 2000. "Dissecting the Black Box: Toward a Model and Measures of Government Management Performance." In Jeffrey L. Brudney, Laurence J. O'Toole Jr., and Hal G. Rainey, eds., *Advancing Public Management: New Developments in Theory, Methods, and Practice*. Washington, D.C.: Georgetown University Press.

Ingraham, Patricia W., and Laurence E. Lynn Jr., eds. 2004. *The Art of Governance: Analyzing Management and Administration*. Washington, D.C.: Georgetown University Press.

Ingraham, Patricia W., Jessica E. Sowa, and Donald P. Moynihan. 2004. "Linking Dimensions of Public Sector Leadership to Performance." In Patricia W. Ingraham and Laurence E. Lynn Jr., eds.. *The Art of Governance: Analyzing Management and Administration*. Washington, D.C.: Georgetown University Press.

Kathi, Pradeep Chandra, and Terry L. Cooper. 2005. "Democratizing the Administrative State: Connecting Neighborhood Councils and City Agencies." *Public Administration Review* 65 (September-October): 559–67.

Keller, Morton. 1977. *Affairs of State: Public Life in Late Nineteenth Century America*. Cambridge, MA: Belknap Press.

Kelman, Steven. 1987. *Making Public Policy: A Hopeful View of American Government*. New York: Basic Books.

Kettl, Donald F. 2000. *The Global Public Management Revolution: A Report on the Transformation of Governance*. Washington, D.C.: Brookings Institution.

Kettl, Donald F. 2002. *The Transformation of Governance: Public Administration for Twenty-First Century America*. Baltimore: Johns Hopkins University Press.

Khademian, Anne M. 2000. "Is Silly Putty Manageable? Looking for the Links between Culture, Management, and Context." In Jeffrey L. Brudney, Laurence J. O'Toole Jr., and Hal G. Rainey, eds., *Advancing Public Management: New Developments in Theory, Methods, and Practice*. Washington, D.C.: Georgetown University Press.

Lane, Charles. 2005. "Justices Rule Spies Cannot Sue U.S. Over Deals." *The Washington Post*, March 3: A03.

Latham, Earl, ed. 1958. *The Philosophy and Policies of Woodrow Wilson*. Chicago: University of Chicago Press.

Link, Arthur S. 1956. *Wilson: The New Freedom*. Princeton: Princeton University Press.

Link, Arthur S., et al., eds. 1966–1994. *The Papers of Woodrow Wilson*, 69 volumes. Princeton: Princeton University Press.

Long, Norton E. 1949. "Power and Administration." *Public Administration Review* 9 (Autumn): 257–64.

Lowi, Theodore J. 1979. *The End of Liberalism: The Second Republic of the United States*, 2nd ed. New York: W.W. Norton.

Lowi, Theodore J. 1985. *The Personal President: Power Invested, Promise Unfulfilled*. Ithaca, NY: Cornell University Press.

Lowi, Theodore J. 1991. "Toward a Legislature of the First Kind." In William H. Robinson and Clay H. Wellborn, eds., *Knowledge, Power, and the Congress*. Washington, D.C.: Congressional Quarterly.

Lowi, Theodore J. 1993a. "Legitimizing Public Administration: A Disturbed Dissent." *Public Administration Review* 53 (May-June): 257–64.

Lowi, Theodore J. 1993b. "Two Roads to Serfdom: Liberalism, Conservatism, and Administrative Power." In Stephen L. Elkin and Karol Edward Soltan, eds., *A New Constitutionalism: Designing Political Institutions for a Good Society*. Chicago: University of Chicago Press.

Lowi, Theodore J. 1995. *The End of the Republican Era*. Norman: University of Oklahoma Press.

Lynch, Thomas D., and Maurice H. Rahimi. 1984. "Woodrow Wilson and the Revolution in Public Budgeting." In Jack Rabin and James S. Bowman, eds., *Politics and Administration: Woodrow Wilson and American Public Administration*. New York: Marcel Dekker.

Lynn, Laurence E., Jr. 1996. *Public Management as Art, Science, and Profession*. Chatham, NJ: Chatham House.

Lynn, Laurence E., Jr. 2000. "Introduction to Part I." In Jeffrey L. Brudney, Laurence J. O'Toole Jr., and Hal G. Rainey, eds., *Advancing Public Management: New Developments in Theory, Methods, and Practice*. Washington, D.C.: Georgetown University Press.

Lynn, Laurence E., Jr. 2001. "The Myth of the Bureaucratic Paradigm: What Traditional Public Administration Really Stood For." *Public Administration Review* 61 (March-April): 144–60.

Lynn, Laurence E., Jr., Carolyn J. Heinrich, and Carolyn J. Hill. 2001. *Improving Governance: A New Logic for Empirical Research.* Washington, D.C.: Georgetown University Press.

Macmahon, Arthur W. 1958. "Woodrow Wilson: Political Leader and Administrator." In Earl Latham, ed., *The Philosophy and Policies of Woodrow Wilson.* Chicago: University of Chicago Press.

Malloy, Timothy F. 2002. "Regulating by Incentives: Myths, Models, and Micromarkets." *Texas Law Review* (February): 531–605.

Maynard-Moody, Steven, and Michael Musheno. 2003. *Cops, Teachers, Counselors: Stories from the Front Lines of Public Service.* Ann Arbor: University of Michigan Press.

Mazouz, Bachir, and Benoît Tremblay. 2006. "Toward a Postbureaucratic Model of Governance: How Institutional Commitment Is Challenging Quebec's Administration." *Public Administration Review* 66 (March-April): 263–73.

Miewald, Robert D. 1984. "The Origins of Wilson's Thought: The German Tradition and the Organic State." In Jack Rabin and James S. Bowman, eds., *Politics and Administration: Woodrow Wilson and American Public Administration.* New York: Marcel Dekker.

Milkis, Sidney M. 1993. *The President and the Parties: The Transformation of the American Party System since the New Deal.* New York: Oxford University Press.

Milkis, Sidney M., and Michael Nelson. 1999. *The American Presidency, 1776–1998: Origins and Development,* 3rd ed. Washington, D.C.: Congressional Quarterly.

Miller, John Perry. 1958. "Woodrow Wilson's Contribution to Antitrust Policy." In Earl Latham, ed., *The Philosophy and Policies of Woodrow Wilson.* Chicago: University of Chicago Press.

Moore, Mark H. 1995. *Creating Public Value: Strategic Management in Government.* Cambridge, MA: Harvard University Press.

Noble, Charles. 1985. "Wilson's Choice: The Political Origins of the Modern American State." *Comparative Politics* 17 (April): 313–36.

O'Toole, Laurence J., Jr. 2000. "Different Public Managements? Implications of Structural Context in Hierarchies and Networks." In Jeffrey L. Brudney, Laurence J. O'Toole Jr., and Hal G. Rainey, eds., *Advancing Public Management: New Developments in Theory, Methods, and Practice.* Washington, D.C.: Georgetown University Press.

Ostrom, Vincent. 1989. *The Intellectual Crisis in American Public Administration,* 2nd ed. Tuscaloosa: University of Alabama Press.

Pfiffner, James P. 2005. *The Modern Presidency,* 4th ed. Belmont, CA: Thomson/Wadsworth.

Rabin, Jack, and James S. Bowman. 1984. *Politics and Administration: Woodrow Wilson and American Public Administration.* New York: Marcel Dekker.

Rainey, Hal G. 1990. "Public Management: Recent Developments and Current Prospects." In Naomi B. Lynn and Aaron Wildavsky, eds., *Public Administration: The State of the Discipline.* Chatham, NJ: Chatham House.

Rohr, John A. 1984. "The Constitutional World of Woodrow Wilson." In Jack Rabin and James S. Bowman, eds., *Politics and Administration: Woodrow Wilson and American Public Administration.* New York: Marcel Dekker.

Rohr, John A. 1986. *To Run a Constitution: The Legitimacy of the Administrative State.* Lawrence: University Press of Kansas.

Rosenbloom, David H. 1984. "Reconsidering the Public Administration Dichotomy: The

Supreme Court and Public Personnel Management." In Jack Rabin and James S. Bowman, eds., *Politics and Administration: Woodrow Wilson and American Public Administration*. New York: Marcel Dekker.

Rosenbloom, David H. 2000. *Building a Legislative-Centered Public Administration: Congress and the Administrative State, 1946–1999*. Tuscaloosa: University of Alabama Press.

Ruskin, John. 1880. *Works*. Boston: Colonial Press.

Schneider, Mark, et al. 2003. "Building Consensual Institutions: Networks and the National Estuary Program." *American Journal of Political Science* 47 (January): 143–58.

Seidelman, Raymond, with Edward J. Harpham. 1985. *Disenchanted Realists: Political Science and the American Crisis, 1884–1984*. Albany: State University of New York Press.

Seidman, Harold, and Robert Gilmour. 1986. *Politics, Position, and Power: From the Positive to the Regulatory State*, 4th ed. New York: Oxford University Press.

Skowronek, Stephen. 1982. *Building a New American State: The Expansion of National Administrative Capacities, 1877–1920*. New York: Cambridge University Press.

Skowronek, Stephen. 1997. *The Politics Presidents Make: Leadership from Johns Adams to Bill Clinton*. Cambridge, MA: Belknap Press.

Skowronek, Stephen. 2003. "Presidential Leadership in Political Time." In Michael Nelson, ed., *The Presidency and the Political System*, 7th ed. Washington, D.C.: CQ Press.

Stid, Daniel D. 1998. *The President as Statesman: Woodrow Wilson and the Constitution*. Lawrence: University Press of Kansas.

Stivers, Camilla. 1998. "The Bureau Movement: Seedbed of Modern Public Administration." In Thomas D. Lynch and Todd J. Dicker, eds., *Handbook of Organization Theory and Management: The Philosophical Approach*. New York: Marcel Dekker.

Sundquist, James L. 1992. *Constitutional Reform and Effective Government*. Rev. ed. Washington, D.C.: Brookings Institution.

Terry, Larry D. 1995. *Leadership of Public Bureaucracies: The Administrator as Conservator*. Thousand Oaks, CA: SAGE.

Terry, Larry D. 1998. "Administrative Leadership, Neo-Managerialism, and the New Public Management Movement." *Public Administration Review* 58 (May-June): 194–200.

Terry, Larry D. 1999. "From Greek Mythology to the Real World of the New Public Management and Democratic Governance (Terry Responds)." *Public Administration Review* 59 (May-June): 272–77.

Thompson, John A. 2002. *Woodrow Wilson*. New York: Pearson-Longman.

Thorsen, Neils Aage. 1988. *The Political Thought of Woodrow Wilson, 1875–1910*. Princeton: Princeton University Press.

Tocqueville, Alexis de. 1988. *Democracy in America*. Translated by George Lawrence, edited by J. P. Mayer. New York: Perennial Library.

Tulis, Jeffrey K. 1987. *The Rhetorical Presidency*. Princeton: Princeton University Press.

Turner, Henry A. 1951. "Woodrow Wilson: Exponent of Executive Leadership." *Western Political Quarterly* 4 (March): 97–115.

Turner, Henry A. 1956. "Woodrow Wilson as Administrator." *Public Administration Review* 16 (Autumn): 249–57.

Van Riper, Paul P. 1984. "The Politics-Administration Dichotomy: Concept or Reality?" In

Jack Rabin and James S. Bowman, eds., *Politics and Administration: Woodrow Wilson and American Public Administration*. New York: Marcel Dekker.

Waldo, Dwight. 1984. "The Perdurability of the Politics-Administration Dichotomy: Woodrow Wilson and the Identity Crisis in Public Administration." In Jack Rabin and James S. Bowman, eds., *Politics and Administration: Woodrow Wilson and American Public Administration*. New York: Marcel Dekker.

Walker, Larry. 1989. "Woodrow Wilson, Progressive Reform, and Public Administration." *Political Science Quarterly* 104 (Autumn): 509–25.

Walker, Larry, and Jeremy F. Plant. 1984. "Woodrow Wilson and the Federal System." In Jack Rabin and James S. Bowman, eds., *Politics and Administration: Woodrow Wilson and American Public Administration*. New York: Marcel Dekker.

Wamsley, Barbara S. 2004. "Technocracies: Can They Bell the Cat?" In Thomas H. Stanton and Benjamin Ginsberg, eds., *Making Government Manageable: Executive Organization and Management in the Twenty-First Century*. Baltimore: Johns Hopkins University Press.

Warshaw, Shirley Anne. 2005. *The Keys To Power: Managing the Presidency*, 2nd ed. New York: Pearson-Longman.

Wilson, James Q. 1989. *Bureaucracy: What Government Agencies Do and Why they Do It*. New York: Basic Books.

Wilson, Woodrow. 1890. *The State: Elements of Historical and Practical Politics: A Sketch of Institutional History and Administration*. Boston: D. C. Heath.

Wilson, Woodrow. 1908. *Constitutional Government in the United States*. New York: Columbia University Press.

Wilson, Woodrow. 1981. *Congressional Government: A Study in American Politics*. Baltimore: Johns Hopkins University Press.

Wolin, Sheldon S. 2001. *Tocqueville Between Two Worlds: The Making of a Political and Theoretical Life*. Princeton: Princeton University Press.

Yates, Douglas. 1982. *Bureaucratic Democracy: The Search for Democracy and Efficiency in American Government*. Cambridge, MA: Harvard University Press.

Index